Working with Beats in Pro Tools®:
Skill Pack

Andrew Hagerman

THOMSON
COURSE TECHNOLOGY
Professional ■ Technical ■ Reference

Working with Beats in Pro Tools®:
Skill Pack

Publisher and General Manager, Thomson Course Technology PTR: Stacy L. Hiquet

Associate Director of Marketing: Sarah O'Donnell

Manager of Editorial Services: Heather Talbot

Marketing Manager: Mark Hughes

Acquisitions Editor: Orren Merton

Marketing Assistant: Adena Flitt

Project Editor/Copy Editor: Cathleen D. Snyder

PTR Editorial Services Coordinator: Erin Johnson

Interior Layout: Judith Littlefield

Cover Designer: Mike Tanamachi

CD-ROM Producer: Brandon Penticuff

Indexer: Larry Sweazy

Proofreader: Gene Redding

Digidesign and Pro Tools are registered trademarks of Avid Technologies, Inc. in the United States and/or other countries. All other trademarks are the property of their respective owners.

Important: Thomson Course Technology PTR cannot provide software support. Please contact the appropriate software manufacturer's technical support line or Web site for assistance.

Thomson Course Technology PTR and the author have attempted throughout this book to distinguish proprietary trademarks from descriptive terms by following the capitalization style used by the manufacturer.

Information contained in this book has been obtained by Thomson Course Technology PTR from sources believed to be reliable. However, because of the possibility of human or mechanical error by our sources, Thomson Course Technology PTR, or others, the Publisher does not guarantee the accuracy, adequacy, or completeness of any information and is not responsible for any errors or omissions or the results obtained from use of such information. Readers should be particularly aware of the fact that the Internet is an ever-changing entity. Some facts may have changed since this book went to press.

Educational facilities, companies, and organizations interested in multiple copies or licensing of this book should contact the Publisher for quantity discount information. Training manuals, CD-ROMs, and portions of this book are also available individually or can be tailored for specific needs.

ISBN-10: 1-59863-327-9

ISBN-13: 978-1-59863-327-6

Library of Congress Catalog Card Number: 2006906798

Printed in the United States of America

07 08 09 10 11 TW 10 9 8 7 6 5 4 3 2

© 2007 Thomson Course Technology, a division of Thomson Learning Inc. All rights reserved. No part of this book may be reproduced or transmitted in any form or by any means, electronic or mechanical, including photocopying, recording, or by any information storage or retrieval system without written permission from Thomson Course Technology PTR, except for the inclusion of brief quotations in a review.

The Thomson Course Technology PTR logo and related trade dress are trademarks of Thomson Course Technology, a division of Thomson Learning Inc., and may not be used without written permission.

Thomson Course Technology PTR, a division of
Thomson Learning Inc.
25 Thomson Place
Boston, MA 02210

http://www.courseptr.com

*This book, my love, and my life are dedicated to
my beautiful Junko-san and our precious daughter Sachiko Elizabeth.*

Acknowledgments

Any book of this kind is a team effort, regardless of the name that happens to be on the cover. The team that brings this title to you is hands down the best one I've worked with, as their fine work shows on every page. My thanks go to Orren Merton for bringing this project to me and coordinating the efforts of the entire team. Cathleen Snyder lends an experienced editorial eye (while at the same time preparing for upcoming nuptials—amazing!). My good friend and colleague kept me honest on the technical points and offered many insightful ideas—thanks! Last but certainly not least, thanks go to Don Gunn for laying a solid foundation for this book.

I'm fortunate beyond words to have found a place working alongside Digidesign—they never fail to amaze and inspire. Special thanks go to John Rechsteiner, Tsukasa Tokiwano, and Andy Cook—I'm deeply appreciative of the faith that each has placed in me. To the Asia and Australia Digidesign team—you're the best, and the example you set has really helped with the writing of this book.

I'm blessed to have the best friends and family a guy could ask for, and if I've done anything of value, it's due to their love and support. My beautiful family buoys me in all ways and has gotten me through the long nights of writing. Brian Smithers and David Oxenreider are both fundamental influences in my life and have both done their part to set me upon this path—thank you, friends. Finally, I'd like to thank the late great Arnold Jacobs (Chicago Symphony Orchestra), who taught me to live with courage (with just one well-placed sentence).

About the Author

Andy Hagerman has been a professional musician (in some form or another) for the majority of his 42 years, beginning with formal training as a classical tuba player (yes, tuba) at the Eastman School of Music and Northwestern University. During his college years, the music technology revolution began to take off (with the invention of MIDI), and Andy was immediately hooked. As the technology evolved over the years, he's kept up with the advancements, constantly amazed at the creative doorways that have opened as a result.

In addition to a career as a performing musician (including Disneyland, Walt Disney World, and Tokyo Disney Sea), Andy has channeled his study of music technology toward compositional pursuits. Particularly active in educational production, Andy has written original music for clients ranging from the American Museum of Natural History in New York City to Caterpillar tractors. He's also had the privilege of teaching others the craft of music technology in a number of situations, including as a lecturer at Full Sail, a media arts college in central Florida.

These days, Andy is busy working, playing, and writing in Tokyo, Japan. He works extensively with musicians, producers, and educators throughout the growing Asia Pacific region and is involved with Digidesign's Training and Education programs. Andy also continues to be active as a composer with Singularity Arts, Inc. (www.singularityarts.com) and creates music for a variety of applications.

Table of Contents

CHAPTER 1 Getting a Stronger Start 1
    Anatomy of a Beat 2
    Why MIDI Matters 7
    What Is a Transient? 12
    Using Rex Files 16

CHAPTER 2 Working Smarter 21
    Working with Edit Playlists 21
    Taking a Second Look at the TCE Trim Tool 28
    TCE Edit to Timeline Selection 35
    Consolidating Regions 38

CHAPTER 3 MIDI and the Beat 41
    Taking a New Look at MIDI: Single Note Height 42
    MIDI Quantize 47
    MIDI Velocity 53
    MIDI Real-Time Properties 54
    Session Linearity 58
    Making MIDI Better: MIDI Track Offsets 60

CHAPTER 4 Editing Power 65
    Bringing Audio and MIDI Together: Identify Beat 65
    Making Grid Mode Work for You 70
    Working with Regions 77
    Tick-Based Audio (and How to Use It!) 82
    New Region Features 84

Contents

CHAPTER 5 **Making the Most of Beat Detective** 95
So What the Heck *Is* Beat Detective, Anyway? 95
Workflow #1: Creating a Tempo Map 97
Workflow #2: Quantizing Audio 105
Beyond the Basics 112

CHAPTER 6 **Mixing Beats** 123
Mixing Drum by Drum 124
Manipulating Sound 129
Working Smarter in the Mix Window 146
Workflow Ideas 152

CHAPTER 7 **Tying It All Together** 159
Stutter and Glitch Edits 159
Loop Trim Polyrhythms 161
"Breaking" the Zero-Crossing Rule 163
Good Luck and Have Fun! 164

APPENDIX **Recommended Shortcuts** 167
Pro Tools 7.0 Keyboard Shortcuts, for Pro Tools|HD, Pro Tools LE,
and Pro Tools M-Powered Systems on Windows 167
Pro Tools 7.0 Keyboard Shortcuts, for Pro Tools|HD, Pro Tools LE,
and Pro Tools M-Powered Systems on Macintosh 173

Index 181

Introduction

The beat, the pulse, the rhythm, the *groove*. They exist by different names and come in thousands of different styles. As a creative musician, you know that a well-crafted rhythm track can not only be the foundation upon which the rest of your music is built, but is often *the* defining characteristic of the musical style you're going after!

In his book *Poetics and Music in the Form of Six Lessons* (Harvard University Press, 1993), classical composer Igor Stravinsky wrote two very notable passages that I've always found inspiring:

> Who of us, on hearing jazz music, has not felt an amusing sensation approaching giddiness when a dancer or a solo musician, trying persistently to stress irregular accents, cannot succeed in turning our ear away from the regular pulsation of the meter drummed out by the percussion?

> This problem of time in the art of music is of capital importance. I have thought it wise to dwell on the problem because the considerations that it involves may help us to understand the different creative types....

Maestro Stravinsky goes on to use terms to describe the visceral feelings that rhythm can induce, including "euphoria" and "dynamic calm," which I think we can all identify with in a variety of musical circumstances. So is my point to discuss Stravinsky's attitudes about rhythm? Not at all (though books can and have been written on the subject)—the point is just that the power of rhythm exists everywhere in music as a fundamental player. The tradition of the beat in musical work is time-honored, it spans styles and generations, and its power is absolutely undeniable.

Here's the bottom line: No matter what music you're into and no matter what you call the beats you create, there's also no denying that how you use them—and how *well* you use them—can make or break your musical work. You're a Pro Tools user (or becoming one) and your goal is to use this application to make better, more creative beats, and to do it with ease and style. You know that if you can use the features in this powerful DAW more comfortably, you'll not only work more efficiently, but you'll also unlock new inspiring ideas and creativity.

Good news: Pro Tools and this book stand at the ready to help you make that creative vision a reality! More good news: New features in Pro Tools, combined with powerful new virtual instruments and plug-in effects, are making Pro Tools more powerful than ever. And even better yet, the same mixing and editing features that have brought Pro Tools to the forefront of the music industry take on even deeper meaning when we look at how to use them with beats.

If you're an inspired creative musician and you're looking to kick your rhythm tracks up a notch, *Working with Beats in Pro Tools: Skill Pack* will be a valuable ally in your quest!

Introduction

Who Should Use This Book

Working with Beats in Pro Tools is a targeted collection of features, tips, and tricks focused on the art and craft of building the perfect beat. With that in mind, the discussions contained within these pages will be made with the assumption of a basic knowledge of Pro Tools. This isn't to say that you need to be an expert user with multiple credits under your belt, but it does mean that you should have a working knowledge of the Edit and Mix windows, basic recording, editing and mixing, and ways to get audio and MIDI into and out of your Pro Tools sessions.

> **NOTE**
>
> If you're completely new to Pro Tools, then you might want to consider making this book part of a multi-level approach to learning this powerful application. I've written another book on Pro Tools LE, entitled *Pro Tools LE 7 Ignite!*, also published by Thomson Course Technology PTR, which can help you get up to speed quickly.
>
> If you're interested in getting up to an expert level on Pro Tools, you might also want to consider turning to the official courses offered by Digidesign (the manufacturer of Pro Tools). Simply, the courses are designed to take a student from the beginning level with the *Pro Tools 101 Official Courseware* book (published by Thomson Course Technology and Digidesign) all the way up to the 310 Pro Tools Expert Certification courses (offered exclusively at Digidesign-sponsored Pro Schools). For more information about these courses, just go to www.digidesign.com/training.

On the music side of the equation, don't worry if you're not a formally trained musician. The beauty of Pro Tools—and computer music in general—is that even untrained (but creative) musicians can enjoy great success in this kind of environment. Of course, any in-depth discussion of beats and their use must include some discussion of their basic musical structure, but the information we cover isn't rocket science and will be valuable knowledge for you to have on hand. This will also include a basic discussion of MIDI (*Musical Instrument Digital Interface*) and how your MIDI tempo comes into play when working with beats, but again, we'll cover what you need to know here in this book. And of course, any general music or audio knowledge you bring to the table is an added advantage, but certainly not a requirement for this book.

How to Use This Book

Music in general is a progressive process, and from creation to performance it's the result of many small steps taken in order. A solid mastery of Pro Tools works much the same way. Though this book is specifically targeted at getting the most out of your rhythm tracks, we'll work from some of the simpler and more general techniques to higher-level ones with more specific uses. We'll also explore how to use multiple techniques in combination to get the results you're looking for.

Introduction

Many "how to" books are designed to take the creative process from start to finish, and though that works for more general books, this one will be laid out a little differently. Each section will be a self-contained discussion on a specific feature or technique. Hopefully this organization will serve you well, and you'll be able to quickly locate the tools you're interested in developing through the book's table of contents and index. Over time, you'll hopefully look over *every* chapter, and I promise you that there is nothing covered here that is exclusive to a specific style or level of usership.

You'll find portions of this book are laid out in a tutorial-style format; there are even tutorial files you use side by side with the book's examples. These exercises, as with the chapters, will be designed to highlight a specific technique, with illustrations in the book to help you on your way. Finally, amongst the text and exercises, you'll see a number of Notes and Tips peppered throughout. Take a look at these to find additional ways to increase your efficiency, additional information on key functions, and even warnings that point out common pitfalls and how to avoid them.

What You'll Need

The goal of this book is to have fun, and thankfully we'll be able to get that job done without breaking the bank. We'll capitalize on one of the greatest strengths of Pro Tools—the fact that the software environments in TDM and LE are nearly identical. The system that I'll be using for this book will be a Pro Tools LE–based system, using an Mbox 2 interface, which is Digidesign's entry-level system these days. For the most part, the plug-ins that I'll use are included with the purchase of your Pro Tools system. The only exceptions to this are a plug-in called "Strike" (a very cool virtual drummer) and the full version of Beat Detective (which is included free in Pro Tools|HD or available for Pro Tools LE through the Music Production Toolkit).

Beyond that, you'll need a host computer, speakers, and a MIDI controller (optional if you want to play some drums!).

> **TIP**
>
> If you want to learn more about the specifications of any Pro Tools hardware, the Digidesign website (www.digidesign.com) is a great place to start. From the Digidesign home page, click on the Products link to view a list of the current Pro Tools products.

> **NOTE**
>
> If you're putting together your Pro Tools system, there is a great resource on the Digidesign website. Digidesign keeps an up-to-date list of compatible hardware on its website. At www.digidesign.com/compato, you can find a list of Pro Tools systems along with their supported operating systems. This page is comprehensive and is constantly being updated to reflect the latest computers and peripherals available. All in all, it's a great resource for Pro Tools users at any level, and whenever you're in doubt about what might work with your system, this page will give you your answer!

Introduction

Plug-Ins You'll Need

To make this book most accessible, I've made sure to use free plug-ins for effects and virtual instruments in the tutorial exercises. Here's what you'll want to have installed for use with the sessions in this book. (Bear in mind that many of these plug-ins and virtual instruments require Pro Tools 7 to run.)

- Xpand! (virtual instrument)
- D-Verb (reverb)
- EQ III
- Dynamics III

You may find that most (perhaps all) of these plug-ins are included with your Pro Tools LE 7 installation disc. If not, it's no problem; you can go to Digidesign's website (www.digidesign.com) and download most of them them for free from the Products → Plug-ins page. The only one you might have a problem with is Xpand! It's not downloadable, but you can get a disc from your reseller or a disc shipped to you from the Dididesign website. (There is a small shipping fee involved.)

There is one plug-in discussed in this book that *isn't* free, named SoundReplacer. We'll talk about it extensively (and in illustrated detail) in the mixing chapter. This plug-in is not essential for the purposes of this book, and you should get a good idea of its operation after reading about it in Chapter 6.

Ready? Let's go!

Getting a Stronger Start

Using beats at a basic level is simple enough—just drag and drop a loop, and off you go. There is a danger in this powerful simplicity, however: Users can create a rhythm track with virtually no understanding of its form or function, and thus be at a loss when wanting to use the track beyond its most basic level. It's a problem, but certainly one with a solution.

The Zen thinker Shunryu Suzuki had an interesting philosophy regarding problems, which was basically a two-phase approach. According to Suzuki, the first step when approaching a problem is to fully *understand* the nature of the problem. With understanding, you are equal to the challenge at hand (and without it, you will be forever at a disadvantage). Once this understanding is achieved, the second phase to solving a problem is taking some sort of action based upon your foundational understanding.

This chapter is all about *understanding* what makes up a beat. Here, we'll dissect a beat on a musical, technological, and physical level. In this chapter, you'll learn:

- How to understand the basics of musical rhythm as it is displayed on a drummer's sheet music and how it translates to views in Pro Tools
- What MIDI tempo is all about and how it can make your audio loops better
- How to recognize the elements of your beats within a Pro Tools audio region
- How *all* of these things come into play with one of the beat-user's best friends: Rex files

> **NOTE**
>
> If you have a strong musical and MIDI background, please feel free to skip over the first half of this chapter and jump to the "What Is a Transient?" or "Using Rex Files" section. If you *don't* have a music and MIDI foundation, I encourage you to read on—you'll be surprised how important these concepts are going forward!

Anatomy of a Beat

If you're out to really get your head wrapped around what makes a beat a beat, it's good to start at the source. If you think about it, all drum loops, even those that are completely created within the computer, can trace their roots back to the performance practices of live human drummers and percussionists. If you dig even deeper, you'll come to find that the way these performance practices were written down and communicated from musician to musician is through the language of written music. That's where we'll start.

The point of this discussion isn't to make expert music sight readers of everyone, but rather to point out the specific aspects of written music that are indispensable to the world of computer-based music creation. Though these concepts are by no means Pro Tools–specific, they certainly will come into play in many of the techniques we'll talk about later in this book.

Tempo

Most folks know that the term *tempo* refers to the speed of a musical piece—how fast or how slow the song is going. The issue of tempo is fairly central to working with beats, and it's an issue that we'll tackle from many angles later in this book, but let's start off by showing how it's displayed in notation-style music.

Tempo is specifically measured in *beats per minute (BPM)*. In this case, when we use the word *beat*, we're talking about how fast you would count the music ("1-2-3-4-1-2-3-4..."). For example, a tempo of 60 BPM means that you have a beat per second (a fairly slow tempo), and a tempo of 120 BPM (Pro Tools' default) has a beat every half second. In printed music, tempo is represented as shown in Figure 1.1.

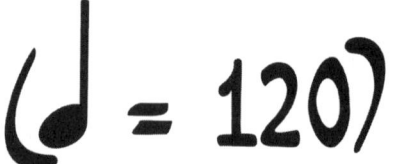

Figure 1.1
A tempo of 120 as shown in printed music. Because tempo is measured in beats per minute, this tempo would have a beat every half second.

> **NOTE**
>
> In this chapter you'll see a number of music notation images. These have been created using an excellent music notation software product called Sibelius. If you're interested in learning more about Sibelius, visit www.sibelius.com.

An easy way to see what tempo your session is using in Pro Tools is to take a quick look at the Transport window, shown in Figure 1.2. Keep in mind that this is the MIDI tempo as specified in Pro Tools and may not be relevant to the tempo of audio regions in your session.

Anatomy of a Beat

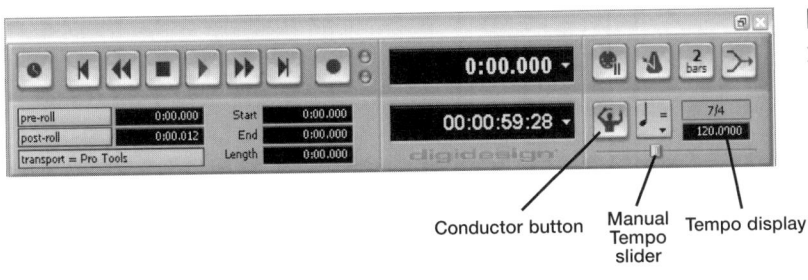

Figure 1.2
Pro Tools' Transport window

- **Tempo display.** You'll find the current tempo displayed here.
- **Conductor button.** This button is commonly called the *Conductor*; if you see it displayed in blue, the Tempo ruler is controlling your session's MIDI tempo. (We'll talk more about this in Chapter 3, "MIDI and the Beat.")
- **Manual Tempo slider.** If the Conductor is not illuminated (as shown here), then the Manual Tempo slider will allow you to control your tempo.

> **NOTE**
>
> If you work with music, you'll want to bring up the Transport window many times every day in your work. Here's a shortcut that will make this *much* easier. To show (or hide) the Transport window, just press Ctrl+1 on a Windows computer or Command+1 (on the numeric keypad) on a Mac. Easy!

Try This: Tapping the Tempo

Even if you're a very experienced musician, it's a time-consuming bother to figure out tempo based solely upon the numeric BPM display. Occasionally, I've lost track of the tempo that I initially had in mind in the process of trying to find that perfect speed by the numbers alone. Here's a tip that should make this process much easier for you. First, make sure that the Conductor isn't illuminated (meaning that your Tempo ruler isn't in control of your session). Next, click on the Tempo display to highlight the numeric field, as shown in Figure 1.3.

Figure 1.3
Ready to tap some tempo!

The rest is simplicity itself—just tap the T key on your computer keyboard at the tempo that you've got in your head. The Tempo display of the Transport window will give you visual feedback as you zero in on that perfect tempo!

3

CHAPTER 1 ■ Getting a Stronger Start

Bars, Beats, Ticks, and Meter

> **NOTE**
>
> These days, the term "beat" has taken on a number of different meanings. (Even in the title of this book, the term could be said to be synonymous with "grooves," "loops," or any number of other catchy words.) In this chapter, however, such vagueness will work against us, so for the purposes of this section, the term "beat" will be used to describe the pulse of the rhythm. In other words, if you count "1-2-3-4-1-2-3-4...," you're in fact counting *beats*.

Going back to notated music, musical notes are organized into regular groups called *measures* or *bars*, in much the same way that words are organized into lines of poetry. This not only gives the musician reading the music a way to keep track of the passage of time, but it also serves as a structural foundation for rhythmic and melodic structure. Figure 1.4 shows what a measure of printed music looks like.

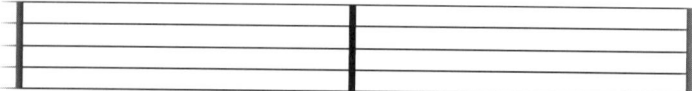

Figure 1.4

Two bars of written music

Pro Tools also uses bars as units of musical measurement, and you can see bars of music displayed on the Bars:Beats ruler (shown in Figure 1.5 above the Min:Secs ruler). In Figure 1.5, you'll see roughly four measures of music.

Figure 1.5

The Bars:Beats ruler, showing measures of music

The way that beats are constructed within a measure is known as *meter*. I'm not talking about meter in the same sense as volume meters, but rather in a way that is also commonly known as *time signatures*. Figure 1.6 shows what a typical time signature looks like; following is a simple description of what the heck the numbers mean.

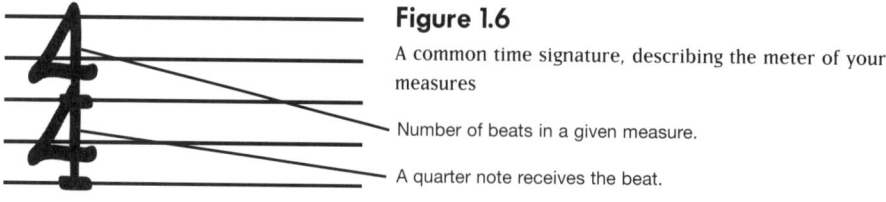

Figure 1.6

A common time signature, describing the meter of your measures

Number of beats in a given measure.

A quarter note receives the beat.

4

- The top number of a time signature describes the number of beats in a given measure. In this case, there are four beats in a measure—this signature is *very* commonly used. If you were working on a waltz (1-2-3-1-2-3...), then this top number would be a 3.
- The bottom number of a time signature tells the musician what sort of written music note receives a beat. In this case, a quarter note gets a beat—again, this is a very common choice. Don't worry if you're unclear about what a quarter note *is* exactly—we'll talk about that in just a moment.

Of course, Pro Tools takes meter into account, and in fact you have a great deal of control here, as you do with tempo. In Figure 1.7, you'll see how meter and metric changes are shown in the Pro Tools Edit window.

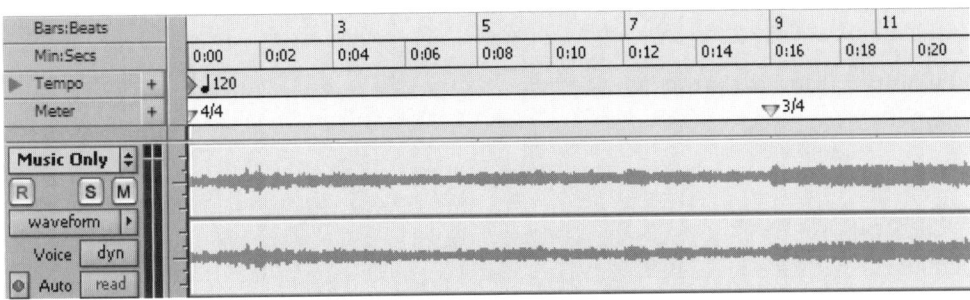

Figure 1.7
This Ruler view shows Bars:Beats in the top ruler, followed by Min:Secs, as we've seen before. Below that is a Tempo ruler showing a tempo of 120 BPM (one beat every half second) and finally the Meter ruler. Note that the Meter ruler shows a change from 4/4 time to a more waltz-ish 3/4 time beginning at Bar 9.

So now we're caught up on what tempo is, how bars are organized, and so on, but what is this "ticks" term all about? Let's take a look at how notes are laid out in a written measure, then put them into a MIDI/Pro Tools context. In Figure 1.8, take a look at a typical measure in quarter notes (keeping in mind that in this case, a quarter note gets a beat).

Figure 1.8
A measure's worth of quarter notes

Now, a musician could play the timing of these notes in a number of different ways (and, in fact, it's nearly certain that a live musician *won't* play them with mathematic precision), depending upon the style of music and other factors. This is second nature to a live musician, but how does a digital medium deal with such variety? With tiny subdivisions of beats called *ticks*, that's how!

Pro Tools divides each beat into 960 evenly spaced *ticks*, as shown in Figure 1.9.

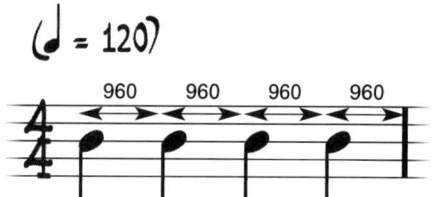

Figure 1.9
Each beat is made up of 960 ticks.

Given this, take a look at Figure 1.10 to see how different note values break down.

- **Whole note.** 4 beats, 3840 ticks.
- **Half note.** 2 beats, 1920 ticks.
- **Quarter note.** 1 beat, 960 ticks.
- **Eighth note.** 1/2 beat, 480 ticks.
- **Sixteenth note.** 1/4 beat, 240 ticks.
- **Thirty-second note.** 1/8 beat, 120 ticks.

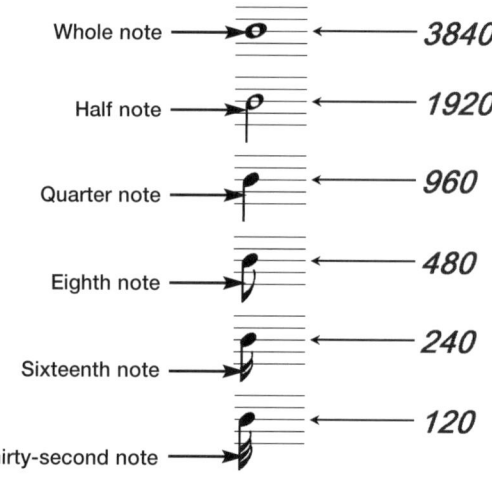

Figure 1.10
Notes of different durations and different tick values

Pro Tools shows this sort of information in a number of different ways. First, if you choose Bars:Beats as your main timescale, you'll see location displayed in Bars|Beats|Ticks in the Main Counter (shown in Figure 1.11), and the selection start, end, and duration displayed similarly to the right of the Main Counter.

Figure 1.11
Bars, beats, and ticks shown in the Main Counter (left) and Edit Selection areas (right)

Also, your grid and nudge values can be set to musical values (in fact, you may use a musical grid almost exclusively in your work!), and in Figure 1.12 you can see not only a notation-style representation of that value, but the value displayed in Bars|Beats|Ticks as well.

Figure 1.12
A grid value of a sixteenth note (240 ticks) and a nudge value of an eighth note (480 ticks)

Now that you understand the notational foundation of music and how it is shown and used in the form of MIDI, how can you use this understanding to make your rhythm tracks shine? Well, in better than half of the techniques we'll work through in this book, MIDI will be a major factor, so let's start that discussion now!

Why MIDI Matters

Through MIDI ticks, Pro Tools can handle fine musical timings, which allows your MIDI to sound more "live." So what if you're not a MIDI musician at all? You'll still be happy that Pro Tools has such accurate musical timing. Powerful tools that we'll work with later, such as Rex files and Beat Detective, rely on MIDI timing to do their thing!

Before we get into the nitty gritty of the more advanced techniques, there's a good bit to talk about just using the basics.

> **NOTE**
>
> In this next section, I'm using a session named "Chapter 1a," which you'll find on the disc included with this book. Bear in mind that you'll need to copy the folder to your hard drive before you'll be able to work with it.
>
> This session contains a single instrument track with drum MIDI data on the playlist. The virtual instrument I've used in creating this data is a great *free* new plug-in called Xpand! brought to you by the Advanced Instrument Research (A.I.R.) group at Digidesign. It is a very usable plug-in (you'll need Pro Tools version 7 or higher) with more than a thousand sounds and a good deal of editability. If you haven't gone to your reseller to pick up a free copy, I'd definitely recommend doing so. You can also order an Xpand! CD online at Digidesign's DigiStore (store.digidesign.com).

There's a commonly held opinion about MIDI that it makes music sound mechanical. I would respond to that by saying that because MIDI is a digital language and works within computerized

CHAPTER 1 ■ Getting a Stronger Start

environments, it is certainly *easy* to make music sound that way. It's a common pitfall to endow MIDI tracks with the sort of superhuman accuracy about which folks complain. In reality, though, the fact that you probably hear MIDI music every day without even knowing it proves that MIDI music doesn't *have* to be that way. The trick lies in the skill of the creative artist—ain't that always the case? Let's talk about some ways to bring your MIDI to life.

Tempo Changes

The trick to working with MIDI beats is to *think like a drummer*. This means a lot of things, of course, but for starters, let's talk about tempo. If you talk to a drummer, you'll learn that the natural inclination—even with excellent drummers—is to bump up the tempo just a little bit in the more exciting sections. These small tempo changes can subtly increase the energy level of the music. Let's take a look (and listen) to a real-world example of how this works.

> **NOTE**
>
> If you're looking at Chapter 1a, you can follow along here.

The session shown in Figure 1.13 is a pretty common scenario—a live drummer playing MIDI drums to a static-tempo click track. The classic problem with this is that even in the more energetic chorus section, the click track has reined the drummer back to a set tempo value.

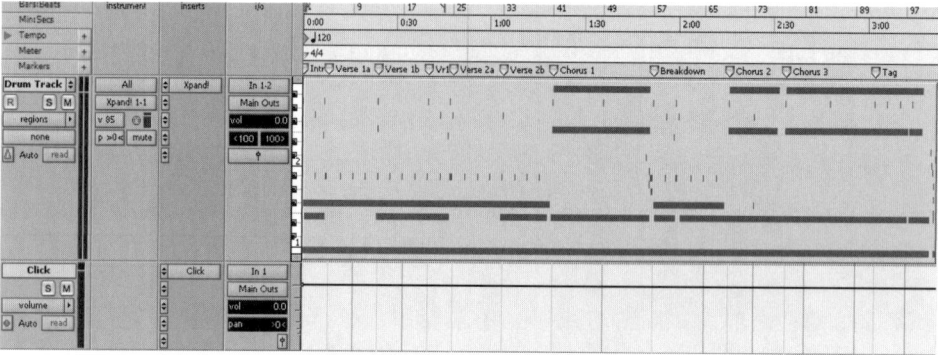

Figure 1.13
Drums and click

Commonly, at a chorus, the energy (and hence the tempo) will increase, and that's what I want to do here. The first step will be to make sure that the Conductor button on the Transport window is selected. When this button is illuminated in blue, the tempo of your session will be managed by the Tempo ruler rather than the Tempo slider, giving you much more control (see Figure 1.14).

Why MIDI Matters

Figure 1.14

The Conductor button (also known as the Tempo Ruler Enable button), which can be found in the Transport window

Once that's done, you'll need to insert a tempo change. Keep in mind that too much of a tempo change will be noticed consciously, and in this case we're looking for a more subtle effect. In this example (shown in Figure 1.15), I'm going to nudge up the tempo by only three beats per minute, from 120 BPM to 123 BPM. My choruses begin at Bar 41, end at Bar 57, then begin again at Measure 69 to the end of the song. Here's how I'm going to insert these tempo changes:

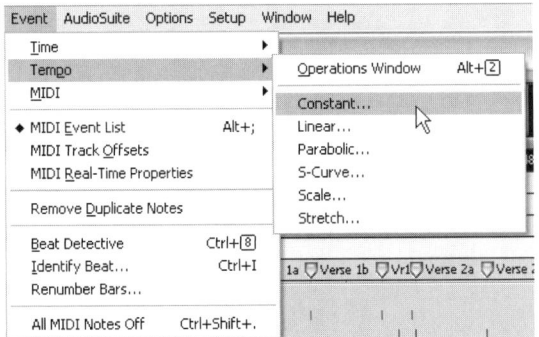

Figure 1.15

The first step to making a tempo change

1. From the Event drop-down menu, choose Tempo, then navigate to Constant. Choosing the Constant option will create an instantaneous tempo change, which is fine for us because the amount of change is so small.

2. In the Tempo Operations window, the rest is simple. First, set your start and end points. (In this case I want to start my first change at 41|1|000 and end it at 57|1|000.) Next, change the tempo—remember, a little change will do the trick. In this case I've changed the tempo to 123 BPM. Finally, because I want the tempo to go back down after the chorus, I'll check the Preserve Tempo After Selection box, which will cause the tempo to jump back down to 120 BPM at the beginning of Bar 57. Figure 1.16 shows what the window will look like.

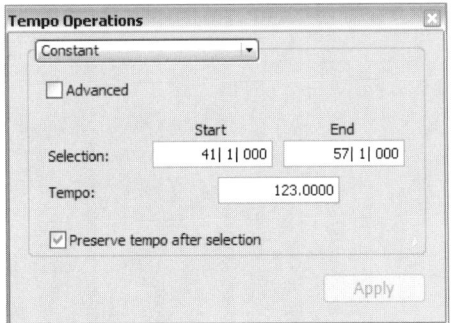

Figure 1.16

The Tempo Operations window for the first chorus

9

3. Finally, I want to bring the tempo back up to 123 BPM from Bar 69 to the end. The process is the same, except that it really doesn't matter much what you choose as your End value (as long as it is after Bar 69). Because you are making this tempo change through to the end of the song, just *don't* check the Preserve Tempo After Selection box, and you're all set!

The Tempo Ruler

The Tempo ruler has got a *lot* of power that you might not be aware of, so let's take a quick look. To see the Tempo ruler's full functionality, just click the Tempo Editor expand/collapse arrow, as shown in Figure 1.17.

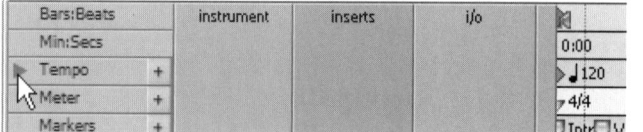

Figure 1.17
Showing the Tempo Editor

The area that will be revealed is a linear representation of your tempo changes. I'll show you how I'd apply the tempo changes I made earlier using this powerful tool instead.

> **NOTE**
>
> If you're following along with the Chapter 1a session, you should go to the File drop-down menu, then choose Revert to Saved. This way, you'll be back to the initial state of the session and ready to redo your tempo changes.

1. The Smart Tool will be helpful for this operation, so please select it now.
2. Select the area that you wish to change—for example, Bar 41 to Bar 57, as shown in Figure 1.18.
3. Move your cursor to the upper area of the Tempo Editor until the tool changes to a downward-facing Trim tool.

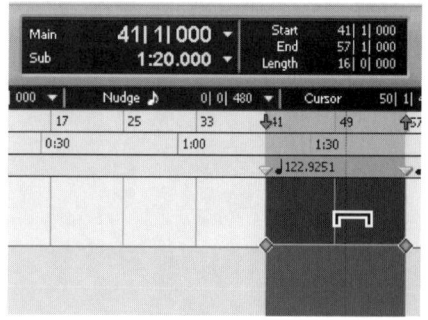

Figure 1.18
Using the Tempo Editor to kick it up a notch!

4. Click and drag up to increase the tempo in the selected area. Note that the resultant tempo value is shown in the Tempo ruler area as you drag upward (see Figure 1.18).

As you might have noted, it can be a little tricky to zero in on specific tempo values. Usually you can get close enough, but if you're an obsessed tweaker like yours truly, you can still get the exact tempo you want by double-clicking the desired tempo change event in the Tempo ruler. (It will appear as a blue triangle, which will open up a Tempo Change window.) Once that's finished, just type the value you want and click OK, as shown in Figure 1.19.

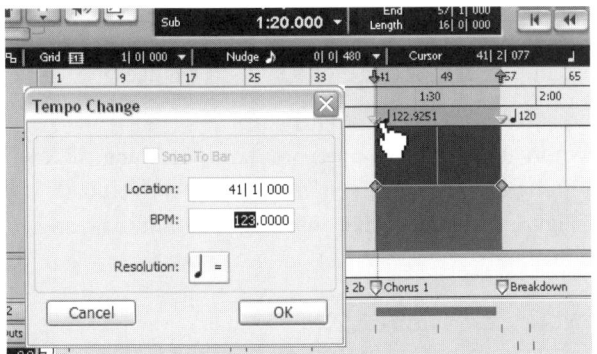

Figure 1.19
Tweakin' tempo

> **NOTE**
>
> Before leaving this section, I've got to mention some different ways of entering data in the Tempo Editor area. In particular, the Pencil tool is a great way to enter tempo data. You have a good number of options with the Pencil tool as well. If you click and hold on the Pencil tool, you'll see a drop-down menu, as shown in Figure 1.20. From the list of drawing options, you can use Free Hand, Line, Parabolic, and S-Curve when drawing tempo. To the right of the list in Figure 1.20, I've shown an S-curve. Parabolas and S-curves will also show blue "handles" that you can use to adjust curvatures. Though this sort of tempo operation is somewhat beyond the scope of this book, it's definitely worth exploring.

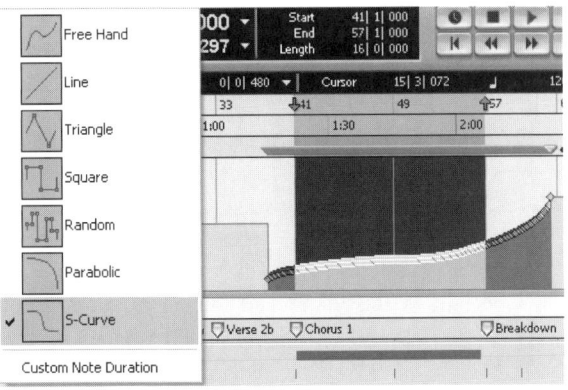

Figure 1.20
Pencil tool options and the Tempo Editor

CHAPTER 1 ■ Getting a Stronger Start

What Is a Transient?

Amusingly enough, even though most professionals (and a good portion of enthusiasts as well) can point out a transient when they see one, it's a tricky concept to put into words. Just on a hunch, I checked my Webster's dictionary, of all things, and I think its definition actually helps. Here's the first, most general definition:

> (adjective) Passing especially quickly into and out of existence

If you think about it, that is exactly what drums do, but if you dig just a little deeper, you'll find an even better definition:

> (noun) A temporary oscillation that occurs in a circuit because of a sudden change of voltage or of load

When you talk about digital audio, voltage is synonymous with volume. So, if you combine the two definitions of what a transient is, you get something like "a sudden change in voltage (volume) that passes quickly into and out of existence." Figure 1.21 shows what that might look like as an audio waveform, in the classic form of a snare drum hit.

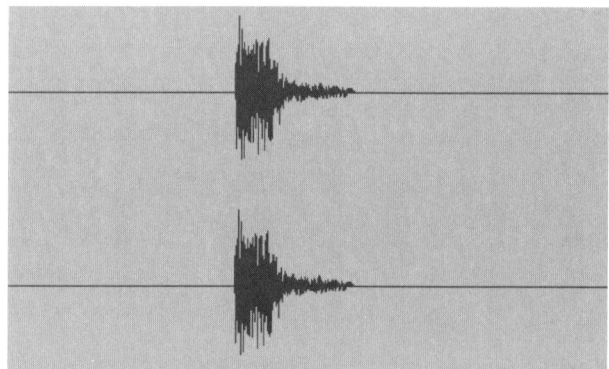

Figure 1.21
A sudden change in volume, a.k.a. a transient

Not only are transients at the very core of what working with beats is all about, but they're something that Pro Tools works with quite well. Let's take a look at some tools that will make your drum editing life *much* easier....

Working with Transients

> **NOTE**
>
> You can follow along with the examples I'll use by launching the session named Chapter 1b, which you'll find on the disc included with this book.

What Is a Transient?

You're probably familiar with the Tab to Transient feature in Pro Tools. (If you're not, we'll be going through its basic functioning here.) However, there are actually a few other dimensions that come into play when you're working with this feature. Let's take for example the very common process of pulling a loopable region from a larger rhythm track. My first job is to listen to a section of the audio and determine roughly the bar(s) that I want to use for my looping region (see Figure 1.22).

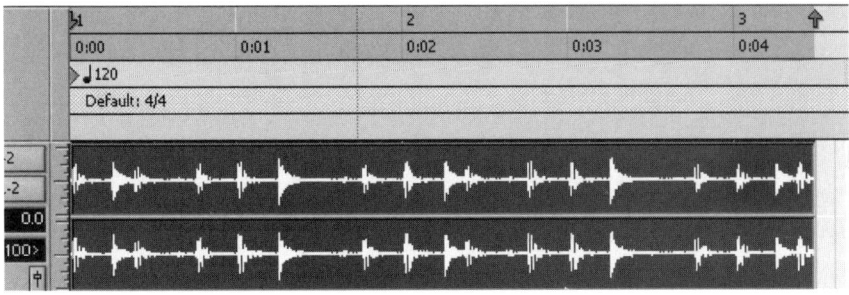

Figure 1.22

My rhythm track, including a usable measure

The next step is to make sure that the Tab to Transient button (located in the upper-left area of Edit window) is activated. The button looks like what you see in Figure 1.23.

Figure 1.23

The Tab to Transient button

Once that's finished, I'll return to the beginning of the track (which is not strictly necessary, but is convenient in this case) and press the Tab key until I reach the first beat of the measure that I want to capture. Next, press and hold the Shift key on your computer keyboard and continue pressing the Tab key until you reach the first beat of the measure that you *don't* want to keep. If you're following along, your selection might look like Figure 1.24. (Take note of the Edit Selection area to help you out.)

Figure 1.24

A loopable selection

13

Of course, you should always let your ear be your guide when making these sorts of selections. When you've got your selection, you have a number of options:

- **Trim Region.** Because you have a selected area, Pro Tools can crop the region to match the selected area. You can find the Trim Region menu item under the Edit drop-down menu, or just press Ctrl+T (Windows) or Command+T (Mac).
- **Separate Region.** This will create region boundaries at the beginning and end of your selection. You can find this option in the Edit drop-down menu as well, or just press Ctrl+E (Windows) or Command+E (Mac).
- **Capture Region.** This will create a brand-new region of your selected area without changing the region that is currently on your track. You'll find this little goodie in the Region drop-down menu or you can just press Ctrl+R (Windows) or Command+R (Mac). You'll be prompted to name your region once you select this menu item.

In this case, I've chosen the Capture Region option because it is very non-destructive, and I want to take a second look at this rhythm track. One of the things I like to do is find loops in unusual places. In this example, there is a second measure that overlaps the measure that was originally captured. Using Tab to Transient once again, I selected another area, as shown in Figure 1.25.

Figure 1.25
A second loop!

If I use the Capture Region option again, I'll have not one, but two good loopable regions in my region list! If you're following along with this session, you'll see the same.

That being said, there is a very common problem that rears its ugly head when doing this sort of work, and there's about a 50-percent chance that it's happened to you. After making your selection, you *may* have found that after playing the area (using loop playback) to check your work, you lose your selection. It's very frustrating! This is actually not a bug or a malfunction (there are plenty of production methods that do use this mode), but the question remains: How do you change the mode so that you don't keep losing your selection? Here's how:

What Is a Transient?

1. From the Setup drop-down menu, choose Preferences.
2. In the Preferences window, navigate to the Operation tab.
3. The first box, named Timeline Insertion Follows Playback, is checked. Simply uncheck it. Problem solved!

> **NOTE**
>
> If you're like me, you will commonly work in *both* modes. Instead of opening the Preferences window all the time, you can just press Start+N (Windows) or Control+N (Mac) to toggle this preference on and off.

There's another neat little feature that comes in quite handy—it's called Separate Region at Transients. This is a variation on the standard Separate Region command, but it will make region boundaries at each transient, as opposed to your selection or timeline insertion. This is very useful for isolating individual hits in a beat and is very easy to use.

1. Select the area that you want to separate at each transient.
2. From the Edit drop-down menu, choose Separate Region (which will reveal a second menu), then choose At Transients, as shown in Figure 1.26.

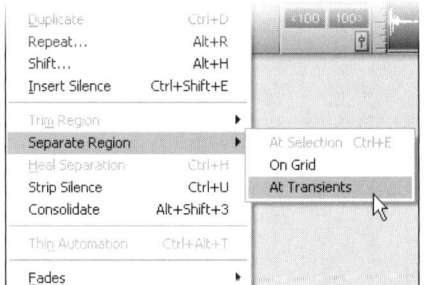

Figure 1.26
Separating your selection at transients

3. The Pre-Separate Amount window that shows up (see Figure 1.27) will allow you to select a pre-separate amount. Here, you have the option of entering a value (in milliseconds), which will move the region boundaries that are to be created before the region. You may need to enter an amount if you find that the leading edges of your transients are being cut off.

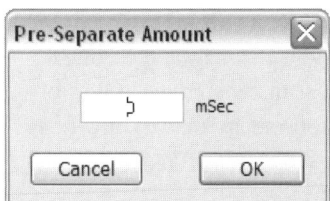

Figure 1.27
Pre-Separate Amount

CHAPTER 1 ■ Getting a Stronger Start

What you'll get when you're finished is a series of regions on your timeline, separated at each transient (see Figure 1.28), plus a number of new regions in your region list. You can now use each individual hit as a brand-new region and modify your beat, or you can create new ones from scratch!

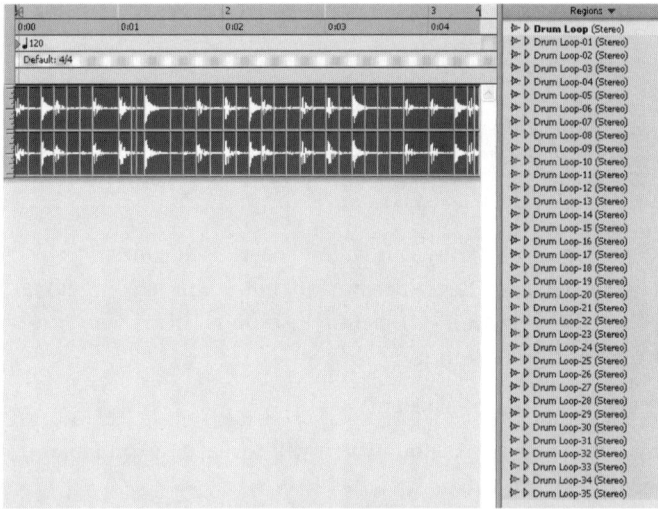

Figure 1.28

After separating at transients

> **CAUTION!**
>
> When we broke down this larger region into many much smaller ones, our edit density increased. High edit density requires more effort from your Pro Tools system and, in extreme cases (many tracks with large numbers of tiny regions and fades), can cause playback problems. If you encounter such problems, consider changing edit playlists (which we'll discuss more in the next chapter) and/or consolidating your regions.

Using Rex Files

Before we leave this chapter behind, I'd like to very quickly talk about Rex and ACID files. Some readers may be well aware of these useful tools (if you're one of them, feel free to skip to the next chapter), but in my travels, I've found that most folks don't know too much about what these beauties can do.

When I try to explain what a Rex file is, the description that works best for me is to call it *intelligent audio*. What I mean is that a Rex or ACID file (most commonly used for beats and other loop-based work) can follow your session's MIDI tempo, even though it is audio through and through. Many people think that this following of tempo is the result of some sort of time compression or expansion, but in reality, that's not what's going on. Good thing, too—too much TCE can adversely affect the sound of your audio.

Using Rex Files

Pro Tools systems these days come with a disc's worth of Rex files as part of their Ignition Pack (the disc is called *Deus Rex Machina*), so you've probably already got a lot of raw material to work with. Just to get you started, I'll run down a very effective way to get Rex files into your session.

> **NOTE**
>
> You can follow along with the examples I'll use by launching the session named Chapter 1c, which you'll find on the disc included with this book.

Let's say that I've got a MIDI or Instrument track with an arpeggiated virtual synth. One of the big advantages of plug-in instruments (such as Xpand!, which I've used in my session) is that the arpeggiator follows my MIDI tempo. Now, what I really want is an audio loop that'll do the same. I also want to import an audio loop that will sound good at the current tempo of my song. (As some of you may have experienced, applying time compression or expansion to an otherwise good-sounding loop can give you a bad surprise.) Previewing your loop is the first place where Rex files will shine.

After opening your Workspace browser, navigate to the location of your Rex files. (I've included one for you to work with, in the Rex File for Chapter 1c folder.) If you take a look at the example in Figure 1.29, you'll notice the name of this particular Rex file is 139 Extra Percussion 1.rx2, which tells me that the loop was created at a tempo of 139 BPM. How will it sound at 120 BPM, my session's tempo? No problem—the Rex file will automatically play back at my *session's* current tempo! Just click the speaker icon to preview the loop (see Figure 1.29).

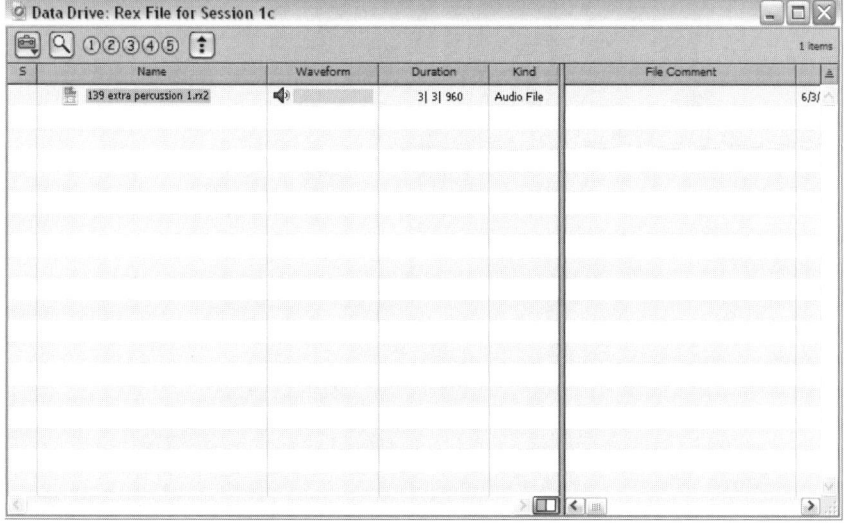

Figure 1.29
A Rex file in the browser

When you find a loop that you like, you'll want to import it into your session. Here's a little tip you might like: Click and hold on the file's icon (your cursor will turn into a hand) and drag your cursor right over to the track list. When you see the gray box in the list, as shown in Figure 1.30, you can let go. This will not only import your audio, but it will also create a new track with your Rex file at the very beginning.

Figure 1.30

Importing to the region list

The next window (shown in Figure 1.31) will ask whether you want to import the tempo of the Rex file (in this case, 139 BPM) into your session or leave your session's tempo the way it is (in this case, 120 BPM) and have the Rex file conform to that tempo. If you like your song's existing tempo, click Don't Import.

Figure 1.31

Rex import options

What you'll wind up with is an audio region that follows the tempo of your session. It gets better, though—if you speed up your song or slow it down, the Rex region will *continue* to track your MIDI tempo. If you're following along with this example, try deactivating the Conductor and adjusting the tempo with the Tempo slider to get a sense of how these files can be used.

> **TIP**
>
> Sometimes, especially in larger facilities, the speakers that you audition with shouldn't be your main speakers. First, it can be distracting to clients who are concerned with other parts of the creative process. Second, if you've turned up the volume of your mains, you could damage your speakers (and your ears!) by blasting an auditioned file. If you have the available outputs (Mbox 2 Pro or greater), you might consider selecting an audition path *other* than your main speakers. It's easy to do: Just go to the I/O Setup window (under the Setup drop-down menu), then navigate to the Output tab. Once there, you'll see Audition Paths in the lower-center area of the window. Simply choose an alternative output for your auditioned files.
>
> Of course, you'll have to have amplification and speakers attached to those outputs to be able to hear your auditioned files, but many find the convenience of separate auditioning speakers well worth the effort!

What makes Rex files so interesting and powerful to use is that they span everything we've covered in this chapter so far. They are clearly audio files, but they are also able to follow your MIDI tempo map and even respond to meter changes, so your understanding of these basic MIDI concepts will serve you well. They do this by somehow linking each individual transient to a musical location, rather than an immutable sample location commonly used by other audio regions. We'll delve even deeper into how this works later in this book, but for now, you should have the tools you need to use Rex files to their advantage.

That's all for the basics. Next we'll look at some ways to work smarter in the Edit window!

2 Working Smarter

Now that the musical and MIDI basics of how beats work are behind us, let's turn our focus toward working *smarter*. There are a number of techniques that, though they've been part of the Pro Tools arsenal for a while, sometimes are not used to their greatest advantage. In this chapter, we'll take a close look at some of those features, with an eye toward adding their power to your beatsmanship. When you're finished, you'll see how beat-making can be done more quickly and efficiently, leaving you with more time for creativity and fun. In this chapter, you'll learn how to:

- Use Edit Playlists to your advantage with both Audio *and* MIDI tracks
- Make the TCE Trim tool work best for beats
- Differentiate between timeline and edit selections, and use this difference to your advantage
- Manage your resources to get the most out of your Pro Tools system

> **NOTE**
> The features described in this chapter will not only help your beat work, but nearly all facets of your creative work!

Working with Edit Playlists

Okay, I'm going to get on my soapbox now (fair warning) and say that Edit Playlists are probably the best-kept secret in Pro Tools. They have been around for quite some time now, and still, too many folks seem to be unaware of them or their power. Let's take a quick look at what they are, and then we'll talk about how you can use them to make your beat-making—and all your work—more flexible.

Simply put, an Edit Playlist is any arrangement of regions on a track. For example, suppose you've got a track named Drums 1, upon which you've put a drum loop that you're thinking of using. You further put a compressor on your drums to punch it up and automate a little volume. That's all

CHAPTER 2 ■ Working Smarter

great, but there's more power to that track than meets the eye. To be technically correct, the name Drums 1 isn't so much the track name (though that term is often used), but more of an Edit Playlist name. In any Pro Tools session (HD, LE, or M-Powered), there is an *infinite* number of Edit Playlists that you can create within a session. So, how do you create them and use them? Let's take a look at a few common ways to work with playlists.

Using Edit Playlists to Create Alternate Edits

> **NOTE**
>
> In this next section, I'm using a session named Chapter 2a, which you'll find on the disc included with this book. Bear in mind that you'll need to copy the folder to your hard drive before you'll be able to work with it.
>
> Here's a session that I used some years ago for some basic website background audio. I've mixed the drums down to a single drum track, plus rendered down some instrumental stems for simplicity's sake.

Here's a common situation: You've got a drum track that works reasonably well with the rest of the music, but you'd like to be able to experiment with some changes *while still keeping your existing work intact*. It'd be even better if you could quickly change between your original track and your modified one (especially if you have an impatient client to whom you'd like to show multiple versions!). In the case of the Chapter 2a session, I'd like to hear this track without the snare hits, just to see how it works. We can easily do this through the use of alternate playlists (with a little help from Separate Region at Transients, which we covered in the previous chapter).

Because I want to keep my track as it is in addition to making my changes, I'm going to start off by creating a duplicate playlist. Essentially, this creates a duplicate arrangement of regions, but in a very special way. Follow along with these steps, and you'll see what I mean.

1. Click the small arrow button to the immediate right of the "track" name, as shown in Figure 2.1. This button, technically called the Playlist Selector, will reveal a menu of Edit Playlist–related functions.

Figure 2.1

The Playlist Selector button

Playlist Selector button

2. From the Playlist menu, choose Duplicate, as shown in Figure 2.2.

Figure 2.2
Duplicating a playlist

3. Once that's finished, you'll see a window that allows you to name your new playlist. In this case, because I'm going to be removing the snare, I've named it No Snare, as shown in Figure 2.3—clever, huh?

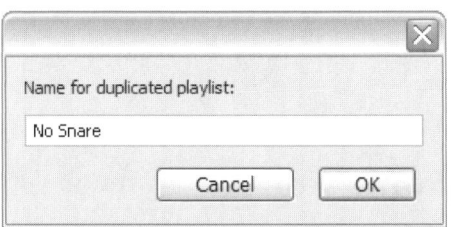

Figure 2.3
Naming your new playlist

You'll see that your "track" name (which we now know is more accurately described as the *playlist* name) has changed to match your new Edit Playlist's name. Now you can have at it! In this case, what I wanted to do was create a track with no snare hits, and here's how I did it.

1. Select the entire drum region.
2. Separate the region at each transient. (For a very quick way to do this, see Chapter 1.)
3. Select each snare drum hit and press the Delete key to remove it.
4. If you listen back to your track, you'll hear clicks as a result of deleting these regions. These are caused by the fact that you didn't cut your regions on the zero volt line. This is something we'll talk more about later, but for now, you can treat these symptoms by fading out each region that precedes a gap (where a snare hit used to be).

> **NOTE**
>
> If you want to see these steps in their completed form, you can open the session named Chapter 2a – Finished.

Here's the payoff to this hard work: You can now change between your original version and your modified versions quickly and easily (and even *during playback*) by going back to the Playlist menu and choosing the desired playlist, as shown in Figure 2.4. It gets even better when you consider that you have an *infinite* number of Edit Playlists in any given Pro Tools session, so you can create *many* different versions of any track (Audio or MIDI)!

CHAPTER 2 ■ Working Smarter

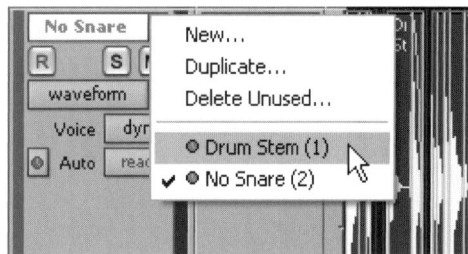

Figure 2.4

Changing between playlists

> **NOTE**
>
> Though you can switch playlists during playback, you'll have to be patient and listen to your previous playlist for a little while before the new one kicks in. This is not a malfunction of Pro Tools, so don't worry!

Using Edit Playlists to Create Alternate Tracks

So you now see the advantage of alternate playlists to create alternate versions of an existing track, but we'll very quickly go one step further and see how you can create brand-new "tracks" while keeping some of your more critical settings intact.

> **NOTE**
>
> In this next section, I'm using a session named Chapter 2b, which you'll find on the disc included with this book. I've used two plug-in effects in this—Compressor/Limiter Dyn 3 (a free download, if it didn't come with your Pro Tools installation disc) and D-Verb.
>
> This session is similar in many regards to the previous session, but notice that a plug-in has been placed on the drum track's insert (compressor), and a send is used to route dry audio over to an Aux track for some reverb. These are both classic examples of how you would implement dynamic-based and time-based effects in Pro Tools.

Here's another real-world example: You've got a drum track in your song and you want to go further than modifying it with some edits—you want a whole new track. Of course, you could create a whole new track (which will use up more of your valuable voices), recreate the routing, and *finally* get to the business of creating the track. You can then go through the process of muting the track that you don't want to hear, but you do run the risk of getting blasted with two drum tracks playing at the same time. Let's do the job more efficiently with playlists.

Because you're not going to be building upon a previously existing playlist, you will choose the New menu item after you click the Playlist Selector button, as shown in Figure 2.5.

Working with Edit Playlists

Figure 2.5
Creating a new playlist

When you're done with that step, you'll be asked to name the playlist, and then you'll immediately see a blank, virginal track. If you're following along with this example, you'll find an audio file in the Audio Files folder called Do You Like This One Better. Go ahead and put it on your new playlist, and you've got a brand-new rhythm track for your song—without losing the old one! You can start playback (the Loop Playback option works well in this example) and switch between the playlists to your heart's content!

If you're following along with this example, you'll find another added benefit to working with playlists in this way, rather than needlessly creating additional tracks. You'll notice that the inserts, sends, I/O assignments, and pretty much everything *except* the regions on the track remain a part of the *track*, regardless of which *playlist* you use on that track!

> **NOTE**
>
> If you want to see what this example should look like completed, you can open the session named Chapter 2b – Finished.

There is one limitation to playlists of which you should be aware. (You *knew* there'd be a catch, didn't you?) Pro Tools' automation remains part of the track, as opposed to being part and parcel of the Edit Playlist. I've taken the liberty of building this aspect into the example session—you'll hear a two-measure fade-in regardless of which playlist you choose. Many times this will work in your favor, but sometimes it won't, and you need to be aware of this condition of tracks and playlists.

That being said, there's an interesting little workaround that you can use in the right circumstances. Read on . . .

Using Playlists on MIDI Drum Tracks

Although it *is* true that Pro Tools' automation (things such as volume, pan, mute, plug-in automation, and so on) is part of a given track as opposed to linked to any particular Edit Playlist, there *is* a way to approach the limitation from a different angle when it comes to MIDI data. The trick lies in understanding that there's Pro Tools automation, and then there's MIDI "automation." Let's take a look at one more session before we leave Edit Playlists behind.

> **NOTE**
>
> In this next section, I'm using a session named Chapter 2c. This will look *very* familiar at this point, except that in this case, we're using MIDI drums on an Instrument track.

If you take a look at the Track View Selector menu (by clicking the Track View Selector button, just below the Record, Solo, and Mute buttons) on an Instrument track, you'll see a segmented list of all kinds of data that can be viewed (see Figure 2.6). The top section of the menu, starting with Blocks and ending with Controllers, lists the kinds of data that are saved with individual Edit Playlists. Of course, Blocks and Regions are included with Edit Playlists as they are in any Audio track, but the other kinds of data in this top section, being MIDI data, are also easily contained in Edit Playlists. The items in the bottom segment of the menu (Volume, Mute, and Pan(s)) are Pro Tools automation and are associated with the track itself, regardless of the Edit Playlist that is currently being used on that track.

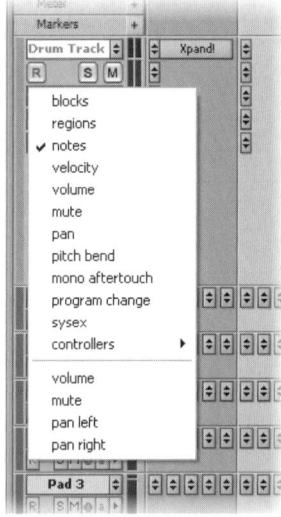

Figure 2.6

Track view options on an Instrument track

You'll note that Volume, Mute, and Pan appear twice on this list. So what's the difference between Pro Tools automation and its MIDI counterparts? On one hand, Pro Tools automation is of a significantly higher resolution than MIDI data, so your values will be more accurate and your transitions smoother if you use Pro Tools automation. On the other hand, though, because data such as MIDI volume is structurally similar to any other kind of MIDI data, you can embed volume changes in the Edit Playlist itself, in a way giving you the ability to change your MIDI mixes with the same ease with which you change your regions. Let's end our exploration of playlists with a quick look at how to get some flexibility with your mixes.

Working with Edit Playlists

In this example, I would like to try out my track with a two-measure fade-in, without losing my original drum track. If you're following along with the example session, create a *duplicate* playlist and name it Drums Fade-In. Once that's finished, change your view format to MIDI Volume, as shown in Figure 2.7.

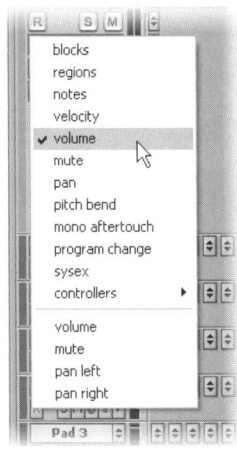

Figure 2.7

Choosing MIDI Volume as a Track view format

Next, I'm going to use the Straight Line option of the Pencil tool to draw a two-bar fade-in. You can use any Pencil tool mode that you like, of course, but if you do happen to use the Straight Line tool, your track should look something like Figure 2.8.

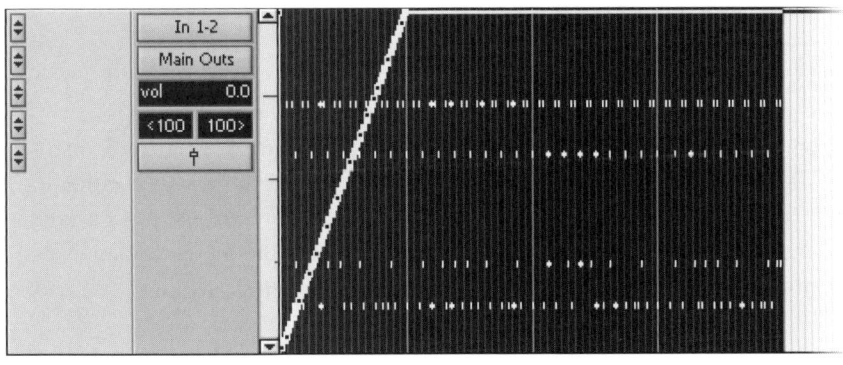

Figure 2.8

A two-measure fade-in using MIDI volume data

There—you're finished! If you change your Edit Playlist on the Instrument track, you'll see that the volume line will change with the playlist—something that *doesn't* happen with regular Pro Tools automation!

27

CHAPTER 2 ■ Working Smarter

Taking a Second Look at the TCE Trim Tool

If you've been working with beats for some time, you've almost certainly used TCE (Time Compression/Expansion) in some situation. Commonly, you can use TCE to match two audio beat segments of different tempos (tempi), or to get a melodic phrase to match a certain beat. In the most basic form, TCE plug-ins can be found in the AudioSuite drop-down menu, by going to the Other submenu. In this submenu, you'll find (at the very least) Digidesign's own Time Compression Expansion plug-in, shown in Figure 2.9.

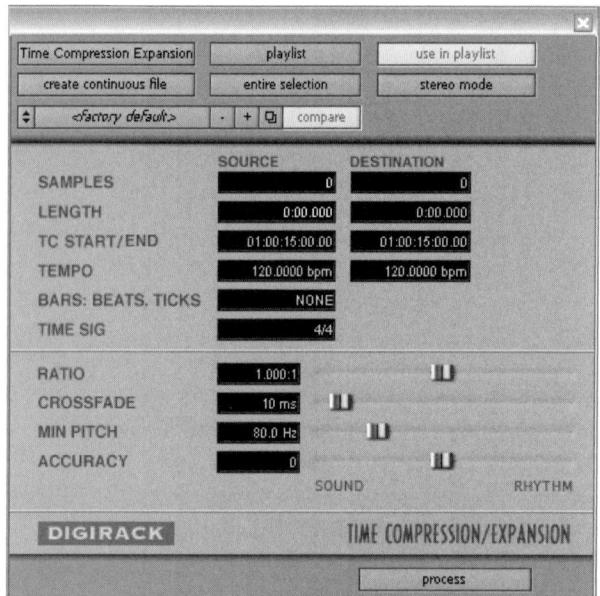

Figure 2.9
The DigiRack Time Compression Expansion AudioSuite plug-in, included with every Pro Tools system

You can use this file-based plug-in to process any selected area of audio, just as you would use any other AudioSuite process, but in the case of TCE, there's another powerful way to use this plug-in—by using the TCE Trim tool. If you haven't used it before, it's easy to access: Just click and hold on the Trim tool at the top of the Edit window and choose TCE from the menu that appears. After you make this selection, your Trim tool will change its appearance, as shown in Figure 2.10.

 Figure 2.10
The TCE Trim tool

The TCE Trim tool now gives you the option to change the speed of your beat with the same ease that you can change region boundaries. This gets especially quick and easy to use when you happen to be in a usable Grid mode of operation. The following example will show some basic—and not so basic—ways to get the job done.

28

Taking a Second Look at the TCE Trim Tool

> **NOTE**
>
> To follow along with this example, launch the session named Chapter 2d, which you'll find on the disc included with this book.
>
> What you'll see in this session is four regions of different lengths. Frustratingly, if you listen to each of these regions individually, you'll hear that each track is eight measures long. What we'll have to do is to conform these regions so that they are all the same length.

In the example, the Piano track is at the desired tempo, so we'll need to alter the Kick, Hi-Hat, and Relaxing Arp tracks to match it. Coincidently, the Piano track is exactly eight bars long (this is a coincidence that we'll look at more deeply in Chapter 4), so we can easily use the Grid mode to our advantage. Just follow these easy steps!

1. Make sure you're in Grid mode by clicking the Grid button in the upper-left corner of the Edit window. This way, your Trim tool will automatically snap to the nearest grid point. Make sure that the Grid button is blue and not purple. (A purple button means you're in Relative Grid mode, which we'll talk about in Chapter 4.)

2. In this particular session, the Grid value is set to 1 second, which is certainly not a music-friendly value. The next step is to change the Grid value to something a bit more relevant. Click the Grid Value pop-up button, as shown in Figure 2.11.

Figure 2.11

The Grid Value pop-up button

3. From there, select Bars:Beats grid format (in the lower section of the menu shown in Figure 2.12).

4. Also in Figure 2.12, you'll see a list of musical grid values at the top of the list from which you can choose. In this particular example, 1 Bar will do just fine.

5. From this point, the rest is simple. Making sure that you're using the TCE Trim tool, just click on a region boundary that you want to change and let the work you did setting up your grid value pay off. Taking a look at Figure 2.13, you'll see the 8-Bars Hi-Hat_01 region being changed to match the 8-Bar Piano_01 region. Because I happen to prefer the tempo of the Piano track in this case, I won't need to apply any TCE to that track. Once I let go of the Trim tool, a progress bar will quickly appear, resulting in a new region on the Hi-Hat track named Hi-Hat-TCEX_01.

CHAPTER 2 ■ Working Smarter

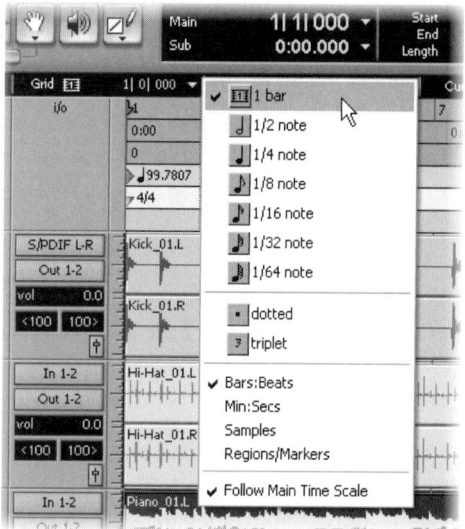

Figure 2.12

Setting an appropriate grid format and value

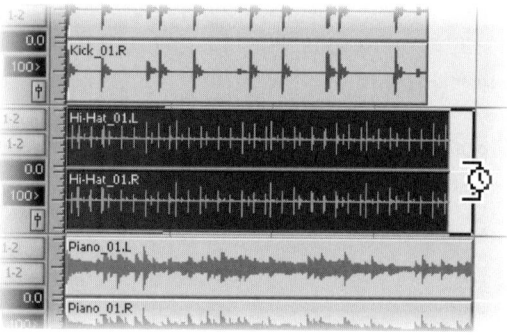

Figure 2.13

Using the TCE Trim tool

Making the TCE Trim Tool Sound Better

Though the TCE Trim tool is a powerful feature, there's no denying that it can have some audible effects that you might *not* like. Most commonly, you might be plagued with a kind of flange type of artifact in the upper frequencies. Is this simply the price to pay for this kind of process, for better or worse? To an extent, yes, but if you dig just a little deeper, you will be able to get the best possible performance from your TCE Trim tool.

The important thing to understand is that the TCE Trim tool is simply another way of accessing an AudioSuite Time Compression plug-in. In a basic Pro Tools system, the program code that drives the AudioSuite plug-in is exactly the same code that the TCE Trim tool taps into. With that in mind, take a second to look at Figure 2.9. You'll see a number of editable parameters. Go ahead, I'll wait. . . .

Taking a Second Look at the TCE Trim Tool

Welcome back. You've seen that this plug-in has a number of parameters at the bottom of the window, which you can tweak to make your AudioSuite TCE-ing sound better. In particular, I've found the bottom parameter (Accuracy) to be very effective in reducing that bothersome flanging sound. Of course, making these changes will affect how the AudioSuite plug-in processes selected audio, but can it make your TCE Trim tool sound better? Actually yes, but you'll have to do a little preliminary work to help out your TCE Trim tool. Don't fret—you'll be able to do these steps quickly once you get the hang of it.

> **NOTE**
> If you've made any changes to the Chapter 2d session, you might want to apply a Revert to Saved at this point to start again from scratch.

1. If you haven't already, switch to Grid mode and set your grid to 1 Bar, as outlined in Steps 1 through 4 in the previous section.
2. The next step is to set some useful plug-in presets in the Time Compression Expansion. Here's an example: After you've got the TCE plug-in window open, move the Accuracy slider fully to the Rhythm extreme. Once that's finished, click the Settings Menu button, as shown in Figure 2.14.

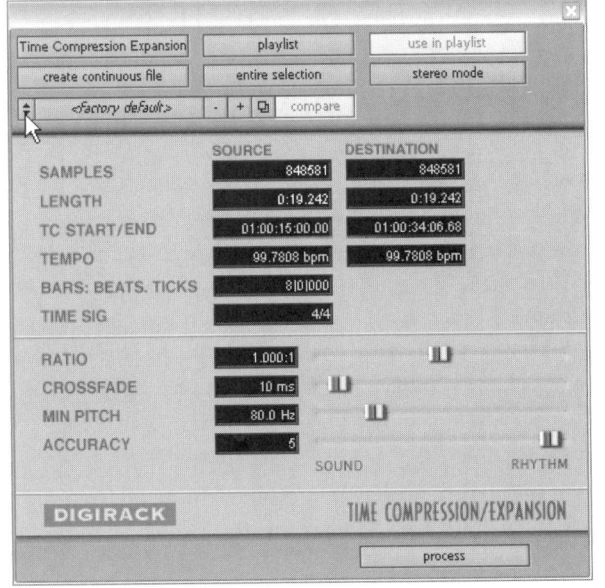

Figure 2.14
Getting ready to save a TCE preset

3. After you click on the Settings Menu button, click Save Settings As, as shown in Figure 2.15. The Save Effect Settings As window will appear.

31

CHAPTER 2 ■ Working Smarter

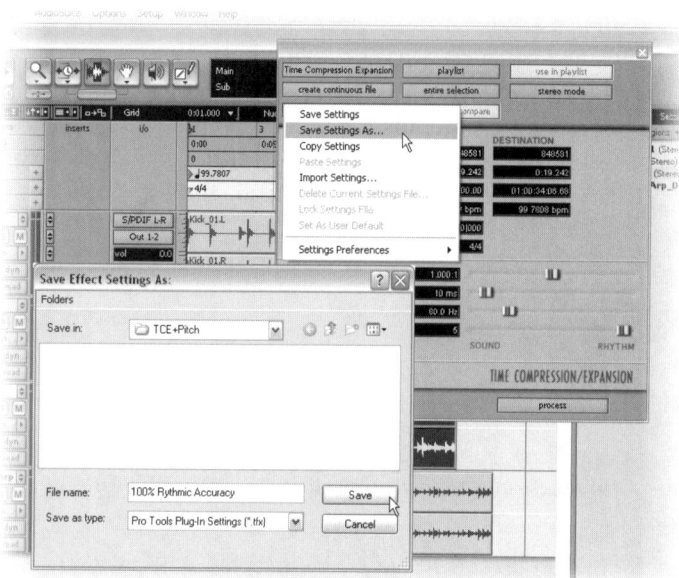

Figure 2.15
Creating a new TCE preset

4. In the Save Effect Settings As window, name your effect descriptively (I chose the name 100% Rhythmic Accuracy), and click the Save button, as shown in Figure 2.15.

5. Repeat Steps 2 through 4, but this time move the Accuracy slider all the way over to the Sound extreme. Remember to name the preset descriptively. For my example, I've chosen 100% Sound Accuracy for this preset name.

> **NOTE**
>
> When you save your effects presets, there are two places where you can store them, and it's important to know where your new presets will be created. Perhaps the most common place to store effects presets is in the Root Settings folder, which is typically a folder located on your computer's internal drive. (This is created automatically by Pro Tools, and though you can change the location of this folder, doing so is beyond the scope of this book.) The advantage of the Root Settings folder is that any session you open on this computer will have access to these presets. On the other hand, you can choose to save your plug-in presets to your Session folder, which will create a plug-in setting subfolder in your current session. This choice has the advantage of being as portable as your session itself and can be particularly handy if you're working in multiple studios using portable drives.
>
> For the purposes of this example, I'd recommend saving your presets to the Root Settings folder. You can access this submenu by clicking the Settings Menu button, as shown in Figure 2.16.

6. You're about halfway done. Now you'll need to let Pro Tools know which preset you want the TCE Trim tool to use. Go to the Setup drop-down menu, and then choose Settings Preferences.

Taking a Second Look at the TCE Trim Tool

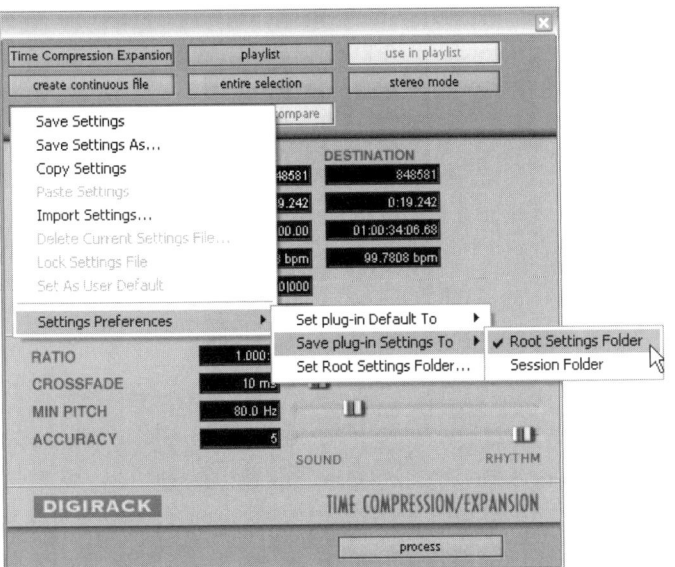

Figure 2.16
Knowing where your plug-in presets are stored is important!

7. When you're in the Preferences window, go to the Processing tab.
8. Click the TC/E Plug-In drop-down menu, as shown in Figure 2.17, and choose the TCE plug-in that you want. The list will show all the different TCE plug-ins that are supported for the TCE Trim tool, with uninstalled products being shown in grey. In this figure, the only installed TCE plug-in available for the TCE Trim tool is the Digidesign TC/E.

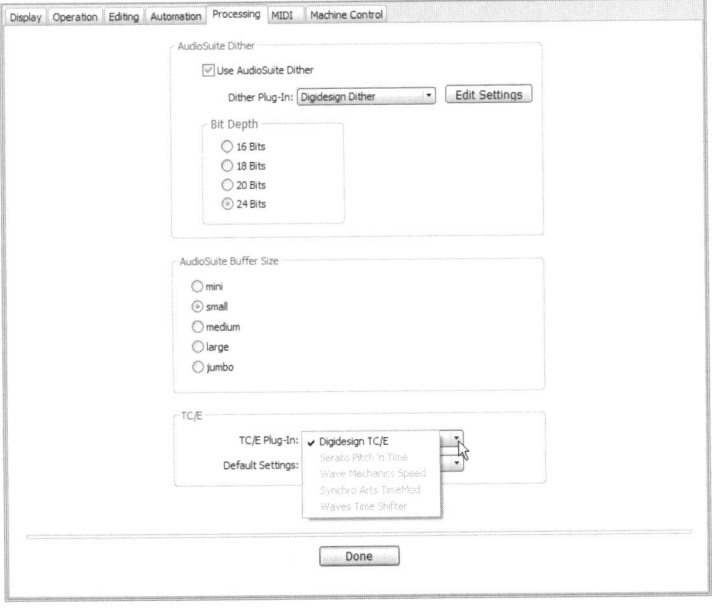

Figure 2.17
Selecting the best TCE plug-in for the TCE Trim tool

33

CHAPTER 2 ■ Working Smarter

9. Now you'll need to choose which preset you want the TCE Trim tool to use. Click the Default Settings drop-down menu (directly below the TC/E Plug-In drop-down menu in Figure 2.18).

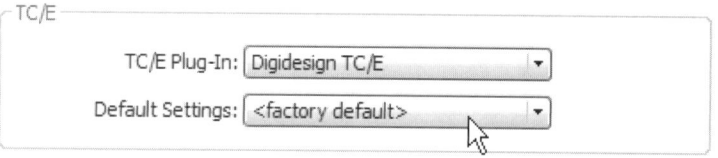

Figure 2.18

Getting ready to pick a preset

10. From the next menu (shown in Figure 2.19), choose the best preset for the work at hand. If your plug-in presets were saved to the Root Settings folder, you'll see them listed in the main menu, directly above Factory Default. If you've saved your presets to your session's Plug-In Settings subfolder, you'll find them in the Session's Settings Folder submenu. If you're following along with the tutorial session, choose the preset that you've created optimized for sound accuracy.

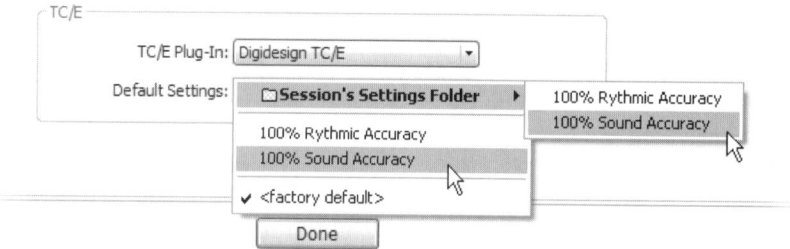

Figure 2.19

Picking a preset

Now you're set to make the TCE Trim tool work at a higher level. If you've followed along with the example, your TCE Trim tool will now use the 100% Sound Accuracy preset, which will minimize any flanging effect. This will be especially well suited to the Relaxing Arp track. When that's finished, you'll want to do some TCE trimming to the Kick and Hi-Hat tracks, but first go back to the Preferences window and switch the preset to 100% Rhythmic Accuracy to ensure that your beat's timing is as tight as possible.

> **NOTE**
>
> To see a completed version of this section, check out the Chapter 2d-Finished session.

TCE Edit to Timeline Selection

> **TIP**
>
> Digidesign is now offering a new free plug-in called Time Shift. (If you don't have it already, you can download it from Digidesign's website.) It is compatible with the TCE Trim tool starting with Pro Tools version 7.2. This plug-in has four distinct algorithms that you can use (Rhythmic is best for percussive beats), plus it has plenty of very usable presets for you to use, as shown in Figure 2.20. This means you won't have to create your own presets—just go to the Preferences window (the Processing tab), choose Time Shift as your TCE plug-in of choice, then pick the appropriate preset (Drums Rhythmic works well for drums).

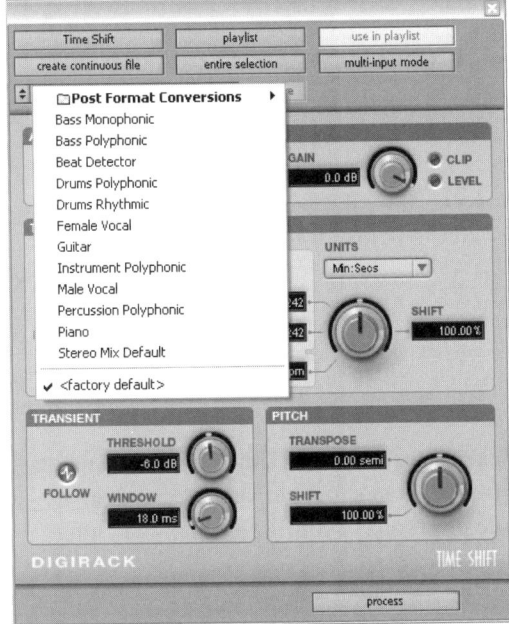

Figure 2.20

Digidesign's new Time Shift AudioSuite plug-in

TCE Edit to Timeline Selection

While we're on the topic of time compression and expansion, let's briefly touch on another variation of this powerful feature. This feature—called TCE Edit to Timeline Selection—is particularly nifty if you are trying to match particularly difficult sections of music (for whatever reason—strange meter, unknown tempo, and so on). Let's take a quick look at how this works.

> **NOTE**
>
> For this section, you can follow the example by launching the Chapter 2e session.

CHAPTER 2 ■ Working Smarter

> **CAUTION**
>
> This particular feature is only available for Pro Tools|HD systems or Pro Tools LE systems with the DV Toolkit 2 option installed. If neither of these applies to you, you'll be unable to follow this section's example.

Here's an example: In the Chapter 2e session, you'll hear a music stem and a drum stem track with a gap in the middle. On the bottom track, you'll hear a drum section that would work in that gap, except for the fact that it is at the wrong tempo (it's too fast). Unfortunately, the session's tempo doesn't match, and even the meter of this particular piece (7/4) would make this a real headache. Of course, I *could* drag the region into the right spot, then TCE trim it manually and hope for the best, but fortunately there's an easier way.

The trick lies in breaking out of a traditional way of working by breaking the connection between your edit selection and your timeline selection. Here's what I mean by this: *Normally*, when you make a selection in a region or track, that selection is mirrored in the timeline, as shown in Figure 2.21.

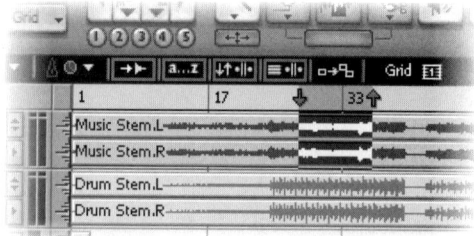

Figure 2.21
Edit and timeline selection—linked

This doesn't have to be the only way that you work, though—just click the Link Edit and Timeline Selection button (in the upper-left corner of the Edit window, and shown in Figure 2.22) so that the blue box disappears, and your edit selection and timeline selection will be completely independent. (Playback will be determined by your timeline selection.)

 Figure 2.22
The Link Edit and Timeline Selection button

Here are the steps to make unlinking your edit and timeline selections work for you.

1. Making sure that your edit and timeline selections are *linked*, select the area that you would like your region to occupy. In the case of the example, use the Selector tool to select the gap between the two instrumental sections.

> **TIP**
>
> You can click memory location #1 (Use This!) to make the correct selection for you.

TCE Edit to Timeline Selection

2. Deselect the Link Edit and Timeline Selection button. The blue box around the button will disappear.
3. Select the region that you want to occupy the selected time. In the case of this example, I've selected the Breakdown Drums_01 region on the Breakdown Drums track, as shown in Figure 2.23.

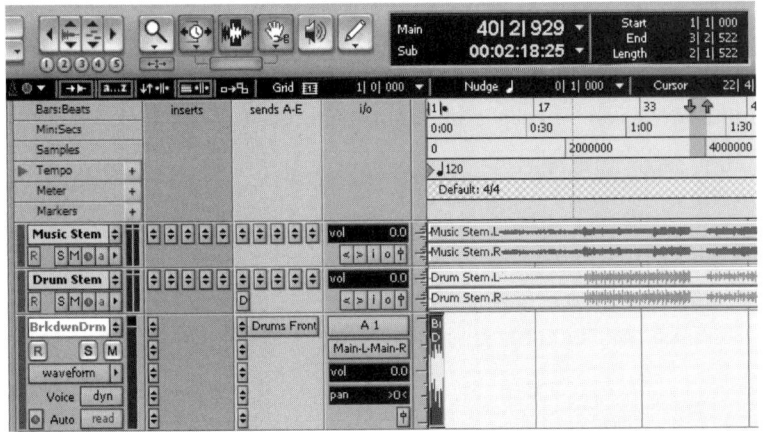

Figure 2.23
Ready to TCE Edit to Timeline Selection

4. From the Edit drop-down menu, choose TCE Edit to Timeline Selection, as shown in Figure 2.24. Your region will be immediately TCE'd and repositioned to conform to your timeline selection, again shown in Figure 2.24.

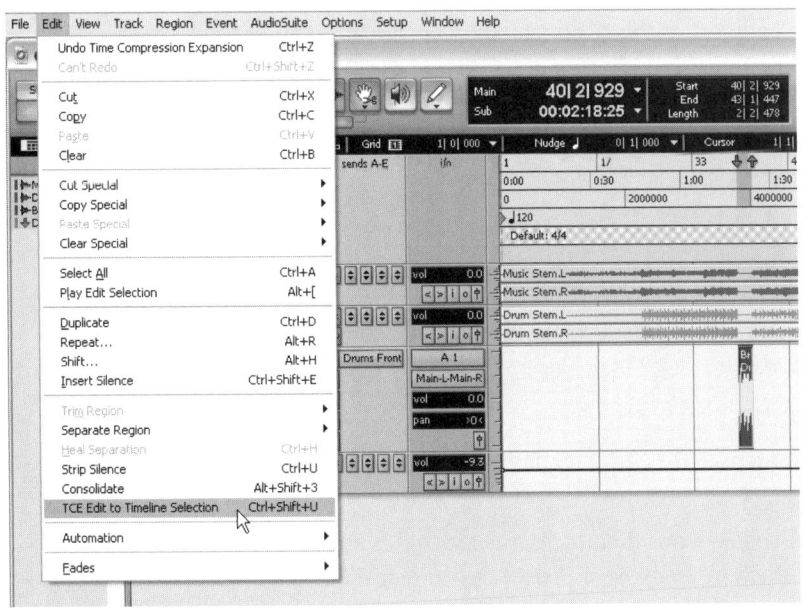

Figure 2.24
After TCE-ing the edit selection to the timeline selection

That's it! Now, only one more thing—make sure to re-enable the Link Edit and Timeline Selection button so that you can get back to working as usual!

Consolidating Regions

During the course of working with drums, you'll frequently find your sessions filling up with numerous tiny regions. Though this is a natural part of the editing process, it can also cause your computer to work harder than it really needs to. The fact is, every time a new region is played, your computer needs to go to your hard drive and retrieve it. The frequency of regions in your session is called *edit density*. Edit density can be caused in a number ways, including:

- Separating regions (including separating at grid points or at transients)
- Using Beat Detective
- Batch fading and edit smoothing (remember, fades are regions too!)

When your edit density reaches critical mass, your hard drive becomes unable to keep pace with the data requests. When it can't keep up, you'll get the friendly little message shown in Figure 2.25.

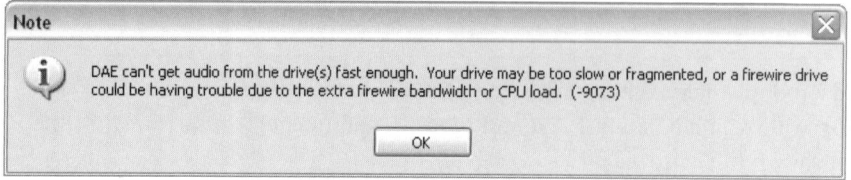

Figure 2.25
Too much edit density!

There's an elegantly simple solution to this problem—the Consolidate feature found in the Edit drop-down menu. Consolidate essentially re-renders a section of a track, including all the regions that might be within that selection, into a single audio file and a single region. Though a consolidated region sounds identical to the original section being consolidated, it can be much easier for your computer to handle. Here's how to do it.

> **NOTE**
>
> Open the session called Chapter 2f (be patient, it'll take a little longer than usual!) to get an example of a highly dense session. It's not much to listen to, but these 32 tracks of silent audio, chopped up every 41 milliseconds, should give your computer a run for its money!

1. Select the sections of dense edits. In the Chapter 2f session, select the entire 10 seconds of all 32 tracks!
2. From the Edit menu, choose Consolidate. Your selections will be rendered into a new contiguous region on a track-by-track basis. You'll notice that all of the original regions are

Consolidating Regions

still in your region list—don't worry, regions that aren't on the timeline don't contribute to edit density.

3. Now try to play your session again. It should perform *much* better!

> **NOTE**
>
> Sometimes, consolidation doesn't quite do the trick all on its own. If you're still getting the message shown in Figure 2.25, try increasing your DAE Playback Buffer. You can find this by going to the Setup drop-down menu, choosing Playback Engine, and selecting a higher DAE Playback Buffer setting, as shown in Figure 2.26. If that doesn't work, you may need to stop work and defragment your hard drive.

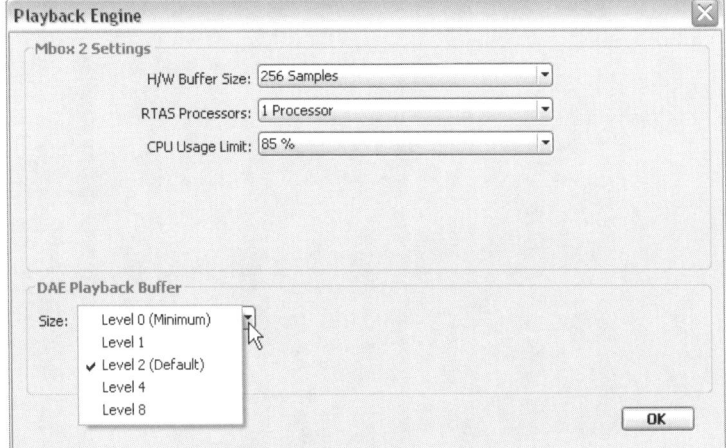

Figure 2.26

Changing the DAE Playback Buffer

> **TIP**
>
> If you take a look at the Chapter 2f-Finished session, you'll see the 32 tracks in their consolidated form. But what if you want to keep your edits, just in case you'll need them in the future? Not to worry—here's where the Edit Playlist skills you learned earlier in this chapter can pay off. Take a look at each track and you'll see the original playlist, complete with high edit density. I did this simply by creating a *duplicate* playlist, consolidating the duplicate, and going from there. Working in this way will give you the performance you need, while keeping your options open for later changes.

That's all for this chapter. Next, we'll take a look at really making the most of your MIDI beats!

39

3 MIDI and the Beat

Sometimes it seems that Pro Tools users fall into one of two camps: those who use MIDI and virtual instruments (along with the other audio features of Pro Tools, of course) and those who *don't*, and who generally avoid working with MIDI. Granted, there are a lot of ways to work that don't really involve MIDI, but even in those cases, a basic understanding of MIDI would occasionally help. When working with beats, MIDI is a key player (though not always an *obvious* one).

In my personal experience, I've found that once the mystery of MIDI is cracked, folks see a level of flexibility and power that in many ways outstrips the power of digital audio. In this chapter, we'll take a look at how to work with MIDI beats in Pro Tools, and you'll learn how to:

- View MIDI drum data in a different (and more powerful) way
- Explore session linearity
- Make quantization work for you
- Work more flexibly using MIDI Real-Time Properties
- Make MIDI sound tighter using Track Offsets

> **NOTE**
>
> For the purposes of this book, a certain basic understanding of how MIDI works within Pro Tools (how to set up tracks, how to use the basic editing tools, and so on) will be assumed. If you are interested in learning more about MIDI basics, you might want to take a look at *Pro Tools LE 7 Ignite!* (Thomson Course Technology PTR, 2005), written by yours truly. How's that for shameless self-promotion?!?

CHAPTER 3 ■ MIDI and the Beat

Taking a New Look at MIDI: Single Note Height

Back in the day, drum machines such as the famous Roland line used a *matrix* style of editor, arranging drum instruments in musical time based upon a sort of graph, as shown in Figure 3.1. Though matrix editors are arguably not the most flexible way of working with drums, the simple visual structure is often a great way to work.

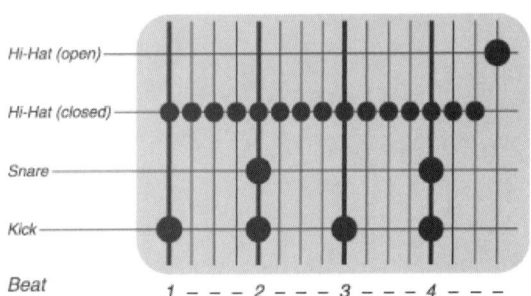

Figure 3.1
Old-school matrix drum editing

So, how do you get the simple beauty of a matrix editor and the power of Pro Tools' MIDI editing? Take a look.

> **NOTE**
>
> For the purposes of this chapter, I've created a simple session (named Chapter 3a) for you to work with. This session has four simple tracks, including one very *badly* performed (by your humble narrator) drum track. Again, for this session, you'll need to have the Xpand! plug-in (free) installed, or you'll need to reconfigure the Instrument tracks with other MIDI instruments.

Typically, MIDI data is viewed in a MIDI or Instrument track on a sort of sideways piano roll (see Figure 3.2). One unique thing about drums, though, is that drum tracks are usually broken down to a small number of different pitches (or MIDI note numbers) on a drum-by-drum basis. For example, in this session the kick drum is C1, the three different snares that I used are C#1, D1, and E1, the closed hi-hat is F#1, and so on. Although this sort of view is very usable when dealing with other kinds of instruments, it can be a bit bothersome with drums.

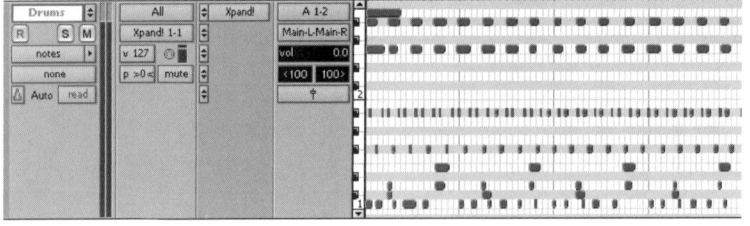

Figure 3.2
A drum kit on a single Instrument track

42

Building a matrix-style environment is a multistep process, but not a terribly difficult one. The first step is to separate each of these pitches (drum sounds) onto their own track.

1. Select the drum region that you wish to split. In the case of this example, select the single region on the Drums track.
2. From the Event drop-down menu, choose the MIDI menu item. From the submenu that appears, choose Select/Split Notes, as shown in Figure 3.3.

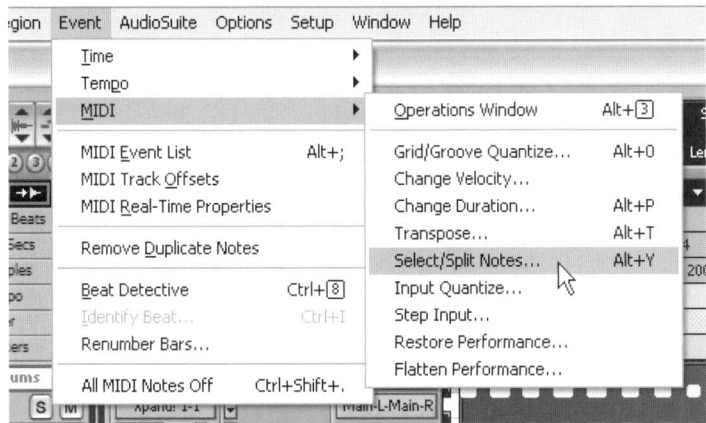

Figure 3.3
Getting ready to split your notes

3. The next thing you'll see is the MIDI Operations dialog box, set to the Select/Split Notes mode, as shown in Figure 3.4. For our purposes, here's how you would set it up:

   - In the Pitch Criteria section, choose All Notes.
   - In the Action section, you need to choose what is to be done. For starters, choose Split Notes.
   - In the leftmost drop-down menu, you will be able to choose whether you want to cut or copy your notes. If you choose the Cut option, the notes will be removed from the original track. Because I might want to have that region to use later, I'm going to choose Copy instead.
   - In the rightmost drop-down menu, you can choose to send your copied notes to the Clipboard (so you can paste all the notes to some other location later), to a new track (meaning a single new track, essentially copying the region), or to a new track per pitch, which is what we're going for, since our goal is to create discrete tracks each with a single drum on it. Please choose this third option.
   - If you have any continuous controller data that you don't want to lose (things such as parameter changes), check the Include All Continuous MIDI Data box.
   - Finally, click Apply. That's it!

CHAPTER 3 ■ MIDI and the Beat

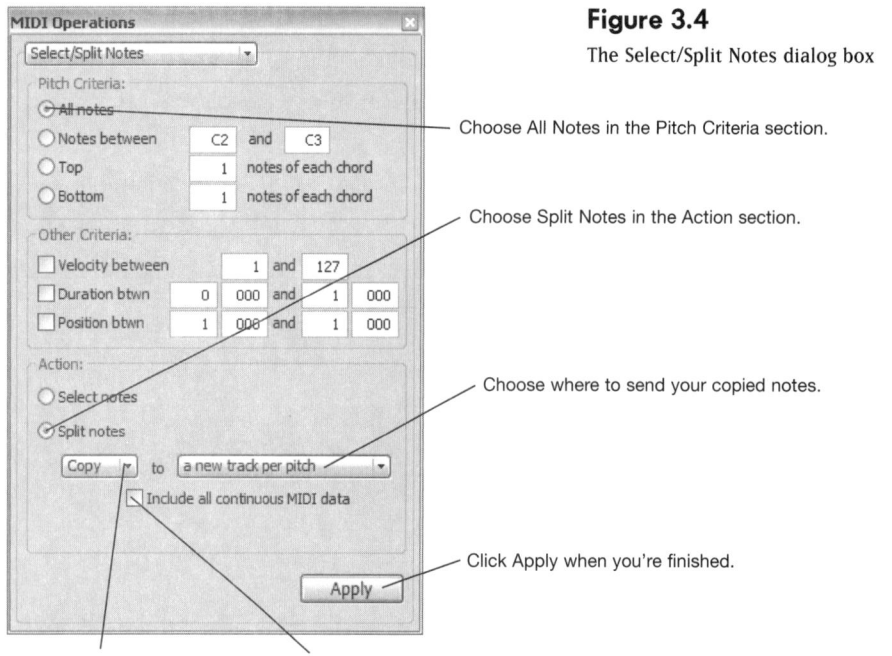

Figure 3.4
The Select/Split Notes dialog box

Choose All Notes in the Pitch Criteria section.

Choose Split Notes in the Action section.

Choose where to send your copied notes.

Click Apply when you're finished.

Choose Cut or Copy. Select this box if you have any continuous controller data you don't want to lose.

4. If you haven't seen a MIDI or Instrument track in Single Note height, you're seeing it (nine times over!) created beneath your original drum track (shown in Figure 3.5). Though it looks like you might be done, there's just a little more you need to do to finish things up.

5. Navigate to the small "o" (for Output) in the instrument column of your Instrument track, as shown in Figure 3.5

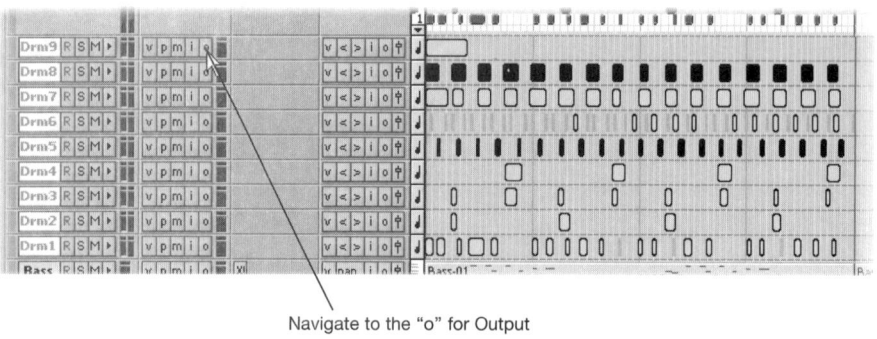

Figure 3.5
Getting ready to change your MIDI output on an Instrument track

Navigate to the "o" for Output

Taking a New Look at MIDI: Single Note Height

CAUTION

When you're working in Instrument tracks, there are actually *two* output selectors—the MIDI Output selector in the Instrument column, and the Audio Output selector in the I/O column. It's important to make sure you're changing your MIDI output and not your audio output. Changing your audio output will have no effect in this example and certainly won't achieve what we're after.

NOTE

Though the example I'm using in this section uses Instrument tracks, you can also split notes with MIDI tracks. In the case of a MIDI track, there is only one output selector, which is located in the I/O column of the MIDI track. If you're splitting a MIDI drum track into individual MIDI tracks, just click the MIDI Output button in the I/O column, as shown in Figure 3.6.

Figure 3.6
Getting ready to change your MIDI output on a MIDI track

6. From the list, choose the virtual instrument (or external MIDI output, if you're using a hardware MIDI device) that you want to hear for this track. In the case of this example, choose XPand! 1-Channel-1 because this is the virtual instrument that is giving you your drum sounds, as shown in Figure 3.7.

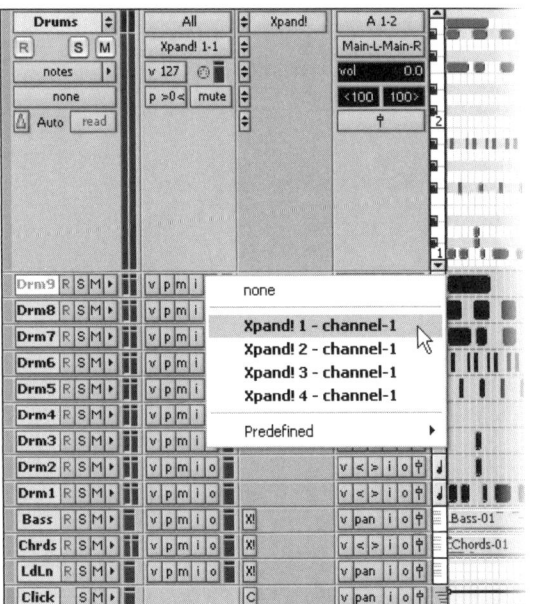

Figure 3.7
Setting your MIDI output

45

7. Repeat this step for all the newly created tracks (in the case of this example, there are nine!), so that all the "child" tracks are outputting to the plug-in on the "parent" track.

> **NOTE**
>
> Here's a way to get the job done faster: Select all the "child" tracks, then hold down Shift+Alt (Windows XP) or Shift+Option (Mac OS X). This will change the output on all selected tracks.

8. There's only one more thing that needs to be done: Because you don't want to hear both your child tracks and the original region, make the original region mute by selecting the region, then pressing Ctrl+M (Windows XP) or Command+M (Mac OS X). Your region will go grey, as shown in Figure 3.8. Be careful to mute your region using this method, rather than muting the entire track. If you do that, you won't hear the drums at all!

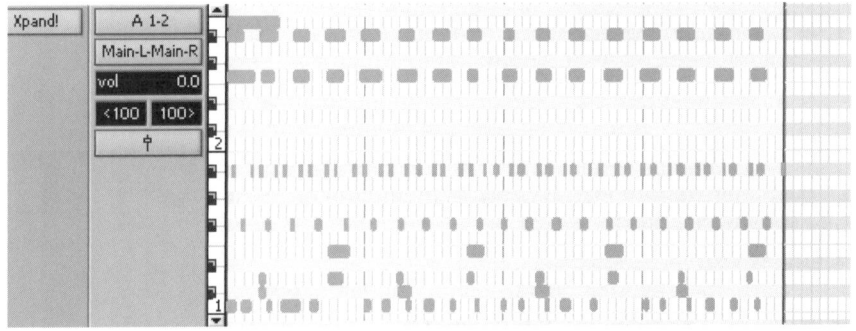

Figure 3.8

Muting your original region

Now you've got a different way of looking at—and working with—your drum kit, and one that just might be more enjoyable. I personally often work this way, and I even go a few steps forward by doing things like the following:

- Solo-safe (Ctrl-click [Windows XP] or Command-click [Mac OS X] the Solo button) the original Drum track so that even if I solo other tracks, the Drum track will not be muted
- Hide the original Drum track
- Rename individual tracks and regions descriptively by drum (kick, snare, hi-hat, and so on)
- Color-code individual tracks

> **NOTE**
>
> To see all of these steps in their completed form, take a look at the Chapter 3a-Finished session.

MIDI Quantize

If you've worked with MIDI beats at all, you've probably used the Quantize feature many times. If you're new to MIDI beats, you're most likely new to the idea of quantization as well. In either case, there's more to this powerful feature than meets the eye. Without spending too much time on this common MIDI process, let's take a look at how Pro Tools gets the job done and see how we can use it to our best advantage for our beats.

> **NOTE**
>
> If you'd like to follow along with the screenshots shown in this section, open up the Chapter 3b session.

If you're new to the Quantize feature, here's how to get to it: From the Event drop-down menu, choose MIDI, then Grid/Groove Quantize. Once you do this, the MIDI Quantize dialog box will open, as shown in Figure 3.9.

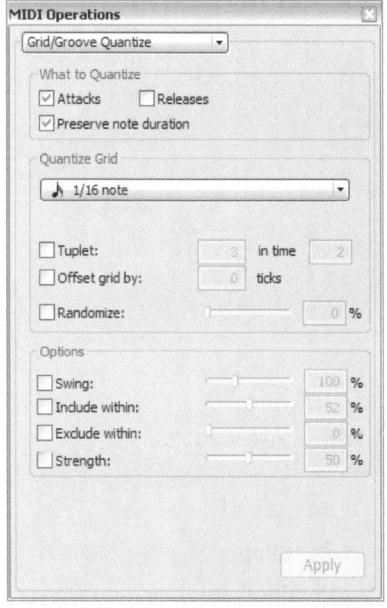

Figure 3.9

The MIDI Quantize dialog box

For those who might be unclear as to what exactly MIDI quantization does, it adjusts the timing of notes by conforming them to your existing tempo. For example, Figure 3.10 shows a sequence of 32 128th notes (very short!) within the space of one beat. This figure shows what the notes look like without any processing. Note that this is an artificially created track, specifically designed to show the finer functioning of quantization.

47

CHAPTER 3 ■ MIDI and the Beat

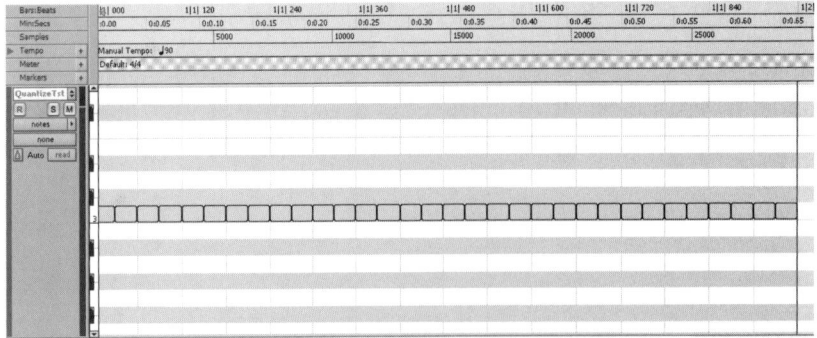

Figure 3.10
The unaltered track

If you take a look at the top section of the MIDI Quantize dialog box—called What to Quantize—it allows you to choose which parts of the note will be conformed to the grid (beginning or end). In this section, we can generally opt for Attacks and move on to the next section.

The next section, Quantize Grid, determines exactly how your notes will conform to the timeline. If you click the drop-down menu, you'll see a menu that looks like Figure 3.11.

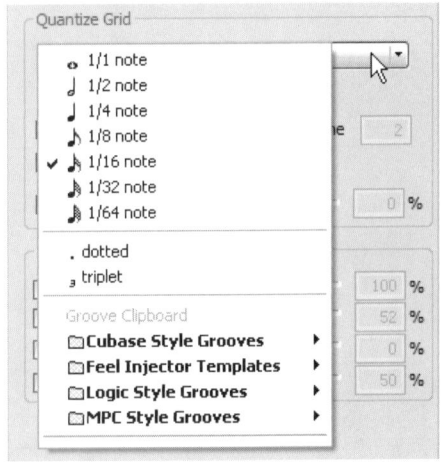

Figure 3.11
Quantization grid options

The top part of this menu refers to mathematically perfect spacing. For example, if you choose to quantize the unaltered track to sixteenth notes (as shown in Figure 3.11), you'll wind up stacking the notes into four neat piles (there are four sixteenth notes per beat), as shown in Figure 3.12. This is particularly useful if you're going for that hyper-accurate electronic feel.

The middle part of your grid allows you to quantize to the nearest triplet or dotted note. These two options modify the selection you make in the upper section of the list, so, for example, if you want to quantize to dotted sixteenth notes (admittedly not a common thing to do!), just select 1/16 Note from the top of the list, then go back to the list and select Dotted. The value you choose will be shown on the Quantize Grid drop-down button.

48

MIDI Quantize

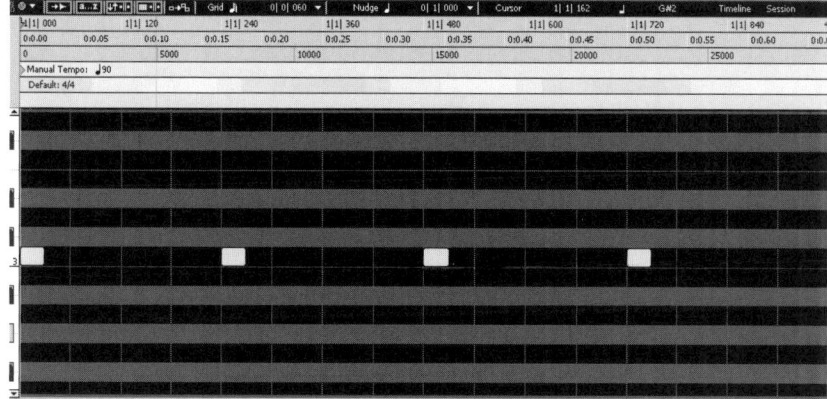

Figure 3.12
A straight sixteenth-note quantization

The bottom section of the Quantize Grid list is a list of groove quantize options. Basically speaking, Groove Quantize will still conform your notes to a grid, just not a mathematically perfect one. This is the way to go if you want to have more of a human feel to your drums. By selecting any of the options at the bottom of the list, you'll open a sub-listing of specific grooves to which you can quantize your selected notes. For example, if I go to the Feel Injector Templates menu item, and then choose Feel Injector 16th Shuffle, I'll see something like Figure 3.13.

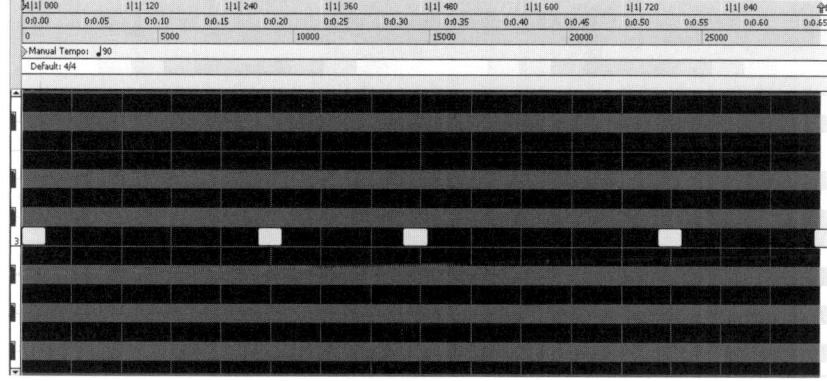

Figure 3.13
Groove quantization

Beyond this list, there are a number of options from which you can choose:

- **Tuplet:** This feature will allow you to fit a certain number of notes into a given space. For example, if you take this example and use the default sixteenth-note quantize and choose to Fit 3 in Time 2, you'll get six evenly spaced notes, as opposed to only four (a 3:2 ratio).
- **Offset Grid By:** This option allows you to set your notes to a fixed point ahead (by entering a negative value) or behind (by entering a positive value).

CHAPTER 3 ■ MIDI and the Beat

> **TIP**
>
> The Offset Grid By feature is particularly useful when working with beats. If you carefully analyze many grooves (such as funk beats, for example), you may find that the snare drum really "lays back" (or plays late relative to the tempo) to get a real sense of a feel. By quantizing your snare notes with a small positive offset (the number of ticks you choose depends on your tempo), you might be pleased with the results!

- **Randomize:** When you add Randomize to your grid quantize, your notes will be freely positioned within a certain percentage of the grid. For example, take a look at Figure 3.14 to see a sixteenth-note quantization with 20% randomization factored in.

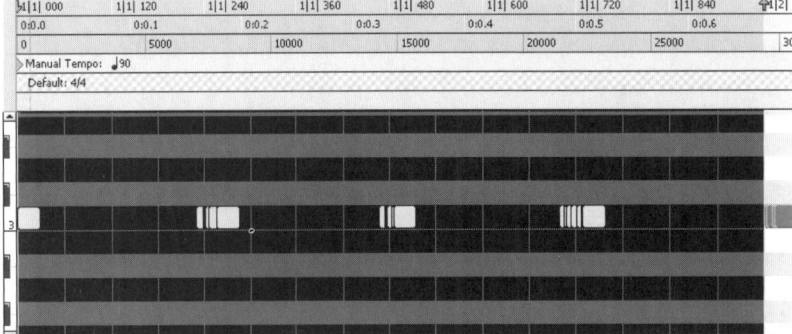

Figure 3.14

Sixteenth-note quantization with 20% randomization

> **CAUTION**
>
> Many folks equate *random* with *human* and put a little randomization into their MIDI to give it that imperfect human feel. That's all well and good, but there are times to use it and times to avoid it. Take drums, for example: When a drummer plays a groove, he is not going to be mathematically "perfect," but *random* isn't what he's doing either. In fact, a good drummer is quite deliberate with regard to the way he pushes and pulls tempo within the confines of a given measure. Applying randomization is certainly not the best way to get this feel.
>
> So if this is the case, when *do* you use randomization when quantizing MIDI? Good question. Personally, I use it anytime multiple humans are being emulated. For example, imagine four trumpet players trying to play a note right on Beat 1 of a given measure. Some will naturally play a little earlier, some later, and one person might just actually nail it dead-on. (If that happens, trust me—it's a coincidence!) In this case, randomizing *does* work in your favor.

The final section of the MIDI Quantize dialog box might seem a bit mysterious to many (I know that it did to me at first!), but it's particularly good for tightening up your MIDI at a higher level.

MIDI Quantize

- **Swing:** Normally, when you quantize, your quantized notes will be evenly spaced (as you've seen in the examples earlier in this section). However, if you use a little swing, your notes will skew in a way. For example, if your notes are quantized to a straight sixteenth-note grid, you'll see four evenly spaced notes, as illustrated in Figure 3.12. However, if you have a swing of 100%, every second grid point will be moved later, giving more of a swing or shuffle feel, as shown in Figure 3.15.

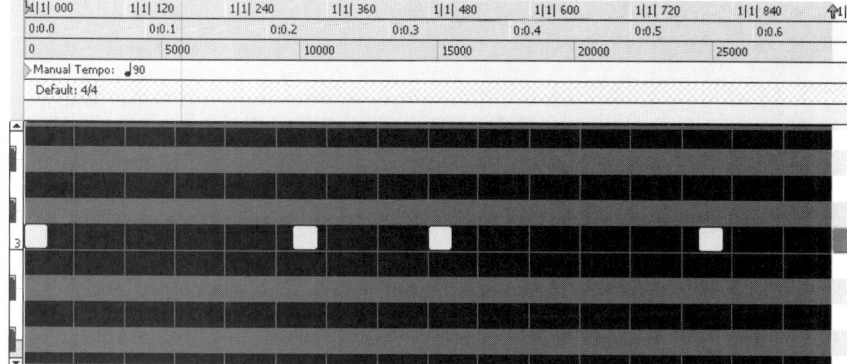

Figure 3.15

Sixteenth-note quantization with 100% swing

- **Include Within:** This one might seem a little confusing at the outset, but it is actually pretty straightforward. Normally, all selected notes, regardless of how far they might be from a grid point, are subject to quantization. When you check the Include Within box and enter any value other than 100%, notes that are particularly far from the grid simply won't be quantized. Let's take the example of quantizing to the nearest quarter note. With the Include Within box unchecked (or checked with a value of 100%), all notes will be quantized—even notes that are half a beat off. If I were to quantize with a 50% Include Within value, as shown in Figure 3.16, then notes that are more than a quarter beat from a grid point would be ignored.

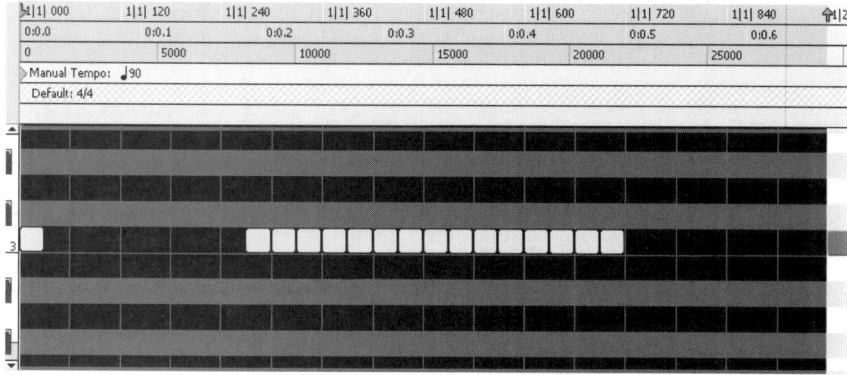

Figure 3.16

Quarter-note quantization with 50% Include Within

- **Exclude Within:** As the name might suggest, this is the mirror image of the Include Within function that we just looked at. In this case, notes that are particularly far from a grid point are the ones that are included. If you take a look at Figure 3.17, you'll see a quarter-note quantize with a 50% Exclude Within value. Basically, the Exclude Within feature allows you to quantize notes that are grossly out of sync with the grid, while leaving notes that are relatively close to the grid alone.

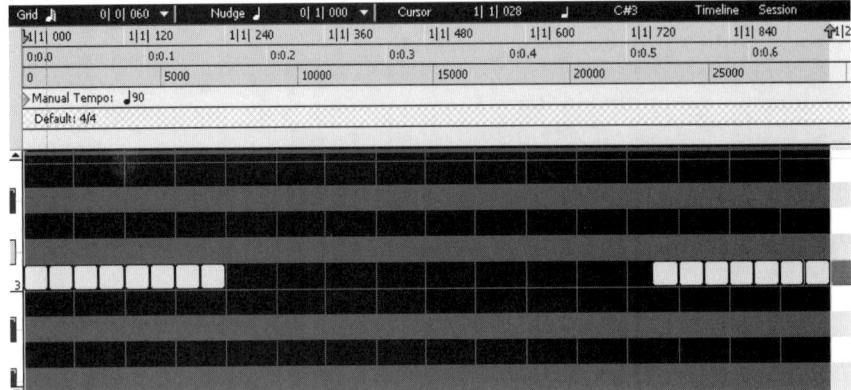

Figure 3.17

Quarter-note quantization with 50% Exclude Within

- **Strength:** Normally, when notes are quantized, they are moved completely to the appropriate grid points. Funnily enough, this even holds true when you groove quantize—it's just that the "grid" that you're using is not a mathematically perfect one. So what if you don't want your MIDI quantize to be so heavy-handed? Try setting your quantize's Strength setting to a value less than the default 100%. Your notes will move toward the appropriate grid point to the extent you specify. For example, if you choose to quantize with 50% strength, your notes' imperfections (timing imperfections, at least!) will be halfway corrected, as shown in Figure 3.18 (which shows our original track quantized to the nearest quarter note with 50% strength).

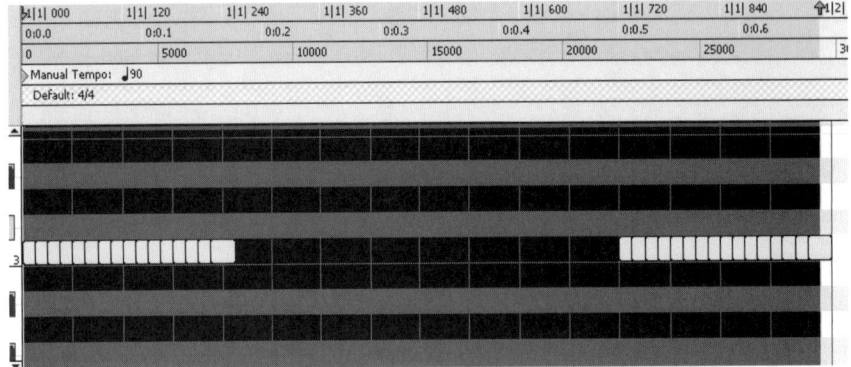

Figure 3.18

Quarter-note quantization with 50% strength

> **TIP**
>
> When dealing with quantization and your drum tracks, the temptation to equate mathematical accuracy with artistic excellence is a common one. I include myself as falling into the quantization-equals-correction trap, especially in the heady early days of MIDI. If you feel the same urge to mercilessly quantize your MIDI, try instead using some of the more subtle effects (particularly Exclude Within and Strength) to more subtly massage your beats. Even if you're into heavily technical styles, try leaving in some "imperfections"—you might be pleasantly surprised at the result!

MIDI Velocity

If you're new to MIDI, the concept of MIDI velocity might seem a bit odd. If you think about what velocity really means though (speed), it does start to make sense.

Essentially, *velocity* refers to the speed at which you strike a key on an instrument, such as a piano. Keyboard-based instruments are particularly good examples for this concept. If you strike a key of a piano slowly, then the note will be played "softly" in terms of volume and tonal color. If it's struck quickly (with a high rate of speed or velocity), the note will not only be naturally loud, but it will have the tonal color of a piano being aggressively played.

> **NOTE**
>
> Bear in mind that the *speed* at which you play a note is completely different from the *force* that you use. Consider this: It is perfectly possible to push a piano's key very hard, but very slowly, in which case the piano would have the softer timbre (tonal color) of a gently played piano.

It's important to keep in mind that *velocity*, though certainly related to volume, isn't volume in and of itself, and once you understand that, you can really tap into a deeper level of MIDI power. Too many users use volume alone to bring out a note (or a selection of notes), which will simply increase the amplitude of the sound without changing the timbre accordingly.

In the case of drum tracks, you can use MIDI velocity data in conjunction with MIDI volume (and in some cases instead of volume data) to bring out subtleties of your drum grooves and more closely emulate how a live drummer would play a drum kit. The trick is not only to increase the loudness, but also to change the color of the sound accordingly, just as a live drummer's kit would sound different (not just louder) when played harder.

If you take a look at Figure 3.19, you'll see some MIDI velocity data in an Instrument track. To see the velocity data, just click the Track View Selector button (just below the Record, Solo, and Mute buttons). You'll see that each individual note has its own velocity stalk. You can easily change the velocity of individual notes by clicking an individual velocity value and dragging with the Grabber tool, selecting notes and scaling the velocity values up or down with the Trim tool, or writing in velocity data with the Pencil tool.

CHAPTER 3 ■ MIDI and the Beat

One more point before we leave our brief discussion of MIDI velocity: When you use the Groove Quantize feature, you should know that timing isn't the only thing that's being changed. Groove templates utilize timing data as well as velocity data to create a more realistic, comprehensive feel. Take a look at Figure 3.19, and you'll see how groove quantization changed not only the timing of the note, but the volume as well.

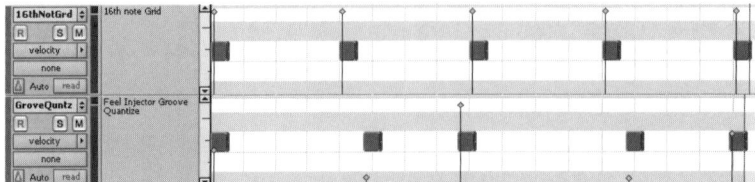

Figure 3.19
The difference between a track quantized to a straight sixteenth-note grid (top) and a sixteenth-note groove quantize (bottom). Notice the velocity changes.

MIDI Real-Time Properties

We've just finished our discussion of matters of MIDI timing and velocity, and if you've followed along, you've probably done a little bit of tweaking of MIDI data. That's fine as far as that goes, but if there's one thing that can really put the brakes on creativity, it is the bothersome process of going down one creative path, changing your mind, and having to undo numerous steps simply to explore another musical option. Of course, using multiple Edit Playlists (discussed in Chapter 2) can be a big help, but there's another feature exclusively available for MIDI data: Real-Time Properties.

Real-Time Properties is a relatively new feature to Pro Tools (introduced with version 7) that allows you to non-destructively modify your MIDI data as it plays (hence the term "Real-Time"). Your MIDI notes aren't actually changed, so it's easy to revert back to the track's original condition and try something new. What's more, you can modify different aspects of your MIDI data (quantize, duration, delay, velocity, and transpose) independent of each other. Let's see how it can work with MIDI drums.

> **NOTE**
>
> If you'd like to follow the example cited in this section, launch the session named Chapter 3c included on the book's disc.
>
> This session (which uses the free Digidesign Xpand! and Compressor/Limiter Dyn III plug-ins) should sound a bit familiar. It includes a slightly edited version of the appallingly lame drum region created by your humble author. Let's see whether we can improve it a bit!

If you haven't used this feature before, you'll have to find it first. There are a couple of ways you can do this:

MIDI Real-Time Properties

- From the View drop-down menu, choose Edit Window, then Real-Time Properties.
- Click the Edit Window View selector (immediately below the Slip mode button, shown in Figure 3.20). From the menu that appears, choose Real-Time Properties.

Either way you choose to do this, when you're finished, you'll see the Real-Time Properties column, as shown in Figure 3.20.

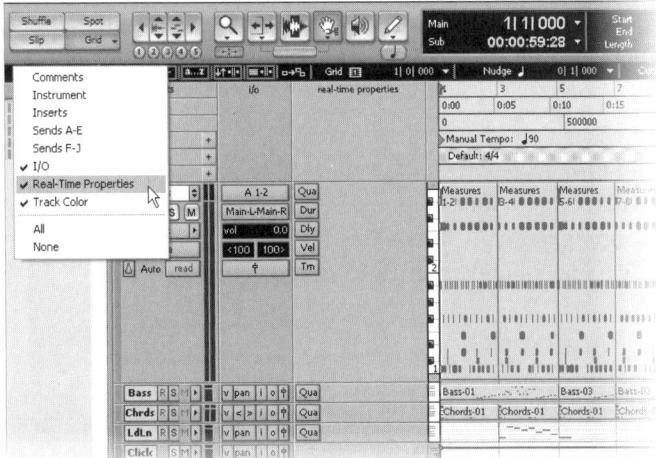

Figure 3.20

Showing the Real-Time Properties column

Believe it or not, the hard work is done! You'll see five buttons in the Real-Time Properties column, reading Qua (Quantize), Dur (Duration), Dly (Delay), Vel (Velocity), and Trn (Transpose) from top to bottom. For the purposes of working with beats, I think that you'll find Quantize and Velocity to be the most useful.

> **NOTE**
>
> If your track height is Mini or Micro (new in Pro Tools 7.3), you'll only see the Quantize button in the Real-Time Properties column. If your track height is set to Small, you'll only see the Quantize and Duration buttons.

The first thing that I want to do to my beat is quantize it, and with Real-Time Properties, I've got a level of flexibility that I haven't had up to now. Here's how you use Real-Time Properties:

1. Click the button that matches the parameter you want to change. In my case, I'll click the Qua button to start real-time quantization.
2. Once a parameter is selected, values will be displayed immediately to the right of the button you just clicked. In the case of quantization, this will show you how your notes are being quantized, as shown in Figure 3.21.

55

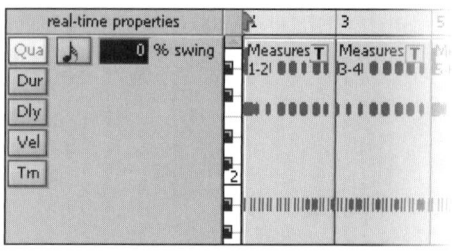

Figure 3.21
Real-time quantization

3. The whole point of a real-time process is that it's happening as you are playing your session, so go ahead and start your session and listen to how your notes sound with quantization.

4. Want to try something different? No problem—you don't even need to stop playback! Just click the Value button, which will reveal a familiar-looking quantization list. Choose the grid or groove that you want to try (personally, I like Feel Injector Templates → 04FeelInjector_16ths). Your drums will immediately change to match your new value.

> **TIP**
>
> Part of the beauty of using Real-Time Properties lies in the fact that you can enable and disable your changes at will. Do you want to hear how your drums originally sounded (without the quantization)? You can do it easily by un-highlighting the parameter button (in this case the Qua button). You'll be able to re-enable your quantize by clicking the Qua button once more.
>
> You will be able to enable, disable, and modify all five Real-Time Properties independently.

If you follow the steps outlined previously, you'll see a small "T" in the upper corner of each region, which signifies that the region is subject to track-based Real-Time Properties. This also means that regions you drag onto the track will also be changed in real-time.

Now let's go a step deeper into MIDI Real-Time Properties. In addition to track-based Real-Time Properties, there are region-based Real-Time Properties that you can employ as well, which are linked to specific regions in your session regardless of the track they're on. For example, suppose I want the drums to be played with more intensity between Measures 5 and 11 in the Chapter 3c session. Here's how I can do this using region-based Real-Time Properties:

1. Select the region(s) that you want to affect. In the case of this example, I select the three drum regions between Measures 5 and 11, as shown in Figure 3.22.

2. From the Event drop-down menu, choose MIDI Real-Time Properties. The floating Real-Time Properties window will open, as also shown in Figure 3.22.

MIDI Real-Time Properties

3. The Apply To pop-up menu will allow you to apply the Real-Time Properties to the selected regions (as shown in Figure 3.22) or to the selected tracks. For our purposes, we'll leave the menu set to change only the selected regions.

4. The rest of the window works just like the Real-Time Properties column. Because I want the drums to be played a bit more aggressively during this section, I will enable velocity as a Real-Time Property and set the value to 200%. Because I also want the same quantize that the rest of the track is using, I'll enable quantization as well.

5. That's it—you can just close the window. You'll note that the selected regions have an "R" in the upper-right corner, identifying that they are subject to region-based Real-Time Properties, as shown in Figure 3.22.

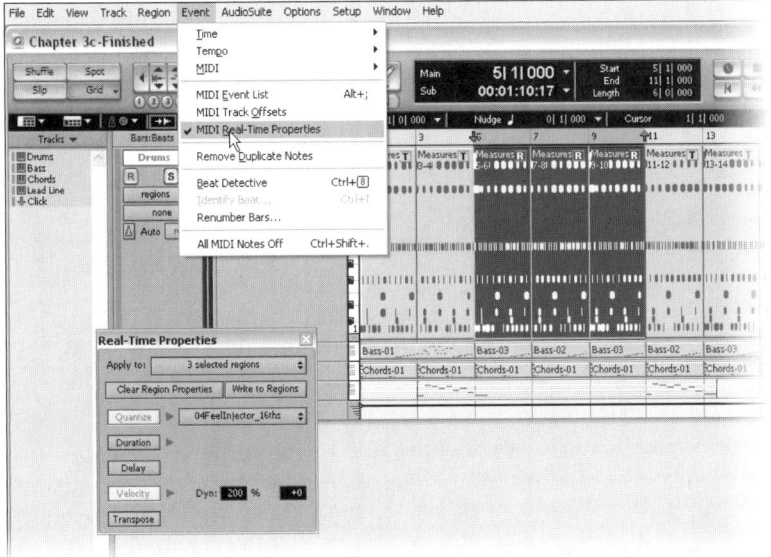

Figure 3.22

Region-based Real-Time Properties

> **TIP**
> Of course, you can use Real-Time Properties on any track that uses MIDI data (MIDI or Instrument tracks). Because I used groove quantize on my drums, I'll also put the same groove on the rest of my MIDI Instrument tracks so they all groove together. You can check out this session in its finished form by launching the Chapter 3c-Finished session.

CHAPTER 3 ■ MIDI and the Beat

> **TIP**
>
> Depending on the setup of your session, you may or may not see any visual change in your notes when you apply Real-Time Properties. You can choose whether you want to see the real-time changes reflected on your timeline by going to the Setup drop-down menu, choosing Preferences, and then going to the MIDI page of the Preferences window.
>
> In the General area of the MIDI page (about midway down the window), you'll see a check box named Display Events As Modified by Real-Time Properties. When this box is checked, you'll see the values you select in the Real-Time Properties area reflected in your region.

Session Linearity

If you haven't explored the session linearity of your session, buckle up! It can be a bit disorienting at first, but once you get the hang of it, you'll find it very useful when working with MIDI music in your session, particularly if your session employs tempo changes.

> **NOTE**
>
> The best way to understand this concept is to do a little hands-on work. Please open the session named Chapter 3d, included on the disc that came with this book.

If you take a look at the Chapter 3d session, you'll see a linear increase in tempo beginning at 68 BPM at the beginning and arriving at 200 BPM at Measure 9. If you take a close look at the Min:Sec, Bars:Beats, and Tempo rulers, you'll note that as the tempo increases, the width of each measure narrows, as shown in Figure 3.23. If you try to drag the first region to the left, you'll see the region change size as you move it in response to the tempo changes. This is probably a familiar phenomenon for most DAW users.

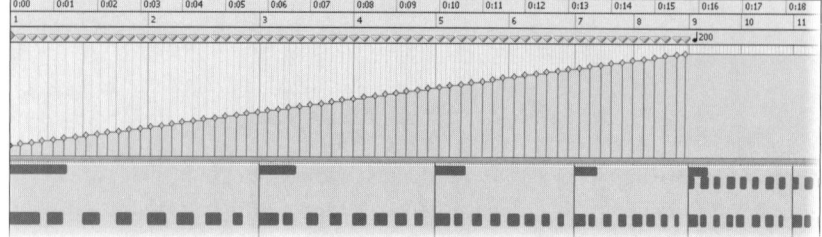

Figure 3.23
Absolute time linearity

The reason this happens is because the Min:Sec timeline (being an absolute measurement of time) is displayed linearly. This means that for any given zoom level, one second is the same distance from the next, and real-time is displayed in a uniform matter. Tempo, on the other hand, is a relative way of looking at time and can change over the course of a song—so songs with tempo changes *can't* be displayed with such a uniform look. Or *can* they?

Of course, there is a way to look at your MIDI data differently (there wouldn't be much point to this section of the book it there wasn't a way!), and one that may suit MIDI musicians much better. Instead of having your session's linearity set to samples (meaning that any absolute time scale will be evenly spaced), set it to a tick-based linearity, meaning that your bars, beats, and measures will be evenly spaced. Here's how to do this:

1. Click the Linearity Display mode down arrow, as shown in Figure 3.24. A menu will appear.

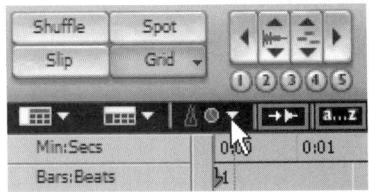

Figure 3.24
Changing your session's linearity

2. Click on the Linear Tick Display menu item. Notice how your screen changes (though the sound of your session does not)—this is only a display change.

You'll notice now that all your measures are evenly spaced, which is sometimes a very handy way to work. (In other words, all your quarter notes, eighth notes, and so on will have a uniform look regardless of tempo.) You'll also notice that because tempo is linear, real time is not! Take a look at the Min:Sec ruler in Figure 3.25, and you'll see what I mean.

A side effect of not having a linear sample display can be a bit jarring at first. If you take a look at the region in the bottom track (10 seconds of silent audio) and drag it to the right (as shown in Figure 3.25), the region will seem to expand! This expansion is visual only, and the audio region (which is sample-based) remains only 10 seconds.

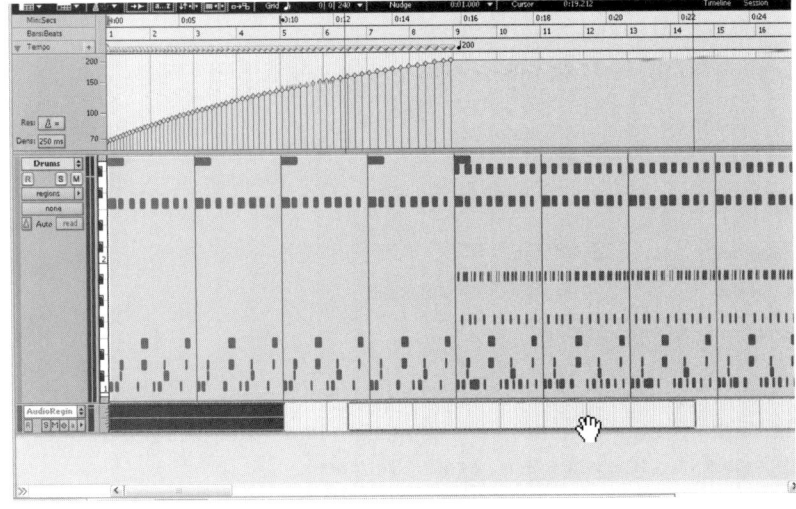

Figure 3.25
Tick-based linearity

59

CHAPTER 3 ■ MIDI and the Beat

It should be mentioned that viewing your session with tick-based linearity isn't a typical way to work for many Pro Tools users. When working with MIDI beats, though, you might find this a very convenient way to work!

Making MIDI Better: MIDI Track Offsets

As I said at the beginning of this chapter, there are people who know and use MIDI and those who don't. That's fine, but it always kills me when somebody says, "I don't use MIDI because it just sounds *bad*." In my opinion, these folks are missing out on a world of creative possibilities, and needlessly.

Of course MIDI doesn't simply sound *bad*. It's being used in virtually every level of the industry, and often so skillfully that the listening public (heck, the *artistic* public) never suspects that the source of the music is MIDI-based! Bottom line: Good work is being done all the time using MIDI.

That being said, MIDI is a fairly old technology with a couple issues that you need to be aware of, some of which we've discussed previously. Here's another one: MIDI's timing isn't perfect. To some extent, there is a degree of latency with even meticulously tweaked MIDI studios. Fortunately, there's a way we can minimize MIDI's timing sloppiness and significantly tighten the sound of our MIDI beats.

The secret lies in MIDI Track Offsets. Basically, what this means is that Pro Tools will trigger a MIDI note before it is meant to be heard (also earlier in relation to the note's visual position in your session). This is a very nifty solution to a nagging problem, and there are two ways to approach it.

Method One

This is pretty straightforward. If you find that your MIDI is uniformly lagging behind your audio, you can globally apply an offset to all the MIDI and Instrument tracks in your session:

1. From the Setup drop-down menu, choose Preferences.
2. In the Preferences window, go to the MIDI tab, as shown in Figure 3.26

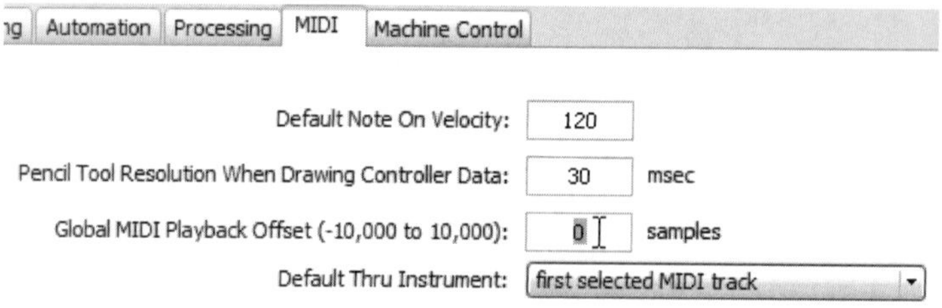

Figure 3.26
Setting your global MIDI offset

3. In the Global MIDI Playback Offset area, enter the samples of latency that you are having in your session (making sure that the value is a negative number).

Making MIDI Better: MIDI Track Offsets

> **NOTE**
>
> If you're going to set a global MIDI offset, it is very common to set the value equal to your hardware buffer size (making sure that the number is *negative*).

This method has the advantage of being easy and covering all the MIDI and Instrument tracks in one fell swoop. If you're a tweaker like me, though, you'll want to take a look at your MIDI timing anomalies (different instruments and external MIDI instruments in particular) on a track-by-track basis. Here's how you can fix your MIDI timing with a high degree of accuracy.

Method Two

> **NOTE**
>
> To follow along with the example shown in this section, open the Chapter 3e session. This session (which uses the Xpand! plug-in) has a single Instrument track with four snare drum hits, plus two empty Audio tracks.

1. The first step is to measure the amount of latency on a given track. In this example, I want to measure the latency of the snare hits of my Instrument track. Using buses, record from your MIDI or Instrument track to an Audio track.
2. Zoom into one of your drum hits (horizontally and vertically) and compare the timing of the note and the timing of the recorded audio. Make a selection between the two different trigger times and note the difference in samples, as shown in Figure 3.27. (Note that the difference between the MIDI and audio is two samples.)

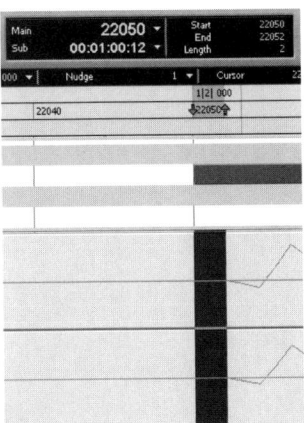

Figure 3.27
Measuring MIDI latency

3. From the Event drop-down list, choose MIDI Track Offsets. The MIDI Track Offsets window will appear, as shown in Figure 3.28.

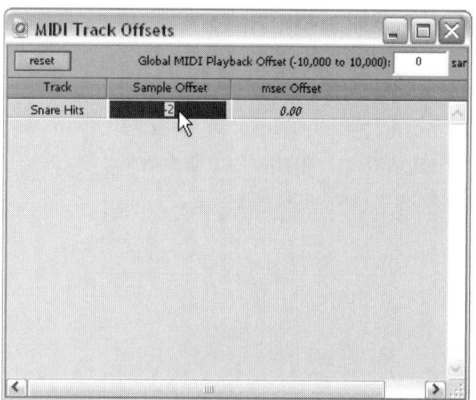

Figure 3.28

Compensating for MIDI latency

4. On the appropriate track, enter the Sample Offset value by entering the number of samples of latency for the track (in my case, two samples) as a negative number, as shown in Figure 3.28. Don't forget to hit Enter to set the value!

That's it! From now on, your MIDI track will play with *much* better timing. To test your work, go ahead and re-record your audio to see how you've done. If you've followed along with this short example, your result should look something like Figure 3.29. (The top Audio track is prior to MIDI offsetting; the bottom track is after you've made your changes.)

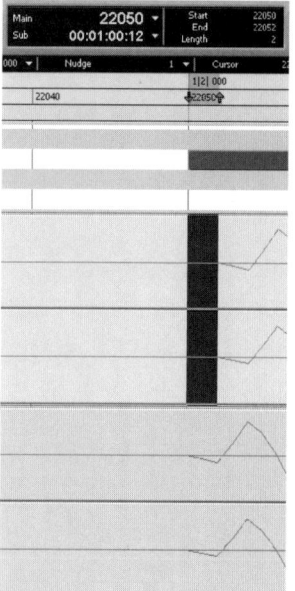

Figure 3.29

MIDI latency—fixed!

> **NOTE**
>
> As for the audio you've recorded in the process of setting and testing your MIDI track offsets, you can delete it. It was only for the purposes of tweaking your MIDI track.

> **TIP**
>
> Before we leave the discussion of MIDI, there's one more cool tool you might want to know about. In the upper-left area of your Edit window, you'll see a little area that looks like Figure 3.30.
>
> The Mirrored MIDI Editing element is a good feature for MIDI drum editing. Very commonly, you will have a single MIDI drum loop that you repeat over the course of your song. When the Mirrored MIDI Editing feature is activated (it'll have a blue box around it), any changes you make to one region will be mirrored to all identical drum regions!

Figure 3.30
Mirrored MIDI Editing button

That's it for our foray into the world of MIDI beats. I hope that you've found some new tricks of the MIDI trade and you've been inspired to take advantage of this powerful ally in musical creation. Next, editing!

Editing Power

Of all the stages of production, I probably spend the most *time* in the editing phase. Perhaps that's because I'm something of a tweaker, obsessing over minutiae that nobody can hear, but I prefer to think that there is just so much editing power in today's DAWs that it demands some serious attention. (My wife, on the other hand, would probably say it's because I'm a tweaker.)

There's a good case to be made that the DAW revolution changed the way we edit more than any other phase of production. The fact that we can now work non-linearly, non-destructively, and with surgical accuracy has changed the way we make music, and even the way the public *hears* music. Of course, this all impacts the way we work with beats as well.

Because you probably know the basics of editing, the goal of this chapter is to help you work *smarter*. In this chapter, you'll learn to:

- Use the Identify Beat feature to help your session work better with loops
- Use Grid modes to your best advantage
- Use powerful new editing tools
- Use tick-based audio
- Use region groups and loops to make editing more efficient and more creative

Bringing Audio and MIDI Together: Identify Beat

As I've mentioned a number of times already (and I will again right now), MIDI—particularly MIDI tempo—plays a huge role in getting the most out of editing beats, even if you're editing *audio* regions. As we go further down the road of editing in this book, this will become more and more evident, but let's start out with a common frustration for many beginners: You import a 4-bar

CHAPTER 4 ■ Editing Power

drum loop that sounds *awesome*, and it loops perfectly, so you don't even need to do any further tweaking. Because you're a savvy Pro Tools user, you set your grid to something very manageable (such as quarter notes or bars) and start dropping regions onto your tracks, and that's when the problems start. For some reason, when you snap your drum loop to the beginnings of measures, there are unwanted spaces or overlaps of your region. How can this be?

You have to understand that even though computers are very *fast* at performing computations, they aren't particularly bright. Though your ears and brain (which are far more complex than the computer!) can clearly hear that this is a 4-measure loop, the computer has no way to make such a subjective determination. You're going to have to help Pro Tools understand the tempo of your beat. After that, life will get *much* easier.

The way to educate Pro Tools about the tempo of your beat is through a handy little feature called *Identify Beat*. If you haven't used it before, you'll find it easy to use and very helpful indeed as we go forward. Let's take a look at two situations in which you might use this function.

> **NOTE**
>
> For this section, open a session called Chapter 4a. Once again, it will use the Xpand! plug-in to supply the bass part.

In the Chapter 4a session, we have a simple but classic example of this problem. You've got a simple MIDI setup with a bass and a click track. Of course, both of these tracks follow the MIDI tempo. The top track (shown in Figure 4.1) shows a cool loop that was imported into the session. Here's the rub: Both the MIDI and the audio regions are four measures long!

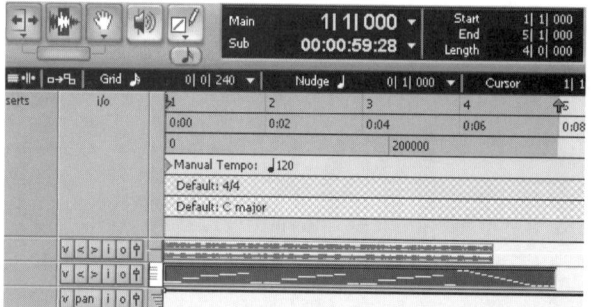

Figure 4.1

Four-bar regions

You can choose to conform the audio region to match the MIDI region or vice versa, but for the purposes of our example, let's assume that you like your drum loop just the way it is, and you want your MIDI to match it. Your job at this point is to clue Pro Tools in on the fact that the audio region is in fact four measures long (contrary to the current Pro Tools tempo). Of course, you can

66

Bringing Audio and MIDI Together: Identify Beat

spend your time hunting for just the right tempo using the Tempo slider, but there's an easier way using Pro Tools' Identify Beat function. Here's how it works:

1. Using the Selector or Grabber tool, select the audio region to which you want to conform your MIDI. (In this case, it is the region on the top track.)
2. If your Transport window isn't already visible, open it now. (You'll find it under the Windows drop-down menu.)
3. If your Tempo Ruler Enable button (also known as the Conductor button) isn't highlighted (in blue, shown in Figure 4.2), click it now. Identify Beat will not be available to you if you are in Manual Tempo Slider mode.

Figure 4.2
Turning on the Tempo Ruler Enable button

4. From the Event drop-down menu, choose Identify Beat. The Add Bar|Beat Markers dialog box will appear, as shown in Figure 4.3.

> **TIP**
> This is a feature that I use quite a bit—you might find that you do too. If so, you might find the shortcuts (Ctrl+I on PCs, Command+I on Macs) real time savers!

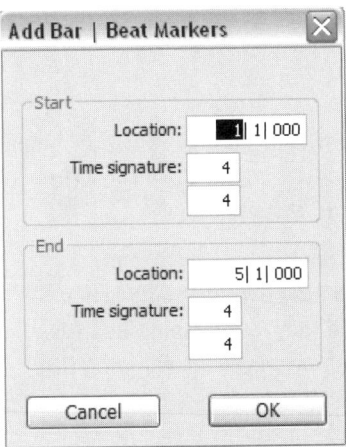

Figure 4.3
The Add Bar|Beat Markers Window, which will appear after you choose Identify Beat

5. The first step is to make any necessary changes to the start location and meter of your selection. In this example, because the region starts at the beginning of the session and is in 4/4 meter (listen and you'll agree), no changes are needed in this area.
6. The last significant step is to set your end location and meter. In our example, we *will* make some changes here. Because I have selected a four-bar region, I will set my end point to be 5|1|000, or the beginning of Measure 5. In this case, we won't need to change the meter, but you do have the option of doing so here if you need to.

> **NOTE**
>
> The audio file used in this example is perfectly trimmed at the proper start and end points—a textbook example. In real-world cases, you may not get such a tweaked example, and you'll have to check and make sure that your loops are properly cropped.

> **CAUTION**
>
> For many new users (yours truly included), the initial temptation might be to set your end point to 4|1|000 for a four-measure selection, but be careful—that would be only three measures long!

7. Click OK.

You will see a change in the visual appearance of your tracks, and for a moment it may appear as though your audio region has been time-expanded, but that's not the case. If you listen to your session, you will hear a change in your MIDI tracks, not your audio loop, and the tempos of both will now be in agreement.

> **NOTE**
>
> To check your work, compare your session to the Chapter 4a-Finished session on the included disc.

There is actually a number of good effects of using this simple but powerful feature. First off, your musical grid will now work *with* you instead of against you, so you will be able to use the Grid mode of editing to your advantage. (We'll talk more about that later in this chapter.)

Also, you can use Identify Beat to help you out with longer drum tracks that change tempo. Consider this scenario: You have a 64-measure live drum track that, being live, drifts in tempo a little bit. After the tracking session, your client decides that he would like to add some Rex files or arpeggiators to the mix. Keep in mind that both Rex files and synth arpeggiators rely on MIDI tempo for their timing. Identify Beat can help you here as well—read on.

> **NOTE**
>
> If you open the session Chapter 4b, you'll see an example of how this works. The session has three drum tracks that start at one tempo, change tempo suddenly after eight measures, then change the tempo again after another eight measures.

Really, the solution to this is just one step from what you've done up to this point. Your first job is to select a segment of audio with a consistent tempo. (In real-world applications, this can vary from just a few beats to quite a long stretch, depending upon the situation.) In the case of the Chapter 4b session, you'll find that the first eight measures have a single tempo.

> **TIP**
>
> Pro Tools' Tab to Transient feature will help you make your selections. (Refer to Chapter 1 for more information on this.) Another helpful tip: The kick track is simply quarter notes.

When you've made that selection, go ahead and use the Identify Beat function just as you did before (making sure that your start point is 1|1|000 and entering an ending point of 9|1|000). You'll immediately see a tempo change at the beginning of your session. (The tempo should be 128.035 BPM if you used Tab to Transient to select eight bars on the kick track.)

The next step is to select from the beginning of Bar 9 (the end of your previous selection) and select the next area of static tempo. In the case of this example, Measures 9 to 17 are all in the same tempo, so you can select eight bars starting at the beginning at Measure 9 and ending at the beginning of Measure 17. Remember, your ears should be your guide, not the existing Tempo ruler. When you've made your selection, go into the Identify Beat window once again and let Pro Tools know that the selection you've made is in fact beginning at 9|1|000 and ending at 17|1|000 (which should result in a tempo change of 137.8848 BPM starting at Measure 9).

If you're following the example Chapter 4b session, the last step is to select the final eight measures (from the start of Measure 17 to the end of the regions) and use Identify Beat to determine the tempo of that selection. If your selection is correct, the resultant tempo should be 128.0362 BPM, and your session's rulers should look something like Figure 4.4.

> **NOTE**
>
> Take a look at session Chapter 4b-Finished to see the steps outlined here in their finished state.

CHAPTER 4 ■ Editing Power

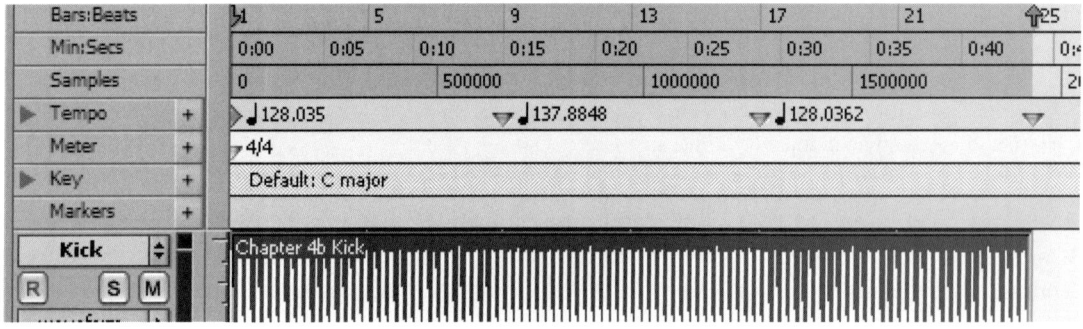

Figure 4.4
Using Identify Beat to create a tempo map

If you listen to your session, you'll now notice that the arpeggio track not only follows the tempo at the beginning of the session, but it changes its tempo based upon the tempo changes that you just created. I've personally used this technique on a number of occasions—particularly in the creation of click tracks after the original session was recorded without a click. (Keep in mind that Digidesign's Click plug-in is essentially a MIDI instrument.)

Making Grid Mode Work for You

Assuming that you're a fairly experienced Pro Tools user, you've no doubt spent some time using the different Edit modes—Shuffle, Slip, Grid, and maybe even Spot. These modes' operations are pretty straightforward, but let's take a closer look at Grid mode.

When you're working with Grid mode, you have the option of using a number of different types of grids. For example, if you're working with film, you would probably use a Time Code ruler or two. When you're working with beats, you'll probably opt for something more suitable, such as perhaps the Bars|Beats ruler, and then select an appropriate resolution—perhaps sixteenth notes (a popular favorite of mine, for some reason).

If by chance you've not used Grid mode much or you are unclear as to how to change the grid settings, here's a little review:

1. Click the Grid Value pop-up arrow, as shown in Figure 4.5.

2. If the grid type section (toward the bottom of the list, as shown in Figure 4.5) isn't set to Bars|Beats, please click that option now to select it. The list will close.

3. Re-open the list (repeat Step 1) and choose the desired grid resolution from the top part of the list (for example, 1/16 Note, as shown in Figure 4.5).

When your Grid mode is set, you're ready to rock! Read on....

Making Grid Mode Work for You

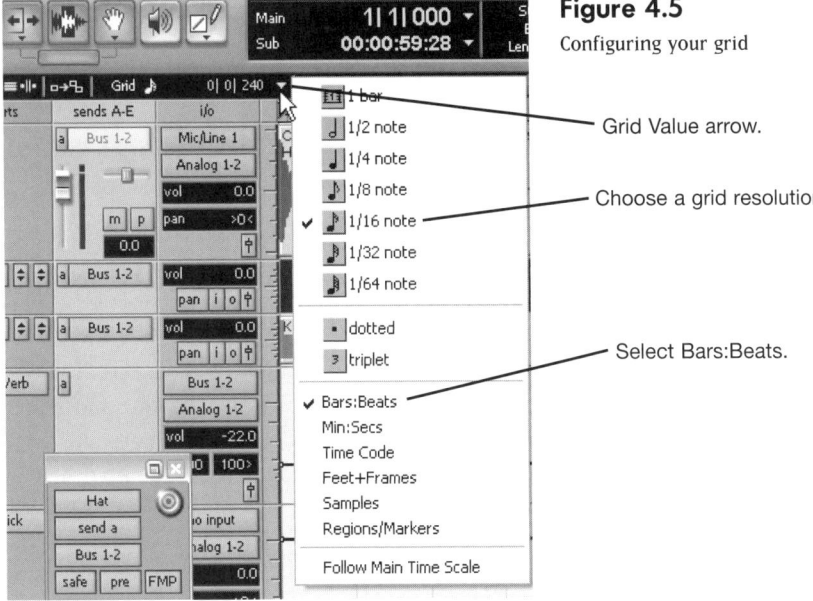

Figure 4.5
Configuring your grid

Relative Grid Mode

The concept of an object snapping to a grid is not a novel one—many DAWs and graphics applications integrate this sort of operation in one way or another. Essentially, this works by having your object—in Pro Tools' case, a region or MIDI note—snap to the nearest grid line as you drag it from one place to another. Not exactly rocket science, right?

Recently, Pro Tools has done this feature one better—a new Grid mode called Relative Grid mode. Instead of snapping objects to a grid point, this mode moves regions by grid values. For example, if you drag a region using normal Grid mode (also called *Absolute Grid mode*), you'll see behavior similar to that shown in Figure 4.6.

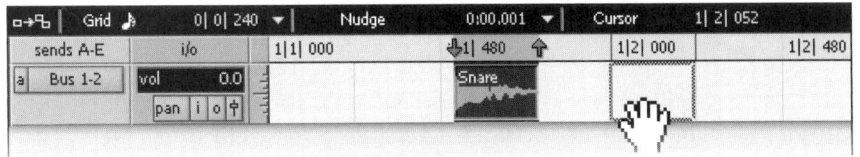

Figure 4.6
Moving a region using Absolute Grid mode

In this example you'll see that the region, originally not on a grid point, will be moved to a grid point. That's all well and good, but what if you happen to *like* the fact that the object is off the grid by a certain amount, and you simply want to move that object to another beat or measure,

71

still maintaining its relative position to the grid? That's where Relative Grid mode comes in—it'll move regions as shown in Figure 4.7.

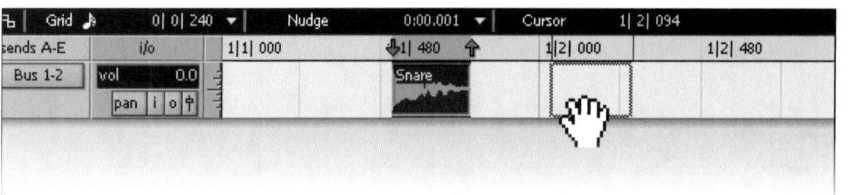

Figure 4.7

Relative Grid mode

Here's a common workflow example of how one might use Relative Grid mode in practice. If you analyze the playing of many drummers, you will find that playing the "up" beats (Beats 2 and 4 in a typical 4/4 measure) gives a certain feeling of being "in the pocket," as many drummers might explain it. This idea is certainly worthy of exploration, and here's how you can use Relative Grid mode to make this exploration easier.

> **TIP**
>
> You can toggle between the Absolute and Relative Grid modes by pressing the F4 key on your computer's keyboard.

> **NOTE**
>
> For this next example, please launch the session named Chapter 4c from the disc included with this book.

In this session, you'll see that we have basic kick, snare, and hi-hat tracks—all Audio tracks. On each of the tracks are individual regions that have been dragged from the region list using Grid mode. (Note that this session's grid setting is set to Bars|Beats with a resolution of 1/16 Note.) A section of half a measure is selected on the timeline (with loop playback). Last but not least, I've unlinked the edit and timeline selection (see Chapter 1) so that we can freely move regions without changing our playback selection. If you listen to the selected area, you'll have to agree that it sounds pretty sterile. If you're looking for hyper-accurate timing for a more electronic feel, that might be fine, but let's see whether we can introduce a little feel by "laying back" on the second beat with the snare track.

Making Grid Mode Work for You

There are a number of ways that you could shift the timing of the selected snare region later.

- Go into Slip mode and move the region using the Grabber tool. This has the advantage of being easy and visual, but it is sometimes not the best way to go if you're looking to move your region by very small amounts.

- From the Edit drop-down menu, choose the Shift menu item. This will launch the Shift dialog box (shown in Figure 4.8), which will allow you to move the selected items to earlier or later amounts. In Figure 4.8, you'll see that the selected region will be moved later by 15 ticks. This method has the advantage of allowing you to be very specific with your changes, but it might not be the most flexible way to work.

Figure 4.8
The Shift dialog box

- Yet another way is to nudge the region, which is a way that I personally like to work for good balance of accuracy and flexibility. Setting up your Nudge value is very similar to setting up your grid. Simply go to the Nudge area (immediately to the right of the Grid area, as shown in Figure 4.9) and choose your nudge scale and your nudge resolution. In this case, I've chosen a nudge scale of Min:Secs, with a resolution of 1 Msec (millisecond). When this is set to your satisfaction, pressing the plus (+) key will move the region later by one nudge increment and pressing the minus (–) key will move it earlier by a nudge value. Repeated pressings will inch the selected region(s) or note(s) by nudge increments.

73

CHAPTER 4 ■ Editing Power

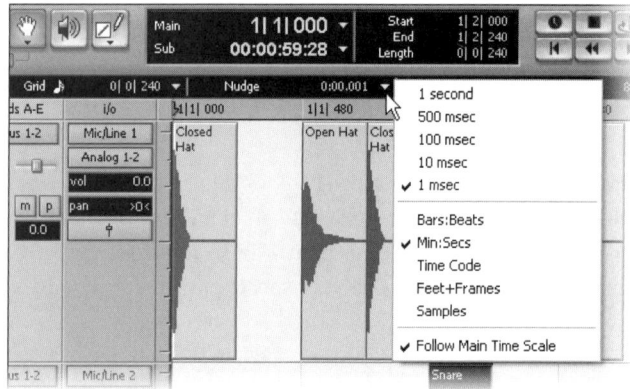

Figure 4.9

Setting your Nudge value

> **NOTE**
>
> Good news! You can make changes using any of the methods mentioned *during playback*, which will allow you to listen to the effect of your changes in the context of your session. Have patience, though—it will take a brief time for your session to implement those changes. In this example, for instance, you need to let the selection loop a couple times before you'll hear your changes take effect.

The degree to which you might shift this snare back is entirely a matter of personal preference, but I would caution you that *a little goes a long way*. The effect that you're looking to achieve here is meant to be felt more on a subconscious level than to be consciously recognized. (In fact, if you can plainly see that the snare is late in relation to the rest of the track, you've almost certainly gone too far!) In my example, I've chosen to shift the snare region back by 11 ticks, which at a tempo of 120 BPM equates to roughly 5 milliseconds.

Now that you've found the timing "sweet spot" for your snare, you will want to duplicate that region to Beat 4 of the same measure and Beats 2 and 4 of the second measure. Here is where Relative Grid mode can help out.

1. Click and hold on the Grid mode button. Soon you'll see a list appear, as shown in Figure 4.10.
2. Choose Relative Grid from the list. The Grid mode button, typically blue, will turn purple, and Rel Grid will be displayed on the button itself. You are now in Relative Grid mode.
3. The rest is easy. Holding the Alt key (for PC-based systems) or the Option key (for Macs), click and drag your snare region to the fourth beat of the first measure. Repeat this step to drag the region to the second beat of the second measure, and finally to Beat 4 of the second measure.

Making Grid Mode Work for You

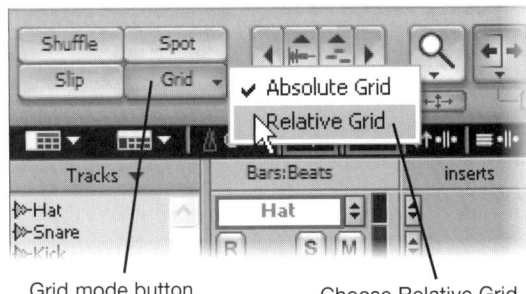

Figure 4.10
Getting into Relative Grid mode

> **TIP**
>
> Holding down the Alt key (for PC-based systems) or the Option key (for Macs) when you're dragging regions is a very quick and easy way to make copies of regions as you're dragging them.

You'll see that each region you've created has maintained a uniform distance from the grid proper. You can even go further and create regions that don't necessarily fall on the upbeats, and all of the snare regions will have this "laidback" feel!

> **CAUTION**
>
> If you're following along with this example, you'll probably want to hear both measures as they loop. Remember that your edit and timeline selections are *unlinked*, and that any selections in your track area will have no effect on the time being played back. Now might be a good time to re-link the edit and timeline selections. (Refer back to Chapter 1 if you're unclear about how to do this.)
>
> To hear just one possible outcome of this exercise, check out the Chapter 4c – Finished session.

Grid Mode Clutch

When working in Grid mode, from time to time you'll want to move regions freely, as if they were in Slip mode. Too often, users will switch modes, make their changes, then switch modes again to get back into Grid mode. Of course, this only takes a second or two, but even so, it's something of a waste of effort.

When teaching classes, I often rely on visual and anecdotal teaching methods, and using clutch is a prime example. Here goes...

CHAPTER 4 ■ Editing Power

In Digidesign terminology, the Ctrl key (on PCs) and the Command (⌘) key (on Macs) have another commonly used name—clutch, which is a great description of the keys' function. If you take the word "clutch" and put it into its better-known automotive context (for those of you with manual-transmission cars), you'll know that engaging the clutch takes the vehicle out of gear. That's exactly what the Ctrl/Command key does to Grid mode—it takes it out of "gear."

It's very simple to use—just hold down the Ctrl key (if you're running a PC) or the Command (⌘) key (if you're running a Mac) as you drag with the Grabber tool. Holding this key will allow you to move regions freely, as shown in Figure 4.11.

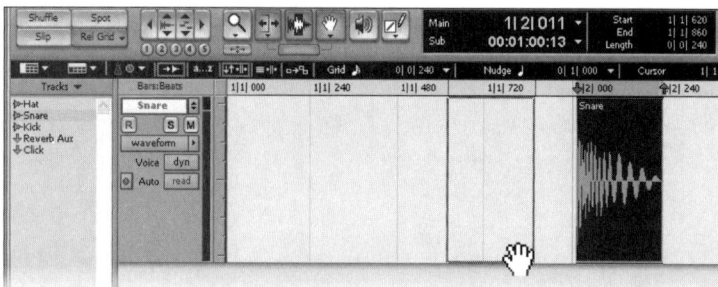

Figure 4.11

Clutching the Grid mode

If you're not using a control surface, applying the clutch to Grid mode is a very straightforward proposal, but it will take a bit of a weird turn when control surfaces are brought into the equation (which is why it gets special mention here).

All of Digidesign's control surfaces have a cluster of four modifier keys (generally located on the right side of the control surface). These four modifier keys include Shift, Option, Ctrl (which often has the word "clutch" next to it), and Comm (which has the Apple key symbol—⌘—next to it). It is important to note that these modifier keys are Mac-centric and are mapped slightly differently when you are dealing with a PC-based system.

- Shift on a Mac is mapped to Shift on a PC—no change.
- Option on a Mac is mapped to Alt on a PC.
- Command (⌘) on a Mac is mapped to Ctrl on a PC.
- Control on a Mac is mapped to Start (Windows) on a PC.

This remapping can get a little bit confusing for those who are using Pro Tools on a PC, but the solution is pretty simple once you get the hang of it: From the control surface, just press and hold the Command (⌘) modifier, which will have the equivalent effect of pressing and holding the Control key on your computer's keyboard. If you're a Mac user, there might be some frustration as well, because many control surfaces (including Control24, Control8, and Digi 002 Factory) list the word "clutch" by the Ctrl modifier key, when in fact the Comm modifier is the one you will want to use to disable the grid. The good news is that the feature works perfectly, even if the labeling is a bit off!

Working with Regions

The art of editing is the mastery of some pretty simple functions and tools. What's so hard about that, you ask? Fair question: The mark of a really excellent editor is that he knows not only *how* to use the tools at his command, but *when* to use them and how to use them in combination to get the desired result.

The next few sections of this book will be all about using a number of editing features to get to a particular goal. Here's the scenario: We have a multitrack drum kit that we want to use for some electronic-style music. The timing of the track doesn't have the sort of mathematical precision that we're looking for, so we'll have to fix that. When that's finished, we want to change the tempo of the drums, but in a way that won't degrade the quality of the audio. Read on . . .

> **NOTE**
> For this next section, please launch the session named Chapter 4d on the disc included with this book.

Strip Silence

The first thing that we'll want to do to reach our goal will be to separate each of the tracks into a number of smaller regions, each with one hit. (More on *why* we're doing this in just a moment.) Strip Silence is particularly good at this job.

It's best to think of Strip Silence as something of a region "gate," similar in effect to a noise gate. Just like a noise gate, Strip Silence removes sections of audio whose amplitude falls below a certain threshold. But wait, there's more!

1. Let's start with the Kick track. First, select the entire Kick region.
2. From the Edit drop-down menu, choose Strip Silence. The Strip Silence window will appear.
3. The first step here is to set the Strip Threshold slider to a value that sufficiently isolates each individual kick drum hit, as shown in Figure 4.12.
4. If you look carefully, you might notice that the boxed area might cut off some of the tail end of the kick. (The higher your threshold setting, the more obvious this will be.) Here's where Strip Silence starts to do more than a simple noise gate. Go to the Region End Pad slider and increase the value so that no part of the kick drum is outside each individual box.

CHAPTER 4 ■ Editing Power

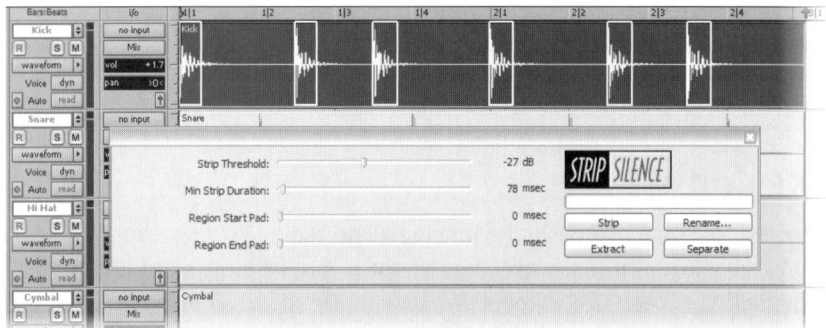

Figure 4.12
Setting the threshold

CAUTION

You will need to be careful when dealing with the Region End Pad slider. Setting a value too high will cause some of your discrete regions to combine, which would defeat the result we're going after.

5. The last part is easy—just click the Strip button in the lower-right area of the window, and you're finished!

NOTE

If you're using Pro Tools 7 or later, you'll notice that the Strip Silence window has a number of buttons in the lower-right corner. Though they're not particularly suited to the job that we're in the middle of right now, they do certainly bear a quick mention:

- **Extract.** This essentially does the opposite of the Strip button—it will leave only the regions of "silence," or the regions of your selection that fall below your threshold and outside your other strip parameters.
- **Separate.** This will not remove any audio from your track, but will rather separate your selected area into regions that would normally be stripped and regions that would normally be extracted.
- **Rename.** After your used the Strip, Extract, or Separate button, you can click the Rename button to assign specific names and numbers to the regions that are inside your selected area. (By the way, this can be used to rename regions in any selected area, and it doesn't necessarily have to be associated with any of the other functions of this window.)

When you're finished with the Kick track, repeat the process for the Snare and Hi-Hat tracks. When you're finished, your tracks should have a sort of checkerboard look, as shown in Figure 4.13.

Working with Regions

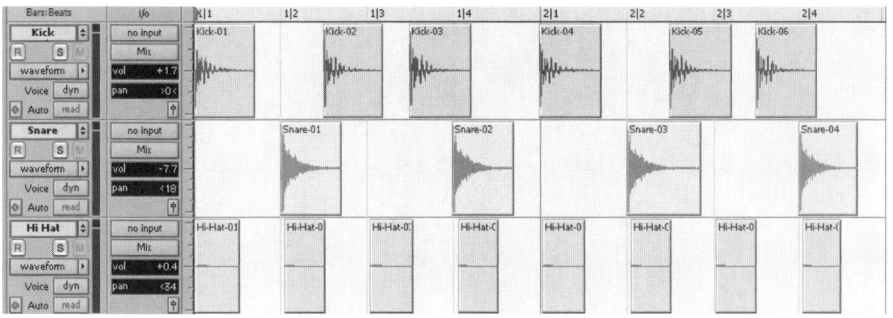

Figure 4.13
After Strip Silence

Separating Regions

Strip Silence is a great tool for this sort of job, but if you take a look (or better, a listen) at the Cymbal track, you'll see that there really isn't any silence to strip! Have no fear; you can use Separate Region to help out in this case.

Separate Region has been around for quite some time, of course, but recently it's had a bit of a makeover, and there's a new option that will really help you out in your work.

1. Select the entire Cymbal region.
2. From the Edit drop-down menu, choose the Separate Region menu item. A second menu will appear, as shown in Figure 4.14.

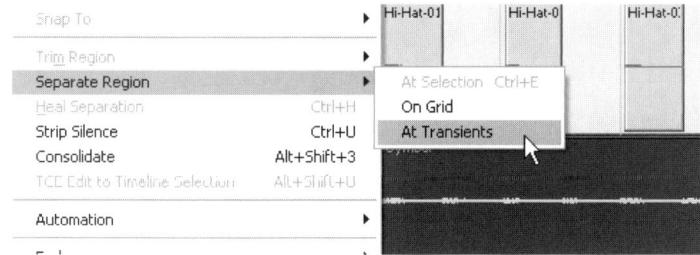

Figure 4.14
The Separate Region submenu

3. Although separating at each grid point might have the effect of isolating individual hits, it probably won't make a separate region at each transient. Choose the At Transients menu option instead. The Pre-Separate Amount window will appear.

4. The Pre-Separate Amount will offset the beginning of each region, moving it away from the transient. For example, if you were to enter a value of 10 milliseconds, the region boundary would be 10 ms before the transient. (Think of it as behaving similarly to Strip Silence's Region Start Pad.) Theoretically, a value of zero will create a region boundary right at the transient, which is what we'll use in this case—just click OK. Your track should be separated, as shown in Figure 4.15.

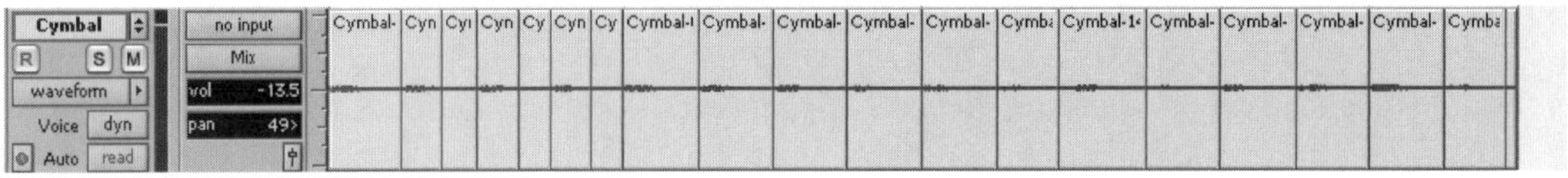

CHAPTER 4 ■ Editing Power

Figure 4.15
Separating regions on the transient

You'll immediately notice that Pro Tools has created a couple of regions where there aren't really any transients, a phenomenon that comes up from time to time and is easily remedied. We'll turn to an old editing friend, Heal Separation.

> **NOTE**
> The Heal Separation feature is only available for separated regions that can be rejoined into contiguous audio. That is to say, if one of the separated regions is moved, even by one sample, the region cannot be seamlessly rejoined, and in this case, Heal Separation will be unavailable.

1. Select the two regions that you wish to rejoin. In the case of this example, the second and third regions of the Cymbal track will need to be combined into one region, as shown in Figure 4.16.

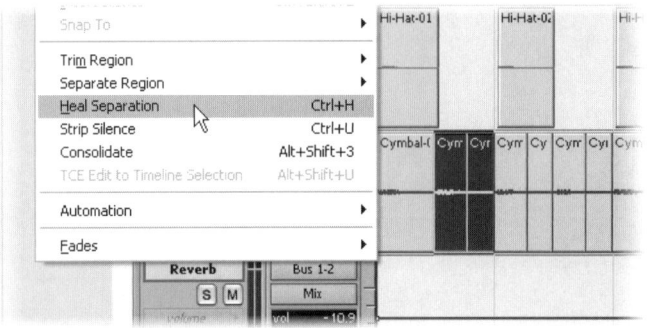

Figure 4.16
The healing touch!

2. From the Edit drop-down menu, choose Heal Separation. The two regions will be combined into one.

3. When you've combined these two regions, continue combining the appropriate regions. (Don't forget the small region at the end of the track.) You'll probably also want to heal the tenth and eleventh regions and re-seperate them manually on the transient. When you're finished, your track should look something like Figure 4.17.

Working with Regions

> **TIP**
>
> You might find that healing separations becomes one of your commonly used editing processes. Using the shortcut key (Ctrl+H for PCs and Command+H for Macs) will make the job go much more quickly! Of course, you can also extend each region's boundaries using the Trim tool.

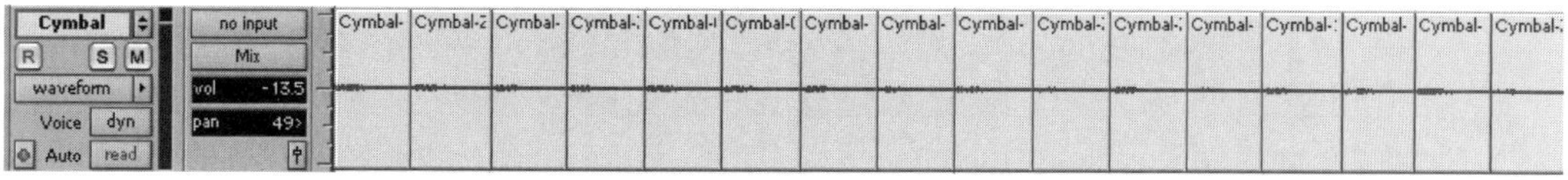

Figure 4.17
The healed track

Though this might seem like a lot of steps just to separate some regions, you will increase your speed with repetition, and the work you've done here will really start paying off in the next sections.

> **NOTE**
>
> **Important!** There's an important general rule among editors, regardless of the program that you might be using: When cutting regions and especially when creating loops, always cut on the zero crossing with the waveform ascending. Essentially, cutting at the zero crossing means separating your regions at the point where the waveform intersects the 0 dB line. This is the point between a wave's compression and rarefaction states and it is similar to a speaker at rest (with no voltage going through it). Adhering to this rule in your work will help you avoid many of the annoying clicks and pops that are sometimes heard at the beginning and end of regions.
>
> As to why we cut with the waveform ascending, that is a bit of a subjective call and is most important when working with looping segments of audio. The idea behind this rule is that when arranging loops end to end, we want to achieve a seamless transition from the end of one region to the beginning of another. If, for example, one region ended with a waveform ascending and was butted up against a region with the waveform descending, the resultant audio would have two consecutive periods of rarefaction, which might sound a bit unnatural. (You'll have to zoom in quite a ways to see this.) The bottom line is that you want your audio waveform to transition smoothly between alternative compression and rarefaction stages.
>
> All this being said, Strip Silence and Separate Region cut regions on the zero crossing, but not necessarily with the waveform ascending. Generally, this is no problem, and it isn't a problem in this situation here (because we're not looping regions), but it is a good fact to keep in mind.

CHAPTER 4 ■ Editing Power

Quantizing Regions

Now that your regions are separated, the next step is to make each hit conform to a perfect mathematical grid. (The style is electronic, remember?) We can do this quickly by quantizing the regions.

1. Select an appropriate grid setting. (If you've been following along with this exercise, you'll have a sixteenth-note grid, which will work fine for this.)
2. Select the region(s) (in the track area, not on the region list) you wish to quantize. In the case of this example, select all the regions on all the tracks of this session.
3. From the Region drop-down menu, choose Quantize to Grid. You'll see that the regions all snap directly to the nearest grid and you'll hear a subtle change in your beat.

> **NOTE**
>
> This feature is of course useful to making an Audio track mathematically perfect, but the power of this simple feature goes even further. If your session has tempo changes—even complex ones that are used to create grooves (commonly created using Beat Detective, which we'll talk about soon)—quantizing your regions will follow these changes as well.

Tick-Based Audio (and How to Use It!)

This next bit is something of a hidden "Easter egg" kind of feature for many folks—a tiny little button in Audio tracks that is rarely clicked. You'll find that when you're working with audio beats, though, working with tick-based audio regions will be a great help.

Typically, Audio tracks and the regions on them are *sample-based* in their timing, which means that their location in time is linked to an absolute sample location. Essentially, this means that if you change your MIDI tempo (which is *tick-based*), the location of the region will not change location, as MIDI regions would tend to do.

Audio tracks don't *have* to be sample-based, though. By switching your Audio track to being tick-based in nature, regions on that track will respond to tempo changes. By using this powerful feature, you'll be able to change the tempo of the drums without any of the sonic artifacts that can occur when you're using time compression/expansion, assuming that you've correctly separated each drum hit.

1. Click the Time Base Selector button on the desired Audio track. (For this example, let's start with the Kick track.) You'll note that Audio tracks' time base is generally set to samples and is shown as a small blue clock on the button, as shown in Figure 4.18.

Tick-Based Audio (and How to Use It!)

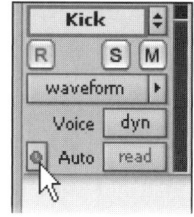

Figure 4.18
The Time Base Selector

2. From the menu that is displayed (see Figure 4.19), choose Ticks.
3. Repeat Steps 1 and 2 for the Snare, Hi-Hat, and Cymbal tracks.

That's pretty much it. From this point on, these tracks' regions will follow tempo changes! To illustrate the point, try opening the Transport window and changing the tempo with the Tempo slider. (Remember, you'll have to disable the Conductor button first.) You'll note that your drum loop now changes speed to match your tick-based tempo settings. Better yet, these changes are made without any of the potentially nasty side effects of the time compression/expansion AudioSuite plug-ins (including the TCE Trim tool).

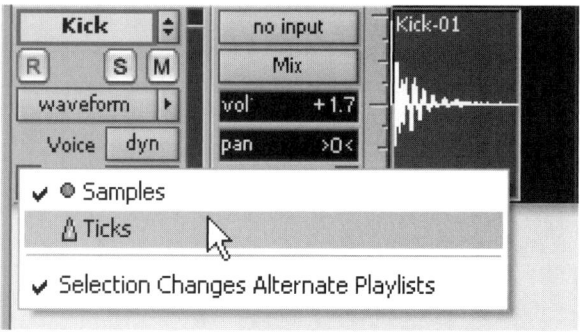

Figure 4.19
Switching to tick-based

Of course, there are things to keep in mind—there's a limit to which this drum kit will sound natural, and generally speaking it will sound better if the speed is increased. (If the speed is decreased, you'll hear gaps in the Cymbal track.) But all in all, it's a great way to get more out of your audio loops!

> **NOTE**
> To hear one possible result of the completion of these steps, take a look at the Chapter 4d-Finished session.

CHAPTER 4 ■ Editing Power

New Region Features

With the advent of Pro Tools 7, there are some new editing features that will help your work, particularly when you're working with beats. Not only that, but there are some welcome improvements to the ways that we can listen to and even preview loops. Take a look. . . .

Region Groups

In older versions of Pro Tools, I have made use of edit groups when working with drums, so that any changes that I made to one member of an active group in the Edit window would be mirrored in all the other members of the group. Though I still use edit groups quite a little bit, much of the role that they played in my workflow has now been replaced with *region groups*, a new feature in Pro Tools 7.

Region groups do just what you think that they do—they group multiple regions into one single object in the Edit window. There are a few very important things to keep in mind when grouping regions:

- Groupings can span multiple tracks.

- Region groups don't have to be on contiguous tracks, but they will include a contiguous block of time. For example, you can select a region on Measure 1 on Track 1, and then additionally select a region on Measure 3 of Track 3. If you group these regions together, no regions on Track 2 will be included in the group, but all regions on those tracks that are within that span of time *will* be included in this list (see Figure 4.20).

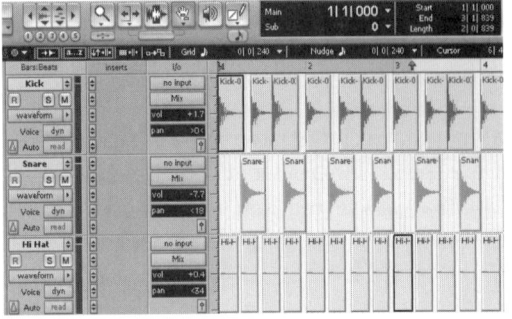 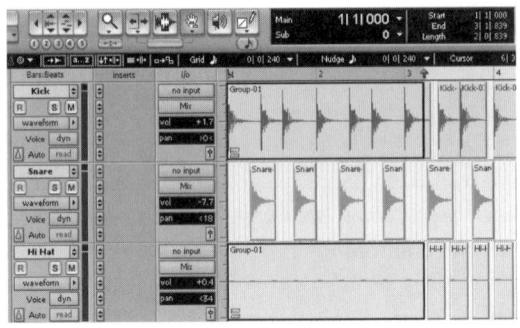

Figure 4.20

Region grouping—before and after

- Region groups may include audio regions, MIDI regions, or any combination of the two.

Here's how we might use region groups with a multitrack drum setup:

> **NOTE**
>
> For this session, please open the session called Chapter 4e. You'll notice that this bears a *very* strong resemblance to the session that you wound up with at the end of the previous section, with the addition of an Instrument track using Xpand!

1. Select the first four measures of the Kick, Snare, Hi-Hat, Cymbal, and Conga tracks. (Note that the Conga track is an Instrument track with MIDI regions.)
2. From the Region drop-down menu, choose Group. The regions selected will immediately become a single object in your track area, as shown in Figure 4.21.

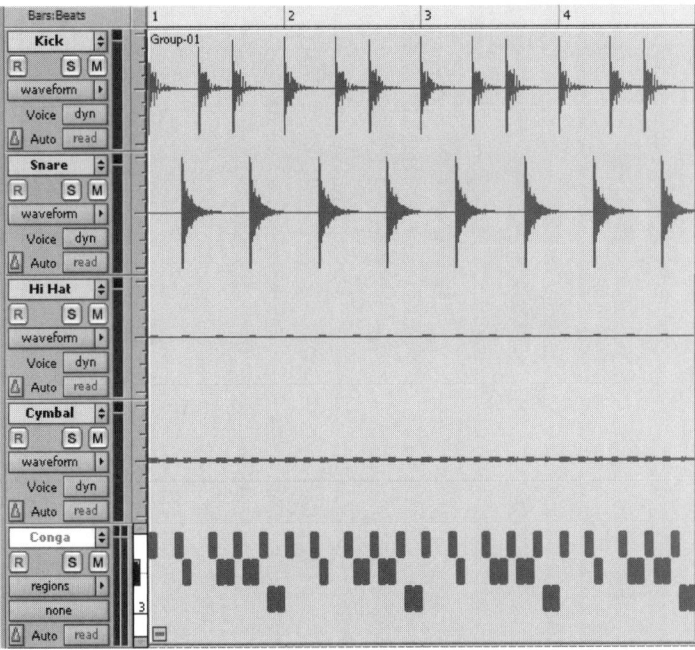

Figure 4.21

Grouping multitrack drums

Note the small icon in the lower-left corner of the region group object. You'll note that the same icon is displayed to the left of the region group as it appears in the region list as well. The icon varies somewhat to indicate what kind of regions might be contained in the group.

Figures 4.22 to 4.25 show the different kinds of region groups.

CHAPTER 4 ■ Editing Power

Figure 4.22
Icon for a region group containing only audio regions

Figure 4.23
Icon for a region group containing only MIDI regions

Figure 4.24
Icon for a region group containing both audio and MIDI regions

Figure 4.25
Icon for a region group in the track area that spans discontiguous tracks

When your region group is created, you'll be able to move and edit all the included regions as a single unit. Better yet, you'll be able to use tools such as the Smart tool on a region group as if it were a single region. Creating fades on a region group is particularly interesting because it will allow you to create a fade that spans many of the component regions, as shown in Figure 4.26.

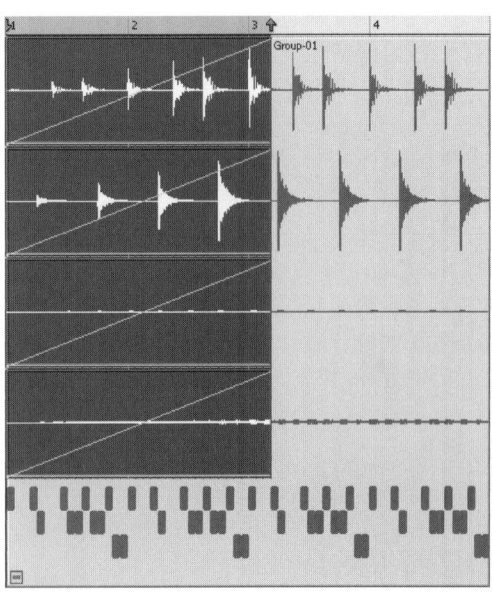

Figure 4.26
Creating a fade on a region group. (Note that a fade is not created for the MIDI component of the group.)

> **TIP**
> If you're like me, you'll use region groups quite a bit once you get the hang of them. The shortcut for creating a group—Ctrl+Alt+G for PCs and Command+Option+G for Macs—will make the job go much more quickly. You can also create a region group quickly by selecting the desired members of that group in your tracks, right-clicking with your mouse, and choosing the Group menu item from the menu that appears.

> **NOTE**
>
> If you take a look at what you've just created, you'll see that it's very similar to a Rex file in most regards—with a few important extras! In fact, a Rex file in Pro Tools is nothing more than a tick-based audio region group. If you import any Rex file, then go to the Region drop-down menu and choose Ungroup, you'll see the Rex region break down into its component drum hits. Of course, what you've just created goes far beyond a simple Rex file because you now have control over individual elements of the drum mix. (You can tweak the edits of specific tracks by ungrouping the group, making your changes, and regrouping.) And, you've combined the power of audio and MIDI regions. Good job!

Region Looping

Now that you've got a four-bar segment of drums that you really like, the next step commonly is to repeat it many times, or "loop" it. Historically, there have been many ways to do this—duplicate region, repeat, or even basic cut, copy, and paste. Now in Pro Tools 7, there's a new feature—Region Loop—that'll do the job more quickly and better!

Working with the session we just used in the last section, let's loop our newly created region group for the duration of our song.

1. Select the region(s) you wish to loop.
2. From the Region drop-down menu, choose the Loop menu item. The Region Looping dialog box will be displayed (see Figure 4.27). Here's a quick rundown of the options that are open to you:

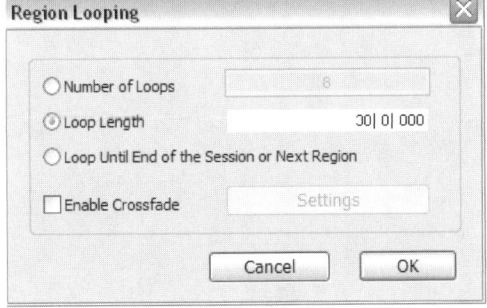

Figure 4.27
The Region Looping dialog box

- **Number of Loops.** Clicking this radio button and then specifying a number of repetitions will cause your region to be repeated a set number of times.
- **Loop Length.** This option will allow you to set a specific length for your loops. Note: The value in the window to the right of the radio button will be displayed in the same format as the Main Time Scale.

CHAPTER 4 ■ Editing Power

- **Loop Until End of the Session or Next Region.** As the name suggests, this option will repeat the selected region until the last event in your session or the next region, whichever comes first.
- **Enable Crossfade.** You can choose to apply crossfades to all the repeated regions, regardless of which of the radio buttons you've selected. Once this option is selected, you will then have the option of configuring the parameters of this crossfade, just as you would with a regular batch crossfade.

> **NOTE**
>
> Be careful of applying crossfades—they can be something of a double-edged sword. If you've not cut on the zero crossing line and you are hearing clicks during your region transitions, a quick crossfade can help minimize this problem by effectively creating a zero crossing for you. However, if you've meticulously edited to maximize the punch of your transients (see more on this in the final chapter), you might find that a crossfade diminishes the punch of the first transient of the region.

3. For the purposes of our example, choose the Loop Length radio button and enter a length of 30|0|000. Your region will be immediately looped for 30 measures. When you're finished, your session should look something like Figure 4.28.

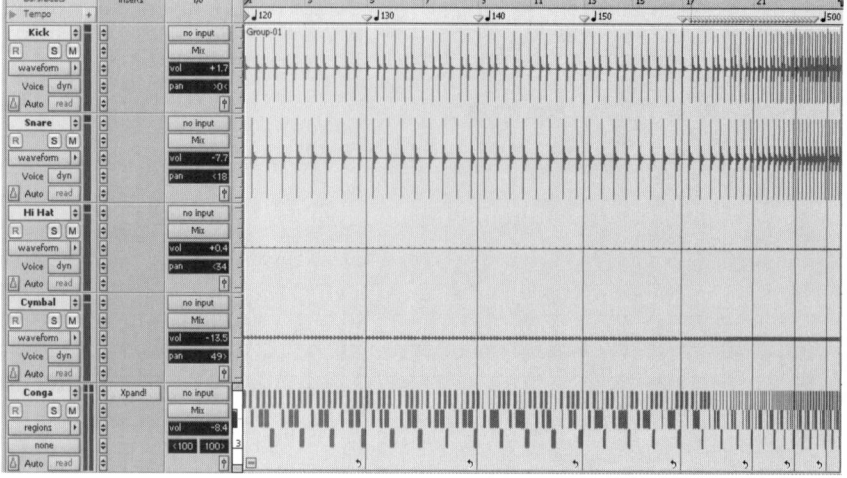

Figure 4.28

After region looping

> **NOTE**
>
> To see these steps in their completed state, just open the Chapter 4e-Finished #1 session.

New Region Features

If you take a look at your session, you'll probably hear the region gain speed (assuming that your Conductor button is enabled in the Transport window). The truth is, I've somewhat booby-trapped the session to illustrate a point: I've placed small tempo changes every 4 measures for the first 16 measures, then a severe linear increase in tempo starting at Measure 17. (I know, I'm a little devil!) Note that because your region group is made up of tick-based audio and MIDI regions, this region group will follow tempo changes as it is looped. Neat, huh?

Here's something else that's neat: There are now *two* ways in which you can trim your region!

If you position your Trim tool on either end of the large region loop object, you can change the beginning or ending of the loop. Note that this will not affect the speed of the loops or change the internal regions in any way; it will just change the starting or ending point of the loop as a whole (see Figure 4.29).

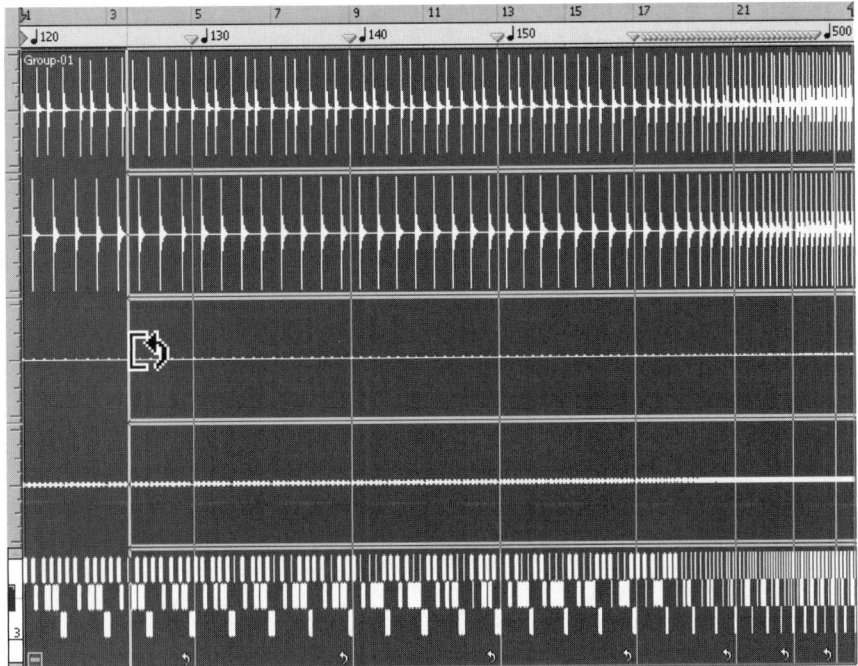

Figure 4.29

Trimming your region loop object

There's also a way to trim the individual regions *inside* the region loop object, but there is a specific way to go about it. Take a look:

1. Select the Trim tool. For this particular process to work, the Trim tool (not the Smart tool) must be selected.
2. Go to the bottom corner of any of the internal regions of your region loop. For example, in Figure 4.30, you'll see that I've chosen the bottom-right corner of the first looped region.

89

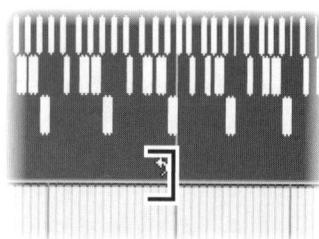

Figure 4.30

Getting ready to trim region loop components

3. Trim the region as normal, dragging right or left. You'll note that you will *not* see the entire region loop change boundaries, but the single component region only, as shown in Figure 4.31.

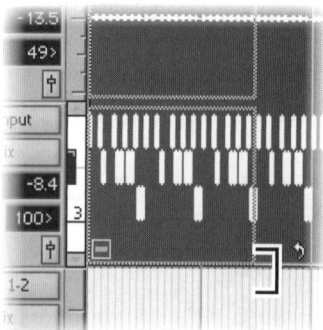

Figure 4.31

Trimming your region loop components

4. Once you release the Trim tool, you'll see two interesting things have immediately happened. First, each component region has altered its boundary to match the changes you've made to the region with which you were directly working. Second, even though you've made changes, the overall duration of your loops hasn't changed. In this particular example, you'll see that the loops are still 30 measures long!

> **NOTE**
>
> If you open the session named Chapter 4e-Finished #2, you'll see just one outcome of this sort of trimming. If you listen carefully, you'll note that I've changed the feel of the region loop from a 4/4 feel to a more waltz-like 3/4 (or 6/8, depending upon how you hear it) loop.

> **NOTE**
>
> If this process intrigues you, take a look at the final chapter's "Loop Trim Polyrhythms" section.

New Region Features

You've covered a good deal of ground in this chapter, and hopefully you've picked up a technique or two in the process. Let's finish this chapter with a very quick mention of a couple of simple but effective new additions to Pro Tools version 7.3.

Dynamic Transport

In previous versions of Pro Tools, checking the loop-ability of a selected area was commonly a time-consuming process, particularly if your loop was a fairly long one. The reason behind this is because loop playback would have to start from the beginning of the selected area, play through the entire selection, and only then loop back to the beginning of the selected area.

With Dynamic Transport those days are over (let the rejoicing begin!), and you can start at any point before, during, or even after a selected area. When working with beats, the benefits are immediate—you can start playback just before the end of your selected area, so you don't have to listen to the entire selection to see whether it loops correctly! Here's how I've come to use this feature with beats:

1. Once you have selected an area that you want to listen to, go to the Options menu and choose the Dynamic Transport item.

> **TIP**
>
> If you're like me and you find yourself using Dynamic Transport frequently, you'll want to start using the shortcut keys—Ctrl+Start+P on a PC or Command+Control+P on a Mac. You can also enable Dynamic Transport by right-clicking the play button in the Transport window and choosing Dynamic Transport from the menu that appears.

2. As soon as you enable the Dynamic Transport feature, two important things will happen. First, your Main ruler (the same format as your Main Counter) will become twice as tall, with a blue triangle in the lower half of the ruler (see Figure 4.32). The second important thing that will happen is that your timeline and edit selection will have been automatically unlinked (also shown in Figure 4.32).

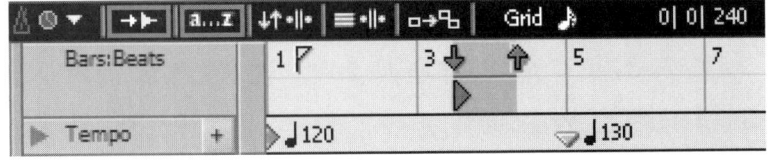

Figure 4.32

Dynamic Transport enabled

3. You can now click and drag the blue triangle (technically called the *Play Start Marker*) to any desired time. Figure 4.33 shows you a common way to use this feature with drums. In this case, once playback starts, playback will begin at 4|3|000, continue until 4|4|000, and then loop back to 3|3|240.

CHAPTER 4 ■ Editing Power

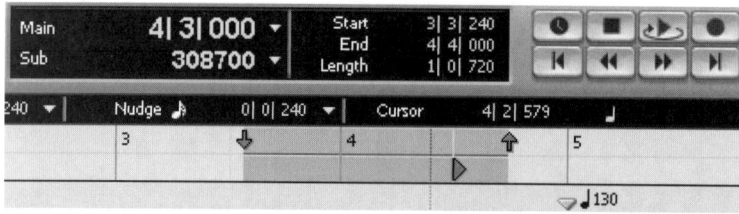

Figure 4.33

A common Dynamic Transport scenario

> **TIP**
> Though enabling Dynamic Transport will automatically unlink the edit and timeline selection, you can easily re-link the selection and continue using Dynamic Transport if you wish. You can re-link the edit and timeline selection in three ways: You can click the Link Timeline and Edit Selection button below the Zoom tool, enable Link Timeline and Edit Selection from the Options drop-down menu, or use the shortcut keys Shift+/ (PC or Mac).

Looping in the Browsers

Last but not least, the browsers. New in the Workspace, Volume, and Project browsers is the ability to preview an audio file *looped*. This means that if you want to preview how a drum audio file will sound repeated, you can now do this in the workspace before importing the file to your session. It's extremely easy, though easy to miss. Here are the two methods of enabling this feature (see Figure 4.34):

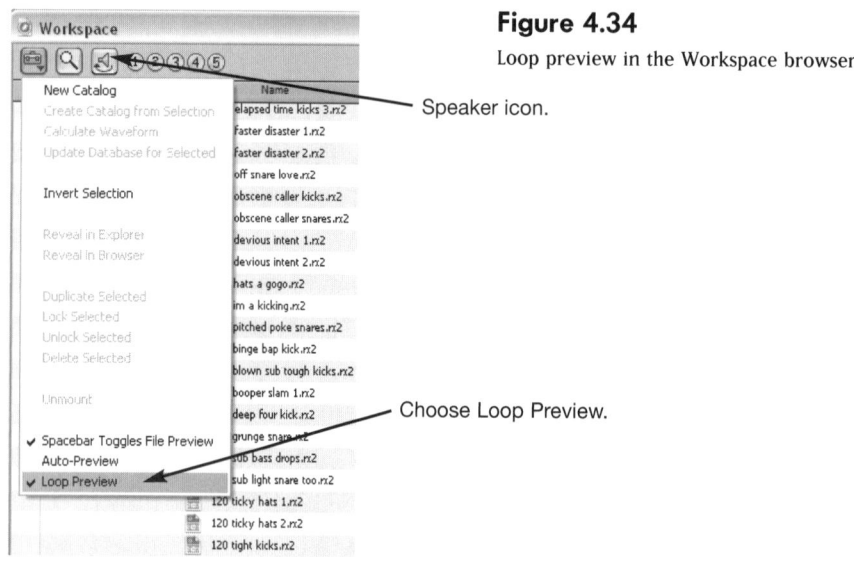

Figure 4.34

Loop preview in the Workspace browser

1. Click the Toolbox icon in the upper-left corner of the browser. In the menu that appears, choose the Loop Preview item to enable loop preview.
2. Start-click (PC), Control-click (Mac), or right-click the Speaker icon to enable loop preview.

When this option is enabled, previewed regions will infinitely loop until the preview is stopped.

Whew, you've done much in this chapter, and if you've found an inspiring trick or two, my job has been successful. Next stop, Beat Detective!

5 Making the Most of Beat Detective

The next couple of chapters will cover some specific features within Pro Tools, and there's really no better place to start than with a great tool called *Beat Detective*. You might find Beat Detective to be a little tricky to operate at the beginning (as I did), but once you understand how this neat little application "thinks," you'll wonder how you ever lived without it! If you're already somewhat familiar with Beat Detective's operation, we'll dig a bit deeper and explore how to really take advantage of its power.

In this chapter, you'll learn how to:

- Use Beat Detective's basic functions with confidence
- Use Beat Detective's more advanced aspects to deal with tricky cases
- Combine your new knowledge of Beat Detective with other concepts already learned, in practical workflow examples
- Use Beat Detective to expand your "toolbox" of grooves

So What the Heck *Is* Beat Detective, Anyway?

Like so much of the best technology these days, Beat Detective isn't simply a self-contained feature, but rather the nexus of a number of technologies. To get the most out of Beat Detective, let's explore how this nexus operates. You'll find that with Beat Detective, a little understanding goes a *long* way!

One very simple way to think of Beat Detective is to think of it as a more advanced form of the Tab to Transient feature in Pro Tools. Like Tab to Transient, Beat Detective analyzes the waveform of a section of audio, makes a determination as to what is a transient and what isn't, and goes from there. In fact, you might say that the fact that Tab to Transient does its job so well contributes greatly to Beat Detective's usefulness.

CHAPTER 5 ■ Making the Most of Beat Detective

Beat Detective goes further than just pointing out transients, however. First, there is a great deal of user input as to what exactly constitutes a *real* transient. After that, Beat Detective has the intelligence to determine the *musical* position of each of the transients (with a little help from you, of course!).

It's this musical analysis that makes Beat Detective really interesting. You see, Beat Detective not only takes Tab to Transient one step further, but it also improves upon what Identify Beat does as well. Whereas Identify Beat calculates tempo based upon the beginning and ending points of a selected area, Beat Detective takes into account its analysis of the transients within that selection. (You'll see how this happens later in this chapter.) In this way, Beat Detective captures not only the *tempo* of a passage, but also the subtle manipulations of time that give us *groove*.

This is all well and good from a conceptual point of view, but it begs the question, "What the heck do you do with it?" Actually, there are a number of commonly used workflows involving Beat Detective.

- **Create a complex tempo map.** In this case, there's no problem with the drum Audio track—in fact, the drum track's feel is perfect as is. The problem is that the MIDI you're using in your session doesn't groove with the drum's Audio track. We'll use Beat Detective in the opposite direction in this case. Instead of conforming the drum audio to a preexisting tempo map, we'll analyze the transients of the drums and *create* a complex array of subtle tempo changes based upon that analysis. This delicate push/pull of musical time is the essence of the drum's groove, and once it has been extracted to the session's MIDI timeline, your MIDI data (which is tick-based to begin with) will get in line with your drum track.

- **"Quantize" an Audio track.** Let's say you've got a live drum track, and at some point in the music, the timing of the playing gets a little sloppy. You'll want to clean up the timing, and Beat Detective is a great tool for this. With Beat Detective, you can analyze the transients within a selection, separate the region at each of the transients, and then conform the individual regions to the MIDI timeline. (Incidentally, you can also use *groove* quantization as well!)

- **Conform one audio beat to another.** This technique takes advantage of both of these aspects of Beat Detective. In this case, you might have a two-bar rock beat on one track and a two-bar shuffle beat on another, and you want to get them to play together nicely. First, you'd decide which of the two feels you want to learn, and then you'd analyze that drum loop and create a tempo map on your MIDI timeline based upon that analysis. Next, you'd analyze the *other* drum loop and "quantize" it to the MIDI timeline (which now reflects the groove of the first region).

This may seem like Greek to you right now, but don't fret—after you go through each of these processes once or twice, you'll find that Beat Detective is actually very easy to use and surprisingly flexible. In the following sections, we'll outline how to get the most out of each of these processes and more.

> **NOTE**
>
> If you've already got some experience with Beat Detective, please feel free to skip to the appropriate sections of interest—I hope that you'll find a few useful tidbits within the exercises. If you're a relative beginner with Beat Detective, I would encourage you to go through all of the following sections in sequence. Between the different examples, we'll cover all the basics of Beat Detective (and then some!).

Workflow #1: Creating a Tempo Map

We'll start with one of the mainstays of Beat Detective used in a very familiar scenario.

> **NOTE**
>
> For this section, please open the session named Chapter 5a, located on the attached disc. You'll need to have Xpand! installed on your system in order to hear the Instrument track.

The session named Chapter 5a presents a fairly common situation in which you might find yourself: You've created or imported a killer drum region (in this case, as shuffle groove) and you want to spice it up with some MIDI. Because you're a savvy Pro Tools user, you've used Identify Beat (which we discussed in Chapter 4) to determine the exact tempo of the loop you're working with, and then created some MIDI. To tighten up the timing, you might have even done some MIDI quantization, but surprise: Try as you might, your mathematically perfect MIDI just doesn't groove with the audio. Play the session and you'll see what I mean—the MIDI and audio have some points where they're noticeably off.

Here's where Beat Detective comes to the rescue. With this tool, it's very quick work to modify your MIDI Tempo ruler (upon which your MIDI data's timing is based) to reflect the particular feel of the drum audio. Whereas Identify Beat is as blunt as a butter knife for this kind of work, Beat Detective is as sharp as a scalpel.

Generally speaking, using Beat Detective is usually a left-to-right process. If you take a look at Beat Detective's window, you'll see what I mean.

Making a Selection

Before you are ready to launch Beat Detective, your first job is to select a region (or a portion of a region) for Beat Detective to work with. In this example, the job will be easy—just select the single four-bar drum region on the Shuffle Drum Loop Audio track. If you listen to this region in Loop Playback mode, you'll note that it loops perfectly—a good indicator that its region is really four measures, no more and no less.

1. From the Event menu, choose Beat Detective, as shown in Figure 5.1. For future reference, the shortcut to Beat Detective is Ctrl+8 (for PCs) or Apple+8 on the numeric keypad (for Macs).

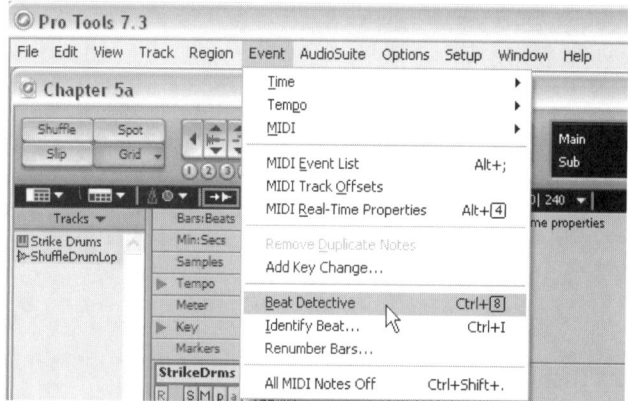

Figure 5.1
Launching Beat Detective

2. You'll see that Beat Detective is laid out in three general areas, with the one on the leftmost side being named Operation. For the job at hand, please choose Audio from the drop-down menu at the top of the Operation area (because we're working with the audio drum track in this case) and click Bar|Beat Marker Generation, because our goal is to create a detailed tempo map.

3. Next, we're on to the Selection area. Now, I can't overstate the importance of this area—in my experience, most confusion about Beat Detective centers around this stage. The first part of this process is to define the beginning and ending points of the selected area (similar to what you might do with Identify Beat). If you listen to the region, you'll find that it is a four-bar segment that begins at the beginning of the session, so you should set your Start Bar|Beat value to be 1|1, and the end point should be the very beginning of the fifth bar, so set End Bar|Beat to be 5|1. Last but not least, you'll need to tell Pro Tools what the Time Signature value of the selection is—in most cases, it'll be 4/4 time, as shown in this example. When you're finished, you should see something like Figure 5.2.

Figure 5.2
Setting your selection

4. Working your way down the Selection area, you'll find the Contains drop-down menu (see Figure 5.3). Here's where you have to use your ears and musical know-how. After listening to the segment of music carefully, you'll need to determine the musical resolution of the beat. In this case, the finest rhythmic value is a sixteenth note, so you should set the value

accordingly. (Just click on the drop-down menu.) In cases where the resolution is based upon a triplet, just click the small box to the immediate right of the Contains drop-down menu. (Just a reminder: We're not working with triplets in this particular example.)

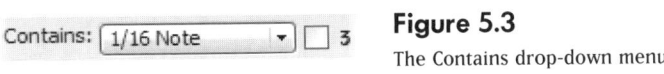

Figure 5.3
The Contains drop-down menu

In this particular example, the tempo of the session (92 BPM) matches the overall tempo of the loop region, and in cases like this you've got an easy way to set your start and end points at your disposal. Simply make your selection (also easy in this case, since the region on the Shuffle Drum Loop Audio track is exactly four measures), then click the Capture Selection button shown in Figure 5.4.

Figure 5.4
The Capture Selection and Tap End B|B buttons

You won't need to use the Tap End BB button for this example, but it does merit an explanation. Let's say for the sake of argument that you've created a selection of audio, making sure that the starting and ending points are right where you want them. You've entered the Start Bar|Beat value, but the problem is that you have no idea as to the actual length of the selection! Let's further assume that the Tempo ruler of the session doesn't match the tempo of the selection, so even the Edit Selection Length display at the top of the Edit window doesn't help.

In this case, just start playback of your session (loop playback is fine for this as well) and click the Tap End B|B button (shown in Figure 5.4) in time with the music. Beat Detective can extrapolate from your entered tempo the duration (in musical terms) of your selection and will automatically fill in the End Bar|Beat value for you. You'll notice that this value may adjust itself as you tap—this is completely normal. Think of this feature as Beat Detective's version of the Tap Tempo feature available in the Transport window (which we talked about back in Chapter 1).

Analysis

At the heart of any use of Beat Detective are a few common aspects. Establishing your selection as described in the previous section is one, and the analysis phase—where Beat Detective actually does *detect beats*—is another. This is pretty straightforward, but it would be good at this point to go into the finer points of this detection process.

1. Click the Analyze button. Immediately, Beat Detective will take a look at the entire selection and determine all of the likely transients at a variety of amplitudes (though if your Sensitivity slider is set to zero, you'll see no visible change).

CHAPTER 5 ■ Making the Most of Beat Detective

> **CAUTION**
>
> Beat Detective does *not* automatically re-analyze audio when a selection is changed. This is something you'll have to do manually. What this means, in effect, is that if you're working on numerous areas in succession, you'll want to analyze each different selection. This can be a little tricky because you will often see beat triggers *without* manually analyzing, but beware—they may well be based upon a previous analysis, and the only way to be sure that Beat Detective will behave as desired is to click that Analyze button!

2. The next step is to gradually raise the Sensitivity slider. You'll notice that markers—called *beat triggers*—will start to appear. The first triggers will appear to signify the loudest transients, followed by softer transient beat triggers being shown as the Sensitivity slider moves to the right. You'll note that beat triggers marking the starts of bars are relatively thick yellow markers, with beats being slightly narrower and sub-beat markers being the thinnest of all.

3. Your goal in using the Sensitivity slider is to capture all of the musically relevant transients, so use your ears. You can play your session when you're using Beat Detective, and even zoom in and out as well. I've found that a value of 43% works well with this example (as shown in Figure 5.5), but do experiment for yourself.

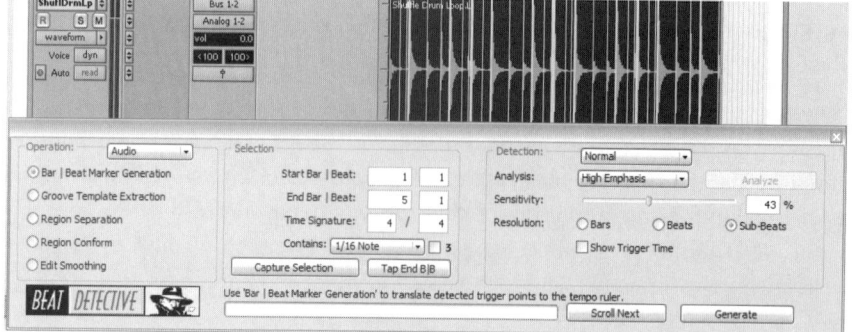

Figure 5.5
Beat triggers

Emphasis

As you experiment with different beats, you might find that the Sensitivity slider doesn't behave quite as you'd like—in other words, beat markers are created in a bad order or certain transients are missed entirely. There are a number of ways to manage this behavior, and probably the easiest is by changing the emphasis of the analysis.

Essentially, the two emphasis modes are different mathematical formulae for detecting and calculating transients. To bias the sensitivity toward the higher frequencies (for example, hi-hat, which is an important element in this example), choose High Emphasis from the Emphasis drop-down menu (to the immediate left of the Analyze button and to the right of the word "Analysis," as shown earlier in Figure 5.5). If your material is more reliant upon lower frequencies (for example, a slap bass guitar track or piano), choose Low Emphasis.

In this example, you'll find that the cymbal content in this beat makes High Emphasis the mode of choice, but by all means, experiment with the two different modes to see how they "think." Please note that you'll have to re-analyze the selection each time you change modes in order to get the desired effect.

Resolution

In some cases, a hyper-accurate tempo map might be more complex than you need—in fact, it could be downright confusing! It's not a problem—just go to the Resolution area to limit the complexity of your tempo map. Directly below the Sensitivity slider, you'll see three radio buttons marked Bars, Beats, and Sub-Beats.

It's pretty simple: If you want Beat Detective to detect only measure downbeats, choose Bars. Choosing Beats will only show beat triggers that fall directly on beats as defined by your time signature. Sub-Beats (arguably the most used mode, and the one that works for this example) will detect transients all the way down to the resolution that you selected in the Contains drop-down menu in the Selection area of Beat Detective.

Working with Beat Triggers

So you're a tweaker—good on ya! Me too, which is why sometimes even the control that we've outlined up to this point just isn't enough! Beat Detective does allow for individual addition, modification, and deletion of beat triggers using the Grabber tool. This way, once you've exhausted the precision of the Beat Detective window itself, you can still go in with sample-accurate precision.

It's up to you, and I know that different people have different working styles, but I find that this sort of work is most efficient when I know what musical values I'm working with. In other words, I want to know exactly what time (in bars and beats) each beat trigger represents. There's a little check box in the Detection area of Beat Detective called Show Trigger Time that will help you with this. When you check this box (as shown in Figure 5.6), you'll see a small bar|beat|trigger label by each beat trigger.

Keep in mind that each of these timing labels signifies the timing that Beat Detective *thinks* the marker is, rather than being a reflection of the timing in relation to the current tempo map. This could be a little confusing at first, but it's sufficient to say that these are the timings of the timing map that you're creating, rather than the one that currently exists. (This will be clear in the next section.)

CHAPTER 5 ■ Making the Most of Beat Detective

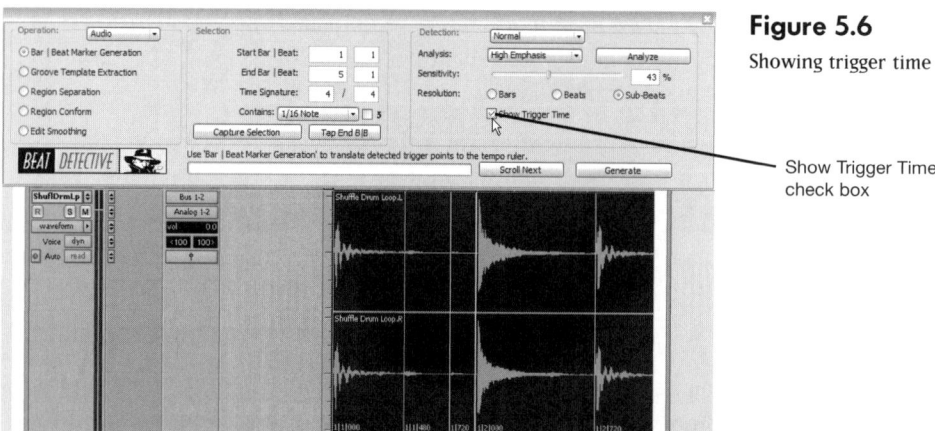

Figure 5.6

Showing trigger time

Show Trigger Time check box

With that out of the way, working with individual beat triggers is simplicity itself. (Before you get into this, you'll probably want to zoom in a bit, so you can see each individual transient clearly.)

> **TIP**
>
> When you're working with beat triggers at this level, you might find yourself zoomed in to a level in which you only see a handful of beat triggers (or maybe even one!). There's a button in Beat Detective that can really save some time when navigating from trigger to trigger. If you look at the lower-right corner of the Beat Detective window, you'll see the Scroll Next button. Each time you click this button, your Edit window will center on the next beat trigger.

- Clicking in an empty area with the Grabber tool will create a new beat trigger.
- Clicking on a pre-existing beat trigger with the Grabber tool will allow you to move it earlier or later in time. (The beat trigger will turn blue to show you that it's ready to be moved.)
- Clicking on a pre-existing beat trigger with the Grabber tool while holding down the Alt key (PC) or the Option key (Mac) will delete the beat trigger. The Grabber tool will have a small minus (–) sign by it to indicate that you're about to remove a trigger, as shown in Figure 5.7.

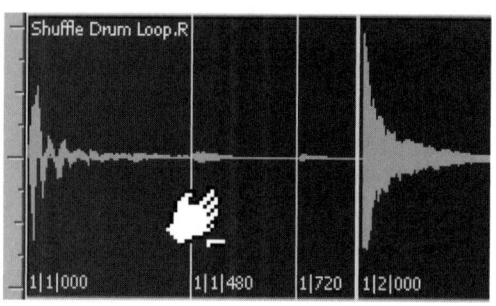

Figure 5.7

Deleting a beat trigger

This will give you enough control over your beat triggers in most cases, but for those special cases, there are two other techniques that you might want to employ from time to time.

Promoting a Beat Trigger

Here's a situation in which you might find yourself: You're dealing with a section of drum audio with a few particularly low-amplitude transients that are crucial to the beat. As you bring your Sensitivity slider value up, more and more transients are progressively marked (as usual), but by the time the low-level transients in question are captured, a number of false triggers have also been created. Basically, Beat Detective has "seen" transients in low-level audio material that are certainly not meaningful transients to your ear.

What to do? Of course, you could delete the unwanted beat markers, but that is more often than not a difficult and time-consuming prospect. It would be really great if you could "fool" Beat Detective into thinking that the low-level transients that you want to capture were actually louder. That's precisely what promoting a beat trigger does, and it's an easy thing to do.

1. While using the Grabber tool, hold down the Ctrl key (PC) or Apple key (Mac). You'll note that there's a small upward-pointing arrow (see Figure 5.8).

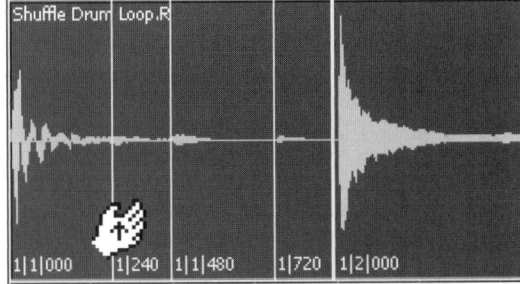

Figure 5.8
Promoting a beat trigger

2. Click on the specific quiet beat trigger(s) that you want to keep. Each time you click a transient, it will be emphasized by a small amount, so you might have to click a given transient multiple times to get the desired result. (This is a feature with which you should definitely experiment.)

3. After you've promoted your beat triggers, you can now *lower* the sensitivity value. Other quiet beat triggers will disappear, but your promoted trigger will stick around a bit longer! By changing the perceived significance of this beat trigger, you are interacting with Beat Detective's analysis at a high level.

Changing the Value of a Beat Trigger

Last but not least, here's one more trigger-related situation and a very easy solution: You listen to your drum segment and analyze it, and all the transients you want are easily detected. However, Beat Detective has assigned a timing to a trigger that you don't agree with (a good reason to check the Show Trigger Time box). Perhaps a transient that you see as being on the second beat is read by Beat Detective as being at Beat 1, Tick 720. It's time to show Beat Detective who's boss and change that trigger's value.

This is *very* easy to do: Using the Grabber tool, double-click on the beat trigger that you want to change. The Identify Trigger dialog box will be shown (see Figure 5.9).

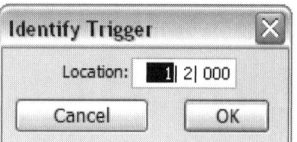

Figure 5.9
The Identify Trigger dialog box

Just enter the value that you feel the trigger *should* be, then click OK. That's it—the label of the beat trigger will be changed. (The position of the trigger will *not* be changed.)

Creating a Tempo Map

Whew—you're almost finished! Truth is, the really hard work is behind you. If you're following the example described here, take one more listen to the way that the Instrument track and the Audio track *don't* groove together.

Now, click the Generate button in the lower-right corner of Beat Detective. The Realign Session dialog box will appear, as shown in Figure 5.10.

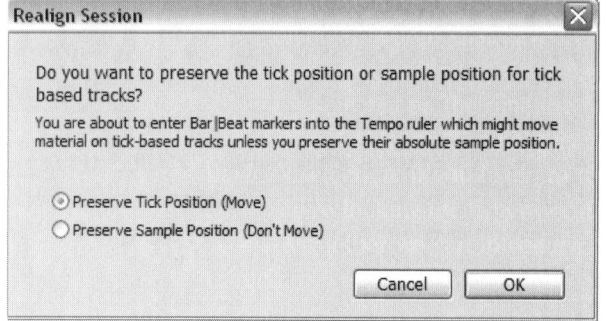

Figure 5.10
The Realign Session dialog box

Thanks to your understanding of sample-based versus tick-based tracks (Chapter 4), this dialog box should make sense for the most part. Essentially, it's stating that because you're about to change the Tempo ruler, you have the option to have your tick-based data (such as the MIDI data on the Instrument track) follow those changes (Move) or stick to its real-time sample position (Don't Move).

Because the point of this particular workflow is to adjust the timing of the MIDI, choose the top radio button, then click OK. You should now see a large number of blue markers appear in the Tempo ruler. If you expand the Tempo ruler (by clicking the triangle to the left of the word "tempo"), you'll see a more graphic representation of the variations of time that make up this particular groove.

More that that, though, you'll hear a significant change in the feel of the bell track! You'll hear it closely follow the timing of the drum Audio track (which you can improve upon even more by setting up a MIDI track offset, which we discussed in Chapter 3). Good job!

> **NOTE**
>
> To see this exercise in its finished form, open the session named Chapter 5a – Finished.

Workflow #2: Quantizing Audio

With the completion of the first workflow example, you've covered most of the basics of Beat Detective operation—the rest of this chapter will be quick by comparison! For this next section, we'll use a (crudely) constructed simulation, designed to show a number of the curves that might be thrown to you in a number of real-world situations. So, with that suspension of disbelief, let's dive in. . . .

> **NOTE**
>
> For this section, please open the session named Chapter 5b, located on the attached disc.

The situation: You've called in a live drummer to lay down a drum beat that you intend to use as a foundation for a song on which you'll be working. Using no click, he laid down a quick couple of bars of shuffle beat, which sounded good at the time, so he packed up and went home.

Being a savvy user, you figured you could just cut the desired loop and use it, but you ran into a few problems the next day.

1. Because you didn't use a click, you have no idea what the tempo of the segment is!
2. The drummer speeds up just a little bit at the end of the two-bar section. You didn't notice it before, but it is significant enough to prevent the section from looping smoothly.
3. The client comes into the studio, listens to the beat, and says, "I don't really like that shuffle feel; can you get rid of that?"

CHAPTER 5 ■ Making the Most of Beat Detective

> **NOTE**
>
> This example is intentionally an extreme case to show the effect of Beat Detective in an easily recognizable manner. In real life, a timing problem that you might more commonly encounter would be a live drum track that rushes or drags a bit. The workflow that we'll show in this section includes the steps you would follow to fix this sort of problem.

With Beat Detective, we can make pretty short work of all these problems.

The mark of a truly high-level user is not only the measure of how many processes one has mastered, but how the person can use *multiple* processes to get more complex jobs done. In this case, we're going to draw upon some skills that we've used before to make our selection and figure out the tempo that the drummer was playing. Just follow these steps, and we'll be able to proceed.

1. First, you'll need to determine the tempo. Though you *could* use Identify Beat (Chapter 4), in this case I'd recommend using Tap Tempo (Chapter 1) in order to create a static tempo throughout the session. When you're finished, your tempo should be about 97 to 98 BPM.

2. Use the Tab to Transient feature (Chapter 1) to move your timeline insertion to the beginning of the beat (after the hi-hat "count off"), as shown in Figure 5.11.

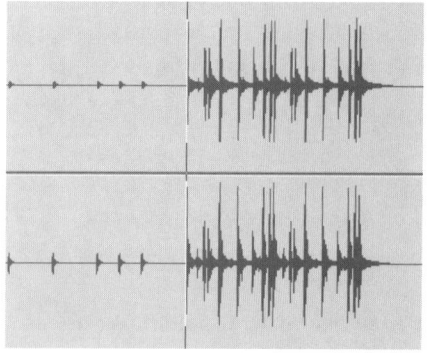

Figure 5.11
The beginning of the beat

3. Still using Tab to Transient, select the entire two-measure segment. Here's a hint: The drummer plays a kick downbeat at the beginning of the third measure, so you have a convenient ending point for the second measure.

4. Now that we're finished with the selection process, let's get rid of the audio that we don't want. This is easy to do by clicking the Edit drop-down menu, choosing the Trim Region menu item, and finally clicking To Selection. Here's a tip: Ctrl+T (PC) or Apple+T (Mac) will do the same thing. When you're finished, you'll have a cropped region on your track.

> **NOTE**
>
> If you're uncertain about the accuracy of your selection, a memory location has been created for your convenience. Just go to the Window drop-down menu, choose Memory Locations, and click memory location #1: Beat Detective Exercise 5b Loop.

Creating Regions with Beat Detective

You're all set to begin the real work behind this workflow, and to do this you'll first need to create separate regions at each important transient. For the most part, you'll find this very similar to the analysis phase that you dealt with when creating a tempo map, with a few important differences. Very quickly, here are the settings that will work in this case:

1. In the Operation area of the Beat Detective window, choose the Region Separation radio button.

2. In the Selection area of Beat Detective, we're going to do something a little different. Keep in mind that in this section, we're telling Beat Detective the musical start and end (and in the process, duration) that we feel the selection should be. Let's say that you want this loop to begin at the start of the session—just set the Start Bar|Beat value to be 1|1. Because it's agreed that this is a two-bar segment, set the End Bar|Beat value to be 3|1. You'll see the result of these choices in just a moment.

3. In the Detection section, a value of 75% using the High Emphasis mode works for our purposes.

4. One more little feature to mention before moving on is a small but useful setting called Trigger Pad, shown in the lower part of the Detection area when in Region Separation mode. From time to time, you might notice the separation process cuts off the beginning of a transient, and setting a Trigger Pad to a value (up to 50 ms) will result in region boundaries being created before the beat trigger. Thanks to sync points (see Figure 5.12), the accuracy of Beat Detective will be maintained. For this example, please set the Trigger Pad setting to 5 ms.

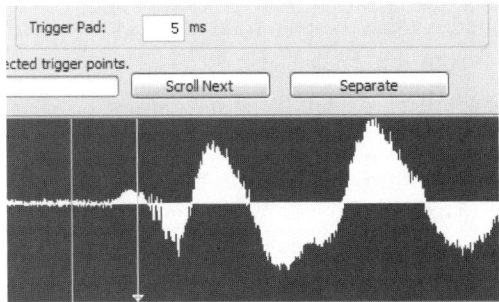

Figure 5.12
The result of a 5ms Trigger Pad

CHAPTER 5 ■ Making the Most of Beat Detective

When you're finished with the preceding steps, your Beat Detective settings should match those shown in Figure 5.13.

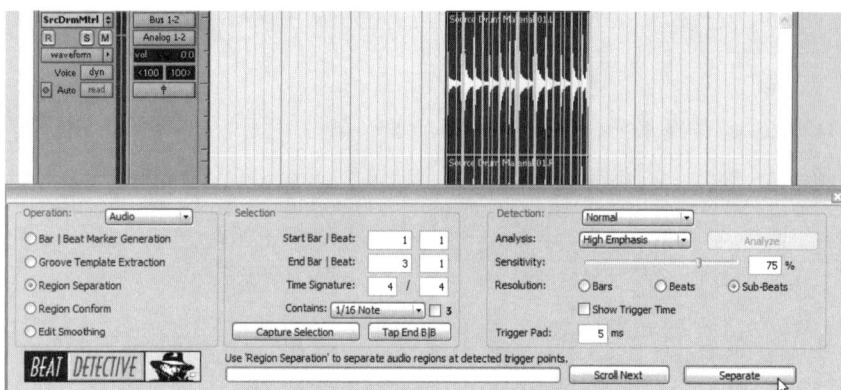

Figure 5.13

Ready to separate regions

All that remains in this process is to click the Separate button (refer to Figure 5.13). Your selection will be separated at each beat trigger. You'll also notice that your region list is immediately populated with the individual regions.

Region Conform

You won't hear any difference as of yet—you've simply cut up a large region into many small slices. Region Conform, a mode that could be thought of as Beat Detective's version of MIDI Quantize, will take the process to the next level by adjusting the timing. This mode is also very straightforward, but before we actually conform the audio, let's take a look at the options available to you.

1. First things first—in the Operation area of Beat Detective, choose the Region Conform radio button. This will take you into the mode of Beat Detective you'll need to fix timing.

2. Because you've already made your selection, the area of the Beat Detective window you'll want to go to is entitled Conform. You'll notice a drop-down menu at the top of this area, giving you two different ways to quantize your audio. Click the menu to choose either of the two Conform modes (Standard or Groove), as shown in Figure 5.14.

    ■ If you take a look at the Standard mode (refer to Figure 5.14), you'll see parameters that look a lot like a MIDI Quantize window. In fact, they do the same thing to audio that the MIDI Grid Quantize window does to MIDI. (For more information on these parameters, refer to Chapter 3.) If you want to adjust Strength, Exclude Within, or Swing, just check the appropriate check box. (Clicking Swing will also enable the radio buttons to allow you to choose an eighth- or sixteenth-note swing.)

Workflow #2: Quantizing Audio

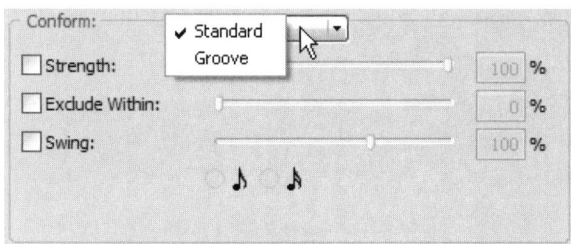

Figure 5.14
Accessing the Conform modes

- Looking at Groove mode (see Figure 5.15), you'll also see some familiar buttons. Below the mode button, you'll see a second drop-down menu that will access the same menu of groove options that you would see in a MIDI Groove Quantize window. There is a Timing slider, which will allow you to choose to what extent the groove will be applied to the audio.

Figure 5.15
Groove mode

> **NOTE**
> In some cases, the timing of your original drums might be off to such a degree that groove-conforming yields undesirable results. In these extreme cases, checking the Pre-Process Using Standard Conform box (refer to Figure 5.15) can really help by applying a standard (grid-style) conform to the audio before applying the groove conform.

3. For the purposes of this example, you can just choose the Standard conform mode with none of the options checked.
4. Click the Conform button in the lower-right corner of the Beat Detective window. Because we've chosen to conform the audio to the first two measures of the session, a message box will appear (see Figure 5.16), asking whether you really want to move the regions. We do, so please click Conform.

You'll finally see and hear a change—and a pretty significant one. The first thing you'll notice is that the regions have moved (conformed) to the first couple measures of the session, a result of the Selection values you entered in Beat Detective. If you listen to the conformed audio regions, you'll hear something as well—the shuffle is gone! That's because you did a standard conform, so

109

CHAPTER 5 ■ Making the Most of Beat Detective

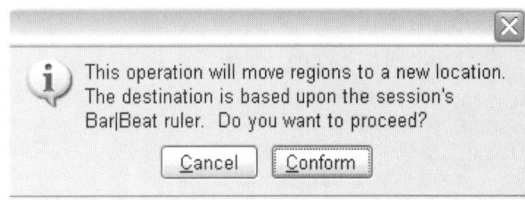

Figure 5.16
To move or not to move, that it the question. . . .

the regions have been quantized to the existing tempo map—in this case, a mathematically perfect 97 beats per minute (see Figure 5.17).

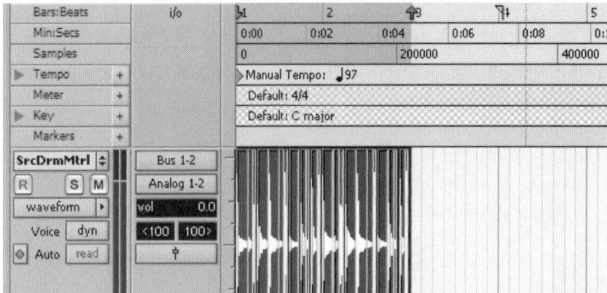

Figure 5.17
The conformed audio

Edit Smoothing

You'll notice that in the process of realigning these small regions, some gaps have been created. Obviously that won't do at all, so Beat Detective has a final mode that will help you finish your work, called *Edit Smoothing*. Here's how it works:

1. Select the area that you wish to "smooth." In the case of this example, you'll want to select the first two measures.

2. In the Operation section, choose the Edit Smoothing radio button.

3. In the Smoothing section (shown in Figure 5.18), you'll see that you have two different ways to smooth your audio. For the purposes of this exercise, we'll listen to what each of these does to our loop.

4. Click the Fill Gaps radio button, and then click the Smooth button (at the lower-right corner of the Beat Detective window). If you take a look at your regions, you'll see that the region boundaries have been adjusted to fill the empty spaces, like an intelligent Batch Trim tool (which is exactly what it is). If you listen closely, though, you might hear a few clicks and pops caused by mismatching waveforms. If you do, then the next step might be more applicable to your situation.

5. Click the Fill and Crossfade radio button. This mode will not only adjust region boundaries like the Fill Gaps mode, but it will additionally add small crossfades between each region boundary to minimize the ill effects of mismatched audio waveforms. When this radio

button is selected, you'll be asked to select a crossfade length—5ms works well in this example. When you've set a crossfade length, click the Smooth button and listen to your selection. Sounds much better, doesn't it?

> **TIP**
>
> You'll notice that a small problem still remains—the last region. If you zoom in, you'll see that even after edit smoothing, there is a gap between the end of the region and the end of the measure, which results in a small gap. This is because there is an unwanted transient that would be revealed, which is obviously something we *don't* want.
>
> The solution to this problem lies in skills you learned in Chapters 2 and 4:
>
> 1. Separate the last region at some point after the end of the crossfade (doing your best to cut on a zero crossing, as discussed in Chapter 4).
> 2. Using the TCE Trim tool in Grid mode (with the grid set to a musical value), drag the end region boundary to the end of the measure. (In doing this, I've found that using the Time Shift plug-in with a Drums Rhythmic setting works best. To learn more about plug-ins and settings for the TCE Trim tool, refer to Chapter 2.)

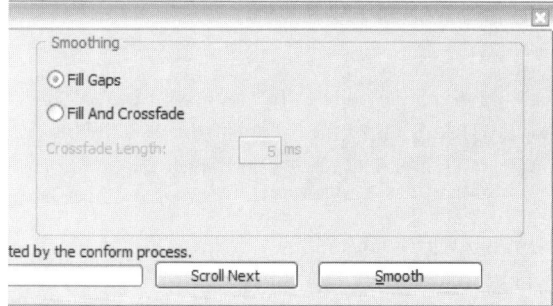

Figure 5.18
Fixing the last region

> **NOTE**
>
> Processes such as Beat Detective can really increase your session's edit density. When you're finished working with Beat Detective, you may well want to consolidate your selection. (Refer to the "Consolidating Regions" section in Chapter 2.) Don't forget—you can also use Edit Playlists to maintain a backup of your separated regions as well. (Refer to the "Working with Edit Playlists" section in Chapter 2.)

> **NOTE**
>
> To see a finished version of these steps, open the session named Chapter 5b – Finished.

CHAPTER 5 ■ Making the Most of Beat Detective

Beyond the Basics

With the completion of the previous section, you've run through the two major uses of Beat Detective, and hopefully you're seeing the implications of this very useful window. These two workflows alone can be combined to conform audio to a MIDI timeline and vice versa. Also, by using both of these processes together, you can create a tempo map based upon one selection of audio, then conform another block of audio to the newly created tempo map!

You've covered most of the aspects of Beat Detective, but there are just a few others that I'd like to briefly touch on before moving on. By the end of this chapter, you'll know more than most do about Beat Detective's operation, and you'll be ready to practice with it and get a feel for how it fits into your creative world.

Working with Multitrack Beats

Beat detective comes in two forms: The Pro Tools|HD version, which is fully loaded with features, and an LE version, which lacks the ability to analyze multiple tracks. (When multiple tracks are selected, only the top track will be dealt with by Beat Detective.) If you have a Pro Tools LE system, a multitrack version of Beat Detective *is* included with Digidesign's Music Production Toolkit.

> **NOTE**
>
> This next section will largely operate under the assumption that you have a full version of Beat Detective. If you *don't* have a full version, check out the "Pro Tools LE, Beat Detective, and Thinking around the Problem" section for a way to get the most out of the limited version of Beat Detective.

At its most basic level, using Beat Detective on multiple tracks is as simple as using it on a single track. Simply make a selection on multiple tracks, and off you go! You can use any of Beat Detective's applicable modes in exactly the same way that you used them earlier in this chapter. Beat Detective will detect transients on all of the selected regions at one time. Really, could it *be* any easier?

Actually, there *are* a couple things you should keep in mind when working with multitrack drums. Read on . . .

> **NOTE**
>
> Though the following sections will provide only general steps and guidelines, you can practice these concepts with the session named Chapter 5c on the included disc.

Overhead and Room Tracks

Very often, when live drums are recorded, a pair of microphones is placed above the drummer, and sometimes a mic or two is even put elsewhere in the room. The purpose of these tracks is to lend a sense of ambience to the close microphone tracks, which you can hear if you play the selected area of the Chapter 5c session.

Because these microphones are farther from the source of the sound than the close microphones, their timing is a little later than that of the close microphones. This is great for creating a sense of space, but it does pose some difficulties for Beat Detective. If you try to analyze these tracks along with the close microphone tracks, you'll be plagued with a slew of double triggers—try it with this session and you'll see what I mean.

The solution to this problem is very simple—just follow these steps:

1. Select the desired area on the close mic tracks *only*, as set up in the Chapter 5c session.
2. Configure Beat Detective's Selection and Detection areas as normal. (Refer to previous sections in this chapter to see how this is done.)
3. Click the Analyze button and adjust the Sensitivity slider as normal.
4. Add the same selected area to the ambience (overhead and room tracks in this case) that you might have in your session. This is most easily done by choosing the Selector tool, holding the Shift key, and clicking in the ambient tracks. You'll note that the beat triggers extend to these tracks as well.
5. You'll note that as soon as you add the relevant track(s), the Analyze button will again be available to be clicked—don't do it!
6. Proceed to the next step in the process (depending upon the workflow you're using at the time) as normal.

If you separate those regions, you'll notice that the region boundaries on the ambient tracks are a bit *before* the actual transient, which is what you want. Now, when you conform your regions, all the regions will conform uniformly, but the transients on the close-miked tracks and the transients on the ambient tracks will maintain their original relative distance, and their ambient effect will remain intact.

Collection Mode

If you take a look at the Chapter 5c session, you'll see that the hi-hat track is significantly softer than the kick and snare tracks (a very common situation). When using Beat Detective, you can see how this might present some difficulties in the detection process—if you analyze all the regions together, you'll likely create unwanted beat triggers on the louder tracks before you capture the ones you *do* want on the quieter tracks. What you need in these circumstances is a way to individually analyze and create beat triggers on a track-by-track basis. Good news—that's what Collection mode is all about!

CHAPTER 5 ■ Making the Most of Beat Detective

In the full version of Beat Detective, you'll see a drop-down menu at the top of the Detection area. Typically, this will be set to Normal (as shown in Figure 5.19). This drop-down menu will allow you to analyze each track individually, but the steps must be executed in the correct order to get the desired result.

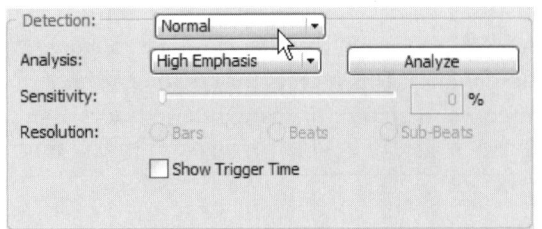

Figure 5.19

Detection modes

1. With Normal mode selected, select the desired area on one track only (for example, the kick track in this session). Adjust the Sensitivity slider so that you mark all of the important transients, just as you would normally do.

2. Now click the Detection mode drop-down menu and switch to Collection mode, as shown in Figure 5.20.

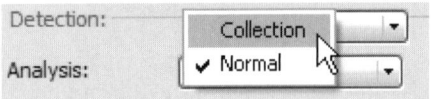

Figure 5.20

Changing to Collection mode

3. When you get into Collection mode, you'll see three options, shown in Figure 5.21.

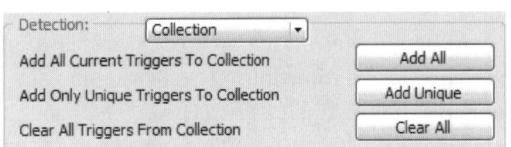

Figure 5.21

Collection mode options

- ■ **Add All Current Triggers to Collection.** Clicking the Add All button will add all current beat triggers to the collected analysis.

- ■ **Add Only Unique Triggers to Collection.** Clicking the Add Unique button will add all current beat triggers to the collected analysis, except those that duplicate preexisting beat triggers.

- ■ **Clear All Triggers from Collection.** The Clear All button removes all beat triggers from the collected analysis.

Because you're just starting out, you should click the Add All button. You'll see the beat triggers appear in the selected area.

Beyond the Basics

4. Switch back to Normal mode and move your selection to the next track (in this case the snare track). Re-analyze the selection (this is very important!), then adjust the Sensitivity slider to mark all desired transients.

> **NOTE**
>
> To easily move your selection from one track to another, you might want to select the Link Track and Edit Selection button, located just below the Trim tool and shown in Figure 5.22. With this option selected, you'll just need to change your selected track, and your selected area will move accordingly.

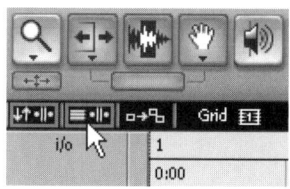

Figure 5.22
The Link Track and Edit Selection button

5. Go back to Collection mode, but this time click the Add Unique button. You'll see your current beat triggers added to the triggers you collected from the first track.
6. Repeat Steps 4 and 5 until you've collected beat triggers from all the desired tracks. (Remember, you should not collect beat triggers from ambient tracks such as the overhead and room tracks in this example.)

That's it—it does take a little time, but it's actually a very easy process. Now that you've collected the desired beat triggers, you can jump onto a more conventional workflow and create your tempo map or conform your audio regions. Neat, huh?

Pro Tools LE, Beat Detective, and Thinking around the Problem

If you are running Pro Tools LE and you don't have the Music Production Toolkit, you'll notice that you don't have the option of analyzing multiple tracks or the Collection mode of detection. There's no denying that this will at some point become a significant limitation, but there is a way that you can think around the problem and squeeze a little extra power out of this form of Beat Detective.

> **NOTE**
>
> To explore this technique, open the session named Chapter 5d from the disc included with this book.

CHAPTER 5 ■ Making the Most of Beat Detective

In this example, I've done a very quick temporary mixdown of the kick, snare, and hi-hat tracks to a track named Drum Mixdown (temp). As the name might suggest, you won't need to use this track in the mixing process, but it *will* give you a composite region upon which Beat Detective can operate. Using this technique, you will be able to create bar|beat markers that represent the kick, snare, and hi-hat tracks. Very quickly, here are the steps to getting the job done:

1. Set up your Beat Detective window to be able to analyze the Drum Mixdown (temp) region. To make the job easier, the settings shown in Figure 5.23 work well!

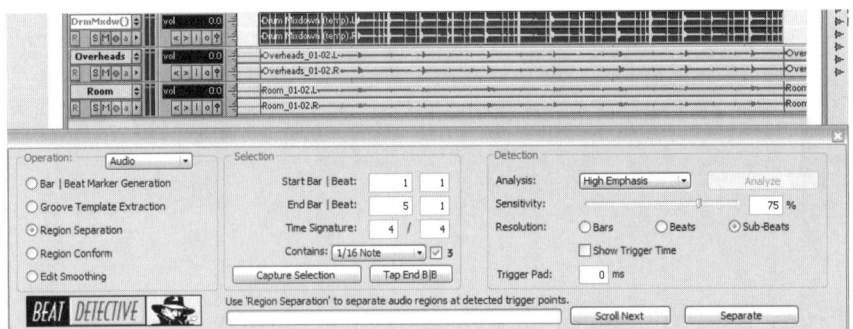

Figure 5.23
Detecting the mixdown

2. If you want to create a MIDI tempo map, you're all set. Generate your bar|beat markers as you would normally do. You won't have the luxury of using Collection modes, but you will effectively have the ability to capture regions from all three drum tracks.

> **NOTE**
>
> Practically speaking, you don't have any similar workaround when you're aiming to separate regions and conform them to a preexisting MIDI timeline. You will, however, be able to process (separate, conform, and smooth) individual tracks one by one and eventually get similar results.

Creating Groove Templates

Got a drum beat that you just love? Wish you could capture its essence and use it to breathe life into your MIDI drums? Boy oh boy, does Beat Detective have a mode for you—Groove Template Extraction. This mode is a fairly simple extension of the work you've already done when you used Bar|Beat Marker Generation. This time, though, you won't be creating a MIDI tempo map; you'll be capturing the timing (and more!) of your beat for use later.

> **NOTE**
>
> To explore this technique, open the session named *Chapter 5e* from the disc included with this book.

1. Click the Groove Template Extraction radio button in the Operation section of Beat Detective.
2. Once again, set up your Selection and Detection fields. (I've found that the settings shown in Figure 5.24 will work well for this example.)

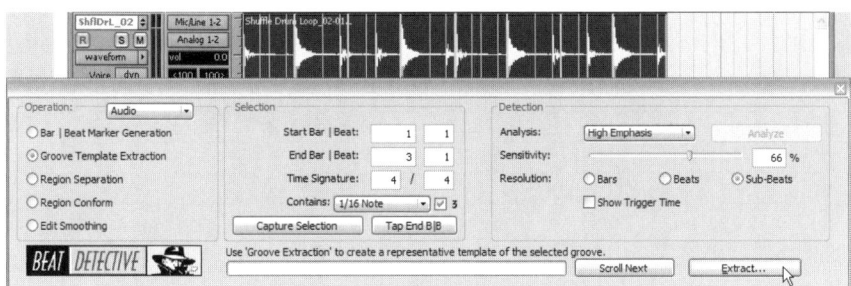

Figure 5.24
Getting ready to extract the groove

3. When you're all ready, click the Extract button.
4. In the Extract Grove Template dialog box that will appear (see Figure 5.25), your first task will be to enter the number of bars that you've analyzed. (In this case, that would be two measures.)

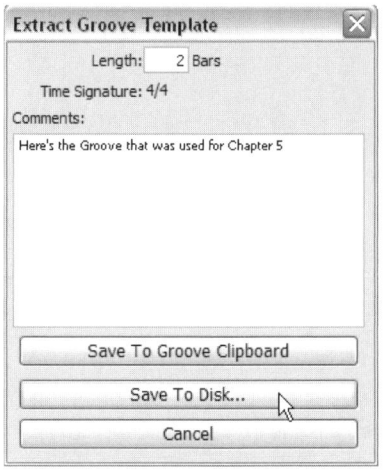

Figure 5.25
Extraction options

5. Enter any descriptive comments that you need to recall the specifics of this groove template.
6. The last stage of this process is to determine how the groove template will be saved. Choose Save to Groove Clipboard if you intend to use the groove template in the short term and not save it in permanent storage. Choose Save to Disk if you intend to save this groove template to a drive and keep it on hand for future use. If you choose to save this

CHAPTER 5 ■ Making the Most of Beat Detective

groove to your hard drive, the Save Groove Template As dialog box will allow you to name the groove and save it in any location you desire. (The window will default to the Grooves folder, as shown in Figure 5.26.)

Figure 5.26
Saving your groove template

You're all set now to apply your extracted information as a groove template to your MIDI, and Figure 5.27 shows just how that's done. All you need to do is select the desired MIDI data and use Groove Quantize as normal. (For a refresher on how to do this, refer to Chapter 3.) If you have saved your groove to the Clipboard, just choose it from the Quantize Grid drop-down menu. If you've saved the groove to disk, as I've done, you'll see the name of the groove added to the list as well. Just choose the desired menu item and apply it in the usual way.

The really cool thing about the way Beat Detective does this is also shown in Figure 5.27. If you take a look at the MIDI data in relation to the source audio data, you'll see that not only has the timing changed to match the timing of the drum track, but the *velocity* has as well, because Beat Detective analyzes the amplitude of the transients and translates the values to a corresponding MIDI velocity value. How's that for doing the job right!

> **NOTE**
> To see this exercise in its finished form, open the session named Chapter 5a – Finished.

Beyond the Basics

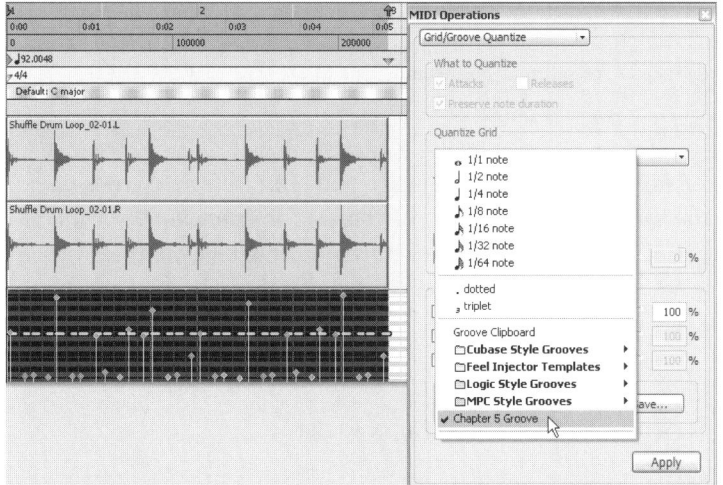

Figure 5.27

Applying the saved groove template and the result

The Other Side of Beat Detective: MIDI Detective

There's just one more thing to touch upon before we move on to more topics, and that is Beat Detective's alter ego—MIDI Detective. Really, what we're talking about here is Beat Detective's MIDI mode of operation, which you can access from the drop-down menu at the top of the Operation section of the Beat Detective window, as shown in Figure 5.28.

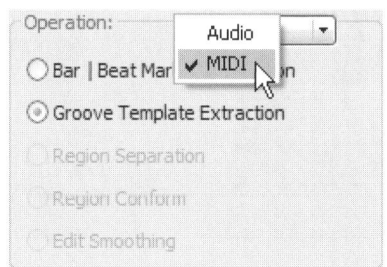

Figure 5.28

Getting to MIDI Detective

One of the big differences that you'll immediately notice when you switch to MIDI mode is that you will have only two operation radio buttons available to you (Bar|Beat Marker Generation and Groove Template Extraction). Though this sounds like a limitation of the feature, the fact is that these are the only two buttons that are relevant to MIDI data.

Beyond that, these modes largely work just like the Beat Detective that you've worked with throughout this chapter, except that the analysis phase and the Sensitivity slider work based upon velocity values rather than transient amplitudes, meaning that as you move the Sensitivity slider from left to right, MIDI notes with the highest velocity notes will be marked first, followed by progressively lesser velocity notes.

119

CHAPTER 5 ■ Making the Most of Beat Detective

> **CAUTION**
> MIDI Detective's Sensitivity slider will only reveal beat trigger markers when the Track view selector is set to Notes.

The only other significant difference between using Beat Detective and MIDI Detective crops up when multiple notes are played as the same time (in the case of chords, for example), but with small timing variations. When using MIDI Detective, the Analysis drop-down menu will give you the means to choose how these situations will be dealt with. Just click the drop-down menu to look at the options available to you (see Figure 5.29).

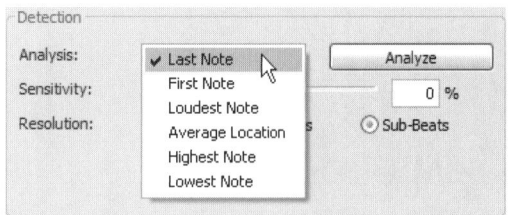

Figure 5.29
MIDI Detective Analysis options

Figures 5.30 though 5.34 show how the various modes work.

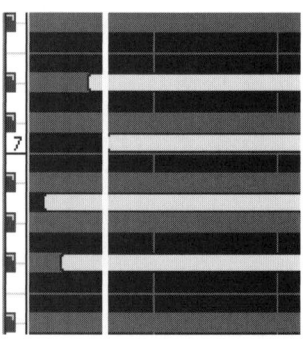

Figure 5.30
Last Note Analysis mode

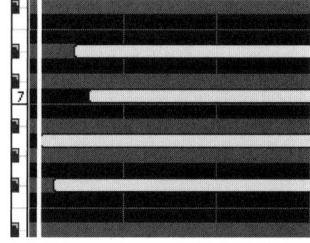

Figure 5.31
First Note Analysis mode

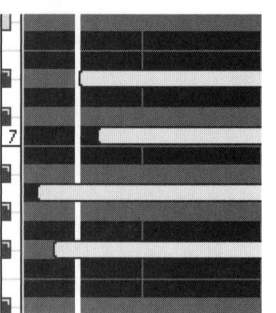

Figure 5.32
Highest Note Analysis mode

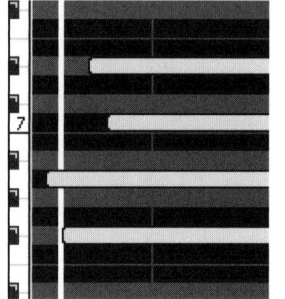

Figure 5.33
Lowest Note Analysis mode

Beyond the Basics

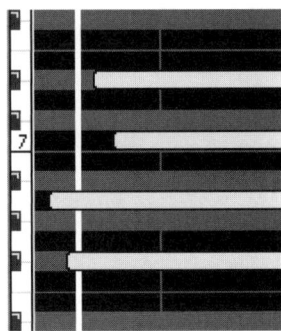

Figure 5.34
Average Location Analysis mode

There's one more Analysis mode (not shown graphically here), called Loudest Note. Choosing the Loudest Note Analysis mode will cause MIDI Detective to mark the note of the chord that has the greatest MIDI velocity value.

Congratulations—you've really gone through the paces of Beat Detective! Now enjoy!

Mixing Beats

Mixing, what a topic. There's probably no more expansive subject in our world, and the varieties of mix philosophies out there are matched only by the passion that people feel for their particular views on the subject. Indeed, mixing is one of the most viscerally artistic things that we do as creative musicians.

This book is a part of a *Skill Pack* series, published by Thomson Course Technology PTR, and it has a great sibling book called *Mixing in Pro Tools: Skill Pack*. This book goes into the topic of mixing in Pro Tools in depth and is highly recommended for those readers who are interested in exploring the vastness of mixing practices in Pro Tools.

That being said, there are some beat-specific aspects of mixing beats that bear mentioning in this book, and that's what we'll concentrate on here. This chapter will focus on how to get the most out of your mixing time by discussing ways to work better and smarter. In this chapter, you'll learn:

- Traditional thoughts on mixing from a drum-by-drum perspective and on the drum kit as a whole
- Commonly used EQ, compression, and reverb techniques
- How to use automation to its greatest advantage
- How to get the most out of your CPU power by mixing *smart*
- More advanced workflows and how to accomplish them in Pro Tools

> **NOTE**
> This book assumes a basic understanding of the layout and function of Pro Tools' Mix window. For more information on how to get around the Mix window, you might want to check out *Pro Tools 101: The Official Courseware* or *Pro Tools LE 7 Ignite!*, both published by Thomson Course Technology PTR.

CHAPTER 6 ■ Mixing Beats

> **NOTE**
>
> I'd like to give a big shout-out to a colleague and close friend, Brian Smithers, who wrote the *Mixing in Pro Tools: Skill Pack* book. His input has been invaluable in preparing this chapter. As mentioned, the scope and purpose of this chapter are not to duplicate the information put forth in *Mixing in Pro Tools: Skill Pack*, so if you really want to dive deep into the world of Pro Tools mixing, I heartily recommend picking up Brian's book!

The art of mixing is a highly subjective land of nuance and shade, so though we'll be talking about some generally accepted schools of thought (and certainly Pro Tools–related issues), the final judge of the quality of the sound is you alone. This means that you'll have to spend some time experimenting with the ideas put forth here and determine for yourself how best to get *your* sound. Becoming comfortable in the mixing phase of production is as much a result of this kind of focused practice as it is an understanding of concepts, so you're strongly encouraged to take your time with each section and experiment.

Mixing Drum by Drum

When mixing multitrack drums, there's a certain duality involved: On one hand, you will need to coax the very best sound out of each individual track. On the other hand, it's also important to never lose sight of how those individual tracks will impact your mix as a whole. It's a delicate balance to maintain, and the ability for the user to think simultaneously on both levels is the sign of a skilled mixer.

To start, let's take a quick look at each drum individually and consider some traditional schools of thought on how to get the most out of them.

> **NOTE**
>
> For this section, a session has been created for you to work with. Please open the Chapter 6a session located on the included disc. If you've got a multitrack drum kit of your own, though, by all means use it instead—the recommendations made here are broadly applicable.

Kick Drum

The kick drum is usually a good place to start when building a good drum kit because it usually doesn't require much work at all. Here are some points to keep in mind when adjusting the tone of the drum:

- Generally speaking, using an equalizer (such as a Digidesign 7-band EQ III) to boost frequencies in the 60–80 Hz range will give your kick more low-end punch.

- Using an EQ to boost frequencies between 4 and 8 kHz will commonly bring out a certain presence (many call it "slap") of the drum. Although it is hard to verbalize the sound of this (as is the case with the field of mixing in general!), to my ears it evokes the sense of the mallet hitting the drum head and is immediately recognizable once these frequencies are emphasized.
- With regard to panning, the kick drum is very simple indeed and is traditionally panned center.

As far as other effects go, the kick drum is kept pretty dry in most cases. If you're noticing a good deal of bleed from the rest of the kit (in other words, if the other drums are being picked up by the kick microphone), you may want to employ the use of a noise gate. (More on this later in this chapter, in the "Manipulating Sound" section.) Also, from time to time, you may choose to put a compressor on the kick drum in order to get more consistent levels for mixing. (Again, we'll talk more about this later in the chapter.) If you do use a compressor on the kick track, you would typically put the EQ *after* the compressor in the signal chain.

Snare

The snare drum is almost as easy to adjust as the kick. Here are some things to try:

- To bring out the body of the snare, try using an EQ to (very slightly) boost the 200- to 300-Hz range. (The actual frequency will depend upon your particular drum, of course—in some rare cases, I've found the magic range to be as low as the 100- to 200-Hz range.)
- The characteristic "crack" of the snare can often be brought out of the track by emphasizing a band in the 4- to 8-kHz range. Most commonly, you'll find the sound you're looking for lurking in the 4- to 5-kHz range. You might want to compare the difference between a high-shelf and a band-pass setting for this high-frequency adjustment. I often find that a shelf gives a more open sound, while a band-pass filter adds more focused presence to the sound.
- As for panning, as with the kick drum, the snare is very commonly panned to the center. On rare occasions, I will pan the snare *very* slightly to the right to match the positioning of the overheads. (You'll see an example of this later in this section.)

In some cases—particularly mixes where your overall kit is going to have a drier sound—you might want to employ the use of a very small amount of reverb to bring out a little of the shimmer of the snare. Personally, I've had good success with a small plate reverb, with about 700–800ms of decay, and about 10ms of pre-delay. Be very wary of using reverb on any individual drum, though, if you plan on using reverb on the kit as a whole. Reverb stacked upon reverb can get very muddy very easily!

Hi-Hats and Cymbals

Cymbals have two very distinctive components to their sound—the impact of the stick on the cymbal itself and the ring ("shimmer" and "sizzle" are commonly used descriptions). You can really breathe life into a dull cymbal sound by finding both of those components with an EQ; here are some hints on where to look:

- To bring out the impact of the cymbal, look for the right frequency around the 200-Hz mark.
- To bring out the shimmer of the cymbal, you'll find it around the 6- to 8-kHz range. A high-shelf setting works well in this case.

Toms

Similar to cymbals, toms are among the more resonant of the drums you'll find in a typical drum kit. As such, they also have two critical components of their sound that you might consider—the impact and the resonance ("ring" or "body") of the drum itself.

One aspect of toms that is different from cymbals is the tuning of the drums, which varies from drum to drum (and drummer to drummer as well). Finding the magic frequencies on your EQ can sometimes be quite a hunt—here are some ideas on where to start:

- The attack sound of many drums can often be found in the 4- to 6-kHz range.
- You can emphasize the resonance of the drum by boosting frequencies between the 100- to 250-Hz range, depending upon the size and pitch of the drum. Be careful that you don't boost those frequencies too much, though. It is very easy to make your drum sound muddy by applying too much EQ.

Ambient Tracks and Panning

Your ambient tracks (for example, you'll find an *overhead* as well as a *room* track in the example session, if you open it) are often the method of choice when going for a sense of reality. Here again, a little tweaking is really all you need to get a good sound from them. Because you're going after a more spacious sound, and given that this sense of space is communicated largely through the upper frequencies, a high-shelf boost (anywhere from 1 kHz and up, depending greatly upon the kit and miking situation) usually does the trick nicely.

If you decide to employ overhead or room tracks, which of the tracks will you use? In the case of the example session, using both tracks together was a bit too much ambience to my ear, so I muted the room track and opted for the tighter sound of the overhead track.

Mixing Drum by Drum

Another thing you must tackle is the issue of panning, and it's a multifaceted issue. The first problem to tackle is one of continuity. If you're like me, you'll want to position (pan) your close-miked drum tracks so that they are in agreement with the ambient track you're using. The next question to ask yourself is just *how* stereo you want your track to be. Consider this: If you're an audience member watching a live band, the drummer is a certain distance from you, and it stands to reason that the farther he or she is away from you, the closer to being a point-source (mono) signal he or she becomes. I'm not a staunch proponent of mono drums per se (though I have panned just this way on occasion), but I do think that if you narrow the spread of the kit, you can put it into the proper context in your overall mix.

This brings up a problem from time to time: The narrower the stereo image of the overhead tracks, the harder it is to place your close-miked tracks in the correct positions to work with them. Here's a nifty little workaround that you might find useful in these cases:

1. With your overhead track (presuming that it's a stereo track) panned out full (hard left and right), adjust your close-miked tracks so they spatially match the overheads. Once that's finished, you might want to set your volume faders so that you have workable rough levels.

2. Change the outputs of all the drum tracks (including the overhead and/or room track) to a pair of unused buses. In the case of the example session, Bus 1 is already used for the snare reverb, and I've chosen Buses 3 and 4, as shown in Figure 6.1.

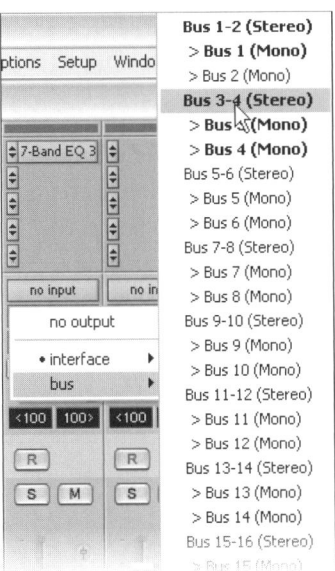

Figure 6.1

Changing the track's output to a bus

127

> **TIP**
> Here's a quick way to change the output of all your drum tracks in one fell swoop: After you select all of the tracks you wish to change, hold down Shift+Alt (PC) or Shift+Option (Mac) and change the output of any one of your selected tracks. The same change will be mirrored on all of your selected tracks.

3. Next, create a Stereo Auxiliary Input track.
4. Set the input of the Aux track to be the same pair of buses that you've selected for the individual drum tracks. This in effect will configure the newly created track to be a subgroup master track.
5. Now you can adjust the overall panning and volume of the entire drum kit with one convenient track. Here's a way to make it even easier: Click the Output Window button, to the immediate right of the Aux track's fader, as shown in Figure 6.2.

Figure 6.2
Opening the output window

6. In the Aux track's output window, click both the Link and Inverse Pan buttons, located directly below the Target button (see Figure 6.3). Now all you'll have to do is move one pan knob, and the other pan knob will mirror its motion, narrowing the stereo image of your entire kit.

Figure 6.3
Focusing your drum kit's stereo image

Manipulating Sound

> **NOTE**
>
> To see the finished version of this section, open the Chapter 6a — Finished session. Note that this session uses the Compressor/Limiter Dyn III, 7-Band EQ3, and D-Verb.

> **TIP**
>
> There are two schools of thought where stereo drum kits are concerned: whether to mix from the perspective of the drummer or the perspective of the audience. This points to another benefit of this method, in addition to ease of use and flexibility—just invert the panning, as shown here in Figure 6.4, and you will effectively change the perspective (from drummer's view to audience's view, or vice versa).

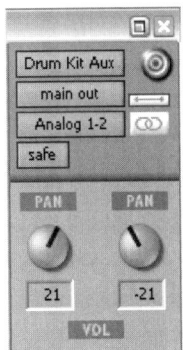

Figure 6.4
Changing perspective

Manipulating Sound

Beyond the basic changes that you can make to an individual track's sound using traditional processes such as equalization and panning, there are a few other tools that bear looking into at this point. These processes aren't necessarily going to bring out the best of the original track, but rather they will change the sound into something else entirely.

> **NOTE**
>
> For this section, you can use session Chapter 6b from your book's disc.

Using Compressors

Compressors are a basic effect, and you'll use them in a number of situations to manage levels and bring out the "punch" in your mix. You'll notice sometimes that if you overly compress audio, you can get quite a change in the sonic quality of the sound, often undesirable. Let's use a compressor beyond the boundaries of good taste to get a change in a snare sound.

The secret to this process is to get a desired character change not simply by overly compressing the sound of the snare, but by combining that drastically changed sound with the original (or "dry") snare. By combining the two, you'll have control over just how much you want your drums to be changed.

1. The first step in the process is particularly easy in Pro Tools. Select the track that you want to work with (in this case it's a snare track, but you could try this with any kind of drum). From the Tracks drop-down menu, choose Duplicate. You'll immediately see Duplicate Tracks dialog box appear.

> **NOTE**
>
> Here's another quick way to duplicate a track: Right-click the track name of the track you want to duplicate, then choose Duplicate from the list that will appear.

2. The Duplicate Tracks dialog box (see Figure 6.5) will allow you to choose which track aspects you want to clone. Because the track we're working with in this example is minimal, you can go ahead with the defaults shown here. If you're working with a track that already has a number of plug-ins, alternate playlists, and so on, you can choose not to copy them here in this dialog box. When you have made your choices, click OK. A copy of the selected track will appear immediately below the original.

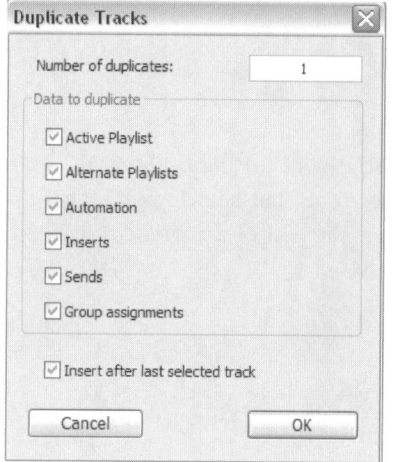

Figure 6.5
The Duplicate Tracks dialog box

3. Solo the clone track so you can hear the changes you're making without the distraction of the other tracks.
4. On the clone track, launch a compressor plug-in (for example, Digidesign's Compressor/Limiter Dyn 3).

Manipulating Sound

> **TIP**
>
> If you don't have the Digidesign Dynamics 3 plug-ins, you can download them for free from the Digidesign website. Just go to the Products page, and then choose Plug-ins → LE and M-Powered Plug-ins → Dynamics III.

5. Though your setting will differ from drum to drum and according to the extent of manipulation that you're going for, you'll generally use more of it than normal. In the example session, you'll find that merciless compression (such as the settings shown in Figure 6.6) will accentuate the decay of the snare and make it sound like a completely different drum.

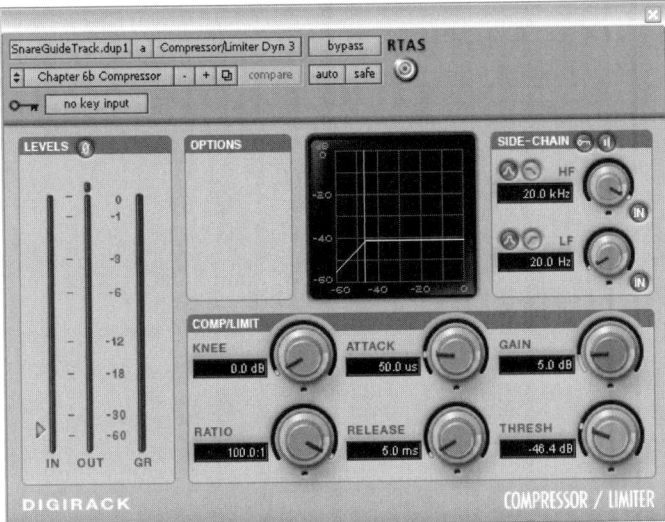

Figure 6.6
A LOT of compression!

> **NOTE**
>
> If you're using the Dynamics 3 compressor shown in this example, a preset has been created for you to experiment with. From the Presets menu, choose Session Settings Folder → Chapter 6b Compressor.

6. When you've got the sound you want for your compressed track, you're ready to start blending it with the original "dry" track. Un-solo the compressed track and adjust both of the tracks so that you get the best parts of both—and something noticeably different from either track alone.

CHAPTER 6 ■ Mixing Beats

> **TIP**
>
> Here's an effective way to get the sound you want out of the two tracks, then get the two to fit into a mix. First, solo just the dry and compressed track. Get the correct balance between the two tracks to get the sound color that you're after. Once you've got the balance, group the two tracks together, then un-solo the tracks and adjust the two tracks so that they blend with the rest of the mix. Grouping the two tracks together will ensure that they maintain their relative balance. (If you're new to groups, we'll discuss them later in this chapter.)

> **NOTE**
>
> To hear one way that this exercise might sound, listen to the session named Chapter 6b – Finished.

Using Gates

A noise gate (often referred to simply as a *gate*) is a particularly useful effect when working with drums—particularly with live drums. A gate allows you to cut signals that fall below a volume threshold that you set and will allow you to minimize or remove bleed from other drums. You can go even further with gates, however, and change the character of a drum's sound. Let's take a look:

> **NOTE**
>
> For this section, you can use session Chapter 6c from your book's disc.

1. Solo the track that you focused on so you won't be distracted by other tracks. If you're practicing with the tutorial session (Chapter 6c), solo the snare track. You'll immediately hear some bleed from other drums—you'll want to get rid of that.

2. Instantiate (Digidesign's fancy word for "launch") your favorite gate plug-in. If you're not familiar with gates, you'll find them in the Dynamics submenu of the plug-in menu.

> **TIP**
>
> For this section, I'm using Digidesign's Expander/Gate Dyn 3 plug-in. If you've downloaded the Dynamics III plug-ins as described in the previous section, you'll have this gate as well.

3. Many gates have a usable snare preset—a good place to start. If you're using the Expander/Gate Dyn 3, try the Snare Gate SC preset. You'll notice two things: First, the unwanted bleed from the other drums is gone. Second, the sound of the drum itself is a little cut off.

Manipulating Sound

4. You can change some of these setting to get a more lifelike sound. First, lower the Threshold setting to get a bit more of the drum's resonance. (At some point, you'll start hearing the noise again—if that happens, you've gone too low with the threshold.) Second, you might get a bit more of a real sound if you lengthen the release (which controls how fast the gate closes once levels go below the threshold). As is usually the case in the world of mixing, let your ears be your guide.

> **NOTE**
>
> If you're using the Expander/Gate Dyn 3 gate, a preset has been created for you to experiment with. From the Presets menu, choose Session Settings Folder → Chapter 6c Snare Gate.

5. Just as you did with the compressor in the preceding section, you can go a step further with gates and get a more synthesizer type of sound. Try setting the threshold higher to give the snare an artificially cutoff sound. Try adding a little time to the attack (increasing the time it takes for the gate to fully open) to soften the initial transient of the drum.

> **NOTE**
>
> If you're using the Expander/Gate Dyn 3 gate, a preset has been created for you to experiment with. From the Presets menu, choose Session Settings Folder → Chapter 6c Snare FX Gate.

> **NOTE**
>
> To hear one way that this exercise might sound, listen to the session named Chapter 6c – Finished. On the snare track, you'll find two instantiations of the gate plug-in—one with each of the settings that we've created here. Try disabling one at a time to hear how each of them sounds in the context of the rest of the drum tracks.

Layering Tracks

Another great way to fatten up a track is to layer it with other complementary sounds. This technique works for beats as well as individual drum sounds, though the process differs slightly. Usually when you combine beats, you simply need to adjust the tempos so that they match and line up the beginnings. When we're talking about syncing up specific drum hits it gets a little trickier, so that's what we'll focus on in this section.

The secret to this process is to get your layered regions to line up with the transients of the original track. It's pretty easy to do with the help of a few of Pro Tools' features.

CHAPTER 6 ■ Mixing Beats

> **NOTE**
> For this section, you can use session Chapter 6d from your book's disc.

Here's the scenario we're working with in the example session: To add a little extra motion to the beat, we want to fatten up the sound of the second snare hit of each measure (the one that hits on Beat 4 of the bar). If you take a look at the session, you'll see five additional snare tracks, each with a single region with a single snare drum on it. Here's how to get them all to line up:

1. Using Tab to Transient (see Chapter 1), move your cursor to the second snare hit on the Snare Guide track.
2. If you take a look at the Snare 1 region, you'll see that the region begins right on the transient, so all you need to do is get the beginning of that region to move to the timeline insertion (which is currently at the second snare hit). You can do it easily by holding down the Start (PC) or Control (Mac) key and clicking on the region using the Grabber tool. The region's start will immediately snap to the timeline insertion!
3. Repeat Steps 1 and 2 for the Snare 2, Snare 3, and Snare 4 regions. (Because they all start on the transient, it's easy.)

Snare 5 is a little trickier. Because there's a little reverse reverb leading up to the transient, the region doesn't start right on the hit. This is no problem, but you'll first have to set up a sync point on the region before conforming it to the snare hit.

Think of a sync point as being a user-definable point of interest within a region. Sync points are used extensively with film dialogue, sound effects, and in this case, conforming musical audio. Setting up a sync point is very easy to do:

1. Again using Tab to Transient, locate the transient in this region. For best results in this exercise, move your timeline insertion to the beginning of the session, then with Tab to Transient enabled, press the Tab key once.
2. Now you're ready to create a sync point, and there are a number of ways you can do it. From the Region drop-down menu, choose Identify Sync Point. If you're inclined to use shortcut keys, Ctrl+, (PC) or Apple+, (Mac) will do the trick. Either way, when you're finished, your region should look something like Figure 6.7.

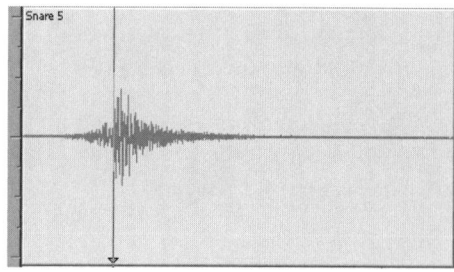

Figure 6.7
Region with sync point

> **NOTE**
>
> If you want to move your sync point, just click and drag with the Grabber tool. To delete a sync point, just hold down the Alt key (PC) or Option key (Mac) and click on the sync point with the Grabber tool.

3. You're almost finished! Using Tab to Transient, move your cursor to the second snare hit on the Snare Guide track.
4. Holding down Shift+Start (PC) or Shift+Control (Mac), click on the region using the Grabber tool. The regions will move, with the sync point aligning to the timeline insertion.

> **NOTE**
>
> To hear one way that this exercise might sound, listen to the session named Chapter 6d – Finished. The important thing is that the regions all line up with the guide track. Now you can blend the different elements until you find a pleasing sound!

When you have the regions all lined up, the fun can begin. Blend the different layers until you have an overall result that you find pleasing. (In this example, I intentionally included some very different-sounding snares, so you can choose what suits you best.)

> **TIP**
>
> Don't forget—each one of the layers of your sound is an independent track, and you can adjust not only the volume of each element, but panning, EQ, and more. Feel free to experiment, particularly with EQ, and use it to bring out the best in each element. Incidentally, this is a great technique when layering entire loops as well—try layering two loops, keeping the low end of one loop and the high end of the other.

Using SoundReplacer

As you've probably noticed by now, I've tried to limit the products discussed to basic Pro Tools LE and free Digidesign plug-ins. The topic of drum *replacement*, however, is important enough that I feel compelled to break this practice just this once. Drum replacement, in a nutshell, is just what it sounds like—it is the exchange of one drum sound for another.

In a practical context, here's a scenario: You get a multitrack drum kit from a client, with a request to "fix" the sound. You notice that although the playing was great, the quality of the recording (or lack thereof) will significantly limit your effectiveness. What you really need is a process that will change the sound, but keep the feel—which is exactly what drum replacement is all about.

CHAPTER 6 ■ Mixing Beats

There are a number of drum replacement plug-ins on the market, but I have two favorites—Digidesign's SoundReplacer and Trillium Labs' TL Drum Rehab. Because the list price for SoundReplacer is more attainable ($395 USD) and because it illustrates the concept so plainly, I've chosen to focus on this one. Don't worry if you don't have this plug-in; there will be plenty of images in this section so you can follow along with the workflow to see whether it suits you.

> **NOTE**
>
> To follow along with this example, just open the Chapter 6e session. No laughing.

This example session, ridiculous-sounding though it may be, is an effective illustration of how *any* source sound can be transformed into a useful beat by using SoundReplacer. Essentially, these two tracks are examples of your humble narrator freestyling. (Please bear in mind that I'm 42 years old, and be charitable.) Let's transform this into a multitrack drum beat.

1. If you're working with regions that incorporate multiple drums (for example, the top track is kick and snare), it's usually a good idea to split the region into individual components. Duplicate the original track, and then use Tab to Transient and Separate Region to create the checkerboard-looking configuration shown in Figure 6.8.

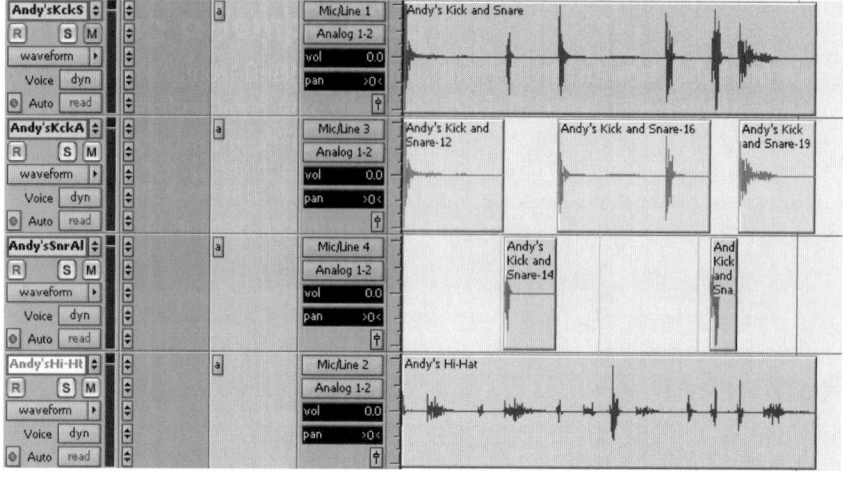

Figure 6.8

Separating the individual component "drums"

2. Let's start with the kick track. First select the drums you want to replace. Once that's finished, go to the AudioSuite drop-down menu, choose the Other category, and then choose SoundReplacer (see Figure 6.9). The SoundReplacer plug-in window will appear.

Manipulating Sound

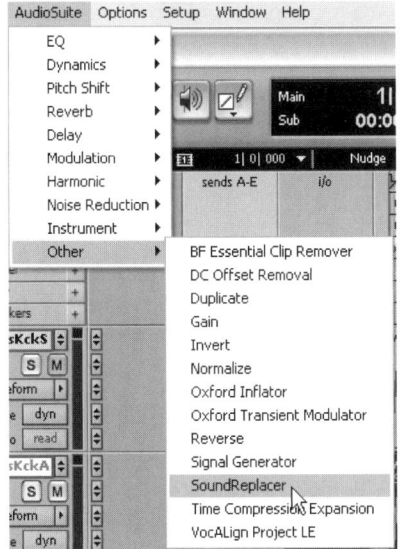

Figure 6.9
Launching SoundReplacer

3. When the SoundReplacer window opens, you'll notice a large blank gray area in the middle of the plug-in. The first thing you want SoundReplacer to do is analyze the audio. Click the Update button (in the upper-right area of the plug-in window), and you'll see a waveform display similar to the one shown in Figure 6.10. Click the Auto Update button to ensure that you continue seeing the correct transient peaks.

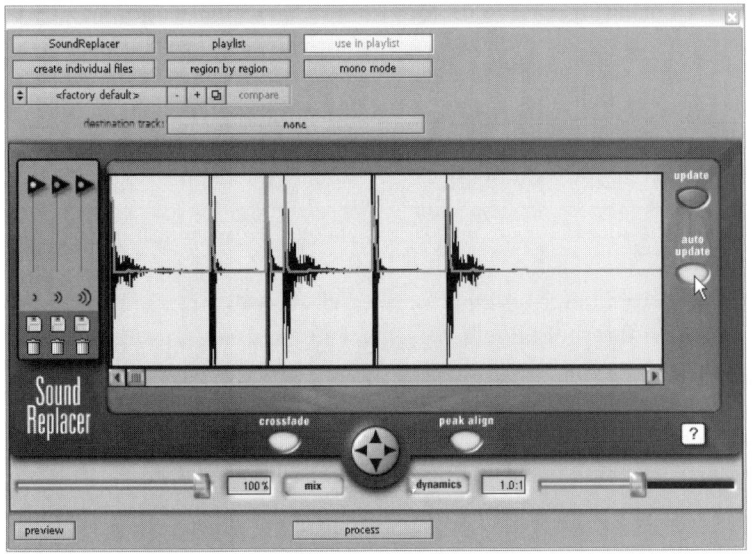

Figure 6.10
Updating the display

4. In the lower center of the SoundReplacer window, you'll see a compass-looking Zoom tool. If you experiment with this one, you'll see that this is an all-in-one Zoom tool. Clicking the right point of the compass will zoom in horizontally, and clicking the left point will zoom out horizontally. The north and south points of the compass will zoom in and out vertically.

5. If you look at the left side of the SoundReplacer window, you'll see three faders, each with a small disc and a trashcan icon below it. Here's where the fun really starts: Click on the disc icon below the yellow (leftmost) fader, as shown in Figure 6.11.

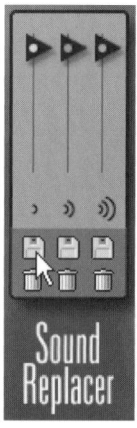

Figure 6.11
Loading a replacement sound

6. The next window that will appear is a fairly basic navigation window, and it is here where you will pick your replacement sound. If you happen to be following with this exercise, you'll find a file called Replacement Kick in a subfolder of the Chapter 6e session named SoundReplacer Files.

> **NOTE**
> If you choose a file, then later decide that you want to use a different one, you can unload that file by clicking on the trashcan icon below the corresponding fader.

7. The next step is to bring the desired fader (in this case the yellow one) down until the threshold (you'll see a horizontal threshold line) intersects with the desired transient peaks. You'll note that as the fader goes lower, vertical yellow lines will appear. This is actually a bit similar to the work that you've done with Beat Detective in that these are triggers (this time *replacement sound* triggers), and the lower you move your fader, the more triggers will be marked. Your task at this point is to lower the fader until all the important notes are marked. When you're finished, the SoundReplacer window will look something like Figure 6.12.

Manipulating Sound

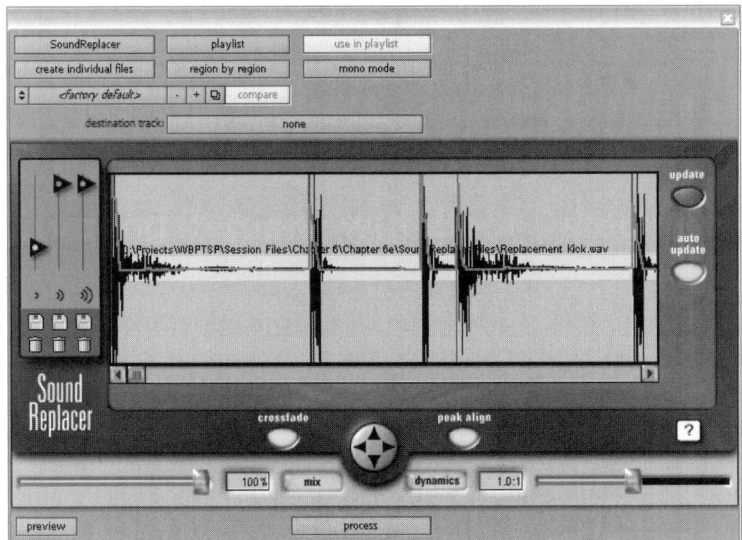

Figure 6.12
Marking the transients

8. You're almost home free, but there are a couple more controls of which you should be aware. First, there's the Mix slider, located in the lower-left corner of the window (see Figure 6.13). This will control the blend between the original sound (0%) and the replacement sound (100%). In this particular example, you really don't need any of the original audio, so you can leave the fader at 100%. In many real-life cases, though, you may well want to blend the two sounds to get a fatter, layered sound. If you click the green Mix button, only the replacement sound will be heard, regardless of the Mix slider setting.

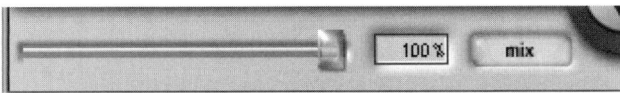

Figure 6.13
The Mix slider

9. On the lower-right corner of the window is the Dynamics slider. By default, the ratio is set to 1:1, which basically means that the replacement sound's volume will match the original sound's volume. If the ratio greater than 1:1 (slider moved to the right of center), the dynamics on the original will be exaggerated with the replacement sound. If the ratio is set to less than 1:1 (slider to the left of center), as shown in Figure 6.14, the dynamic range of the replacement sound will be less than that of the original audio. This second kind of setting is very commonly used to tame an extremely dynamic original track.

139

CHAPTER 6 ■ Mixing Beats

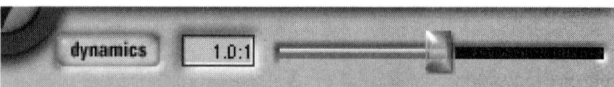

Figure 6.14
The Dynamics slider

> **NOTE**
>
> If you click the Dynamics button to the left of the Dynamics slider, you will un-highlight it, and the dynamic ratio will automatically be 1:1. This is very useful for comparing your Dynamics slider settings to a dynamically neutral setting.

10. There's one more button to be aware of when tweaking your replacement sound—the Peak Align button. When active (its default state), SoundReplacer automatically detects the transient peak of your replacement audio and matches that peak with the trigger points (in this case, the yellow vertical lines). In most cases, this is exactly what you want, but in some cases (particularly with some more synthetic-sounding drums), the peak comes a little later in the replacement file's sound, and this sort of peak alignment doesn't gel with the original track's timing. No problem—just turn Peak Align off by clicking it (the green light will go off), and the beginning of the replacement region will be matched to the trigger line instead.

Figure 6.15
The Peak Align button

At this point, you're ready to process your audio, and you can do this in a number of ways. Assuming that you've got some experience with AudioSuite plug-ins (and if you're new to AudioSuite, don't fret—they're pretty straightforward), the most common question to address is whether to create one large contiguous region or individual regions that match the regions within your selected area.

In this case, I'd recommend choosing to process Region by Region (as opposed to Entire Selection), which will in effect create individual files instead of one continuous file (see Figure 6.16). Going this route will give you individual regions that you can reposition independently.

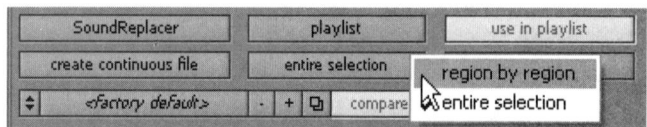

Figure 6.16
AudioSuite processing options

There—you're done, and as soon as you press the Process button (in the lower center of the AudioSuite window), new files will be put into your region list, and your kick track will now actually sound like a kick and look like Figure 6.17.

Manipulating Sound

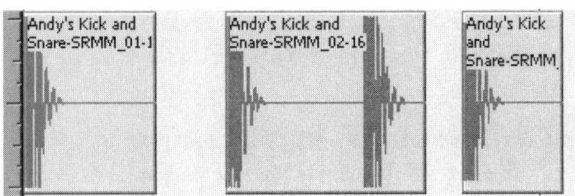

Figure 6.17
The replaced kick track

Now that we're finished with the kick track, the next step is the snare. You'll go through almost identical steps, except that in this case the replacement file should be a snare sound (for example, the Replacement Snare file in the SoundReplacer Files subfolder of the Chapter 6e session). Just before you hit the Process button, your SoundReplacer window should look something like Figure 6.18 . . .

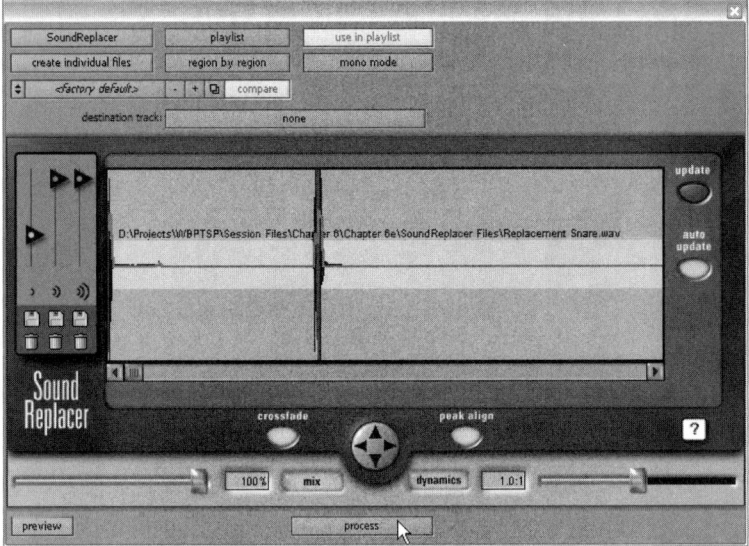

Figure 6.18
Ready to replace the "snare" with a real snare sound!

. . . and your resultant snare track should look something like Figure 6.19!

Figure 6.19
The final snare track

On a basic level, that's how SoundReplacer (and drum replacement in general) works. There are a couple of common curves that can be thrown at you with this sort of work, and I've somewhat reproduced these with the Hi-Hat track.

The original Hi-Hat track that I created was done at a relatively low volume. This is similar to the kind of problem that you might run into with a drum track in which the microphone has been placed too far from the drum itself, and the combination of low drum volume and high bleed from other drums makes isolating only the triggers that you want very difficult, as shown in Figure 6.20.

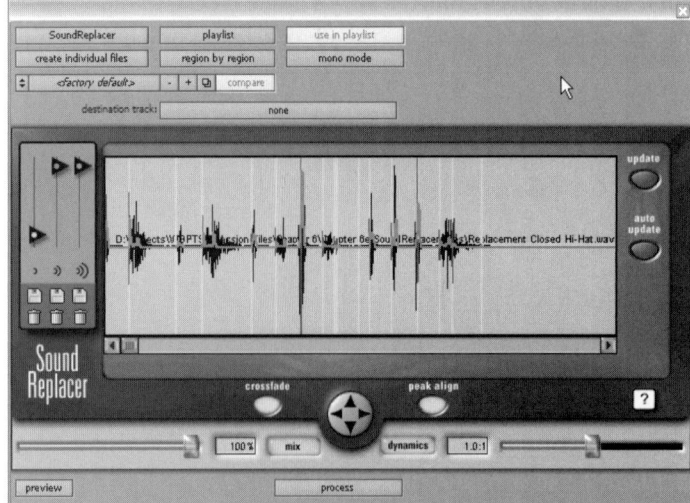

Figure 6.20

SoundReplacer and a problematic track

A lot of conventional wisdom suggests applying a noise gate to the audio before using SoundReplacer, but I tend to recommend a different method—Strip Silence (which we discussed in Chapter 4). Don't worry about going extreme with the settings—your goal in this case is not to catch the duration of the individual hits, but rather to make sure that you catch the beginnings of each hit, because that's what will determine the trigger marker times. In fact, in most cases, I'll use Strip Silence, and then further shorten the regions to make sure that I avoid tempting SoundReplacer with any stray transients!

Figure 6.21 shows the Hi-Hat track with very aggressive Strip Silence, and though it sounds a bit rough, it's now ready for SoundReplacer.

> **NOTE**
>
> If you open the Chapter 6e – Finished session, you'll see an alternate playlist on the Hi-Hat track named Andy's Hi-Hat after Strip Silence, so that you can see and hear what I've done to the original track to help SoundReplacer work a bit better. For more on playlists, please refer to Chapter 2.

Manipulating Sound

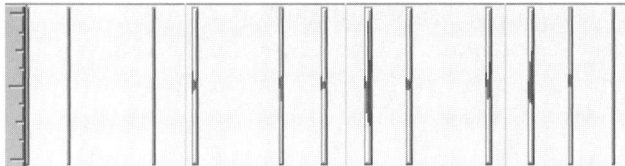

Figure 6.21
A modified track to maximize SoundReplacer's effectiveness

Now you're ready to select your hi-hat regions, making sure to click the Update button so that you can see your selected waveforms. Now we're going to make use of the faders on the left side of the SoundReplacer window.

The three different faders are analogous in principle to velocity zones in a sampler. In the case of SoundReplacer, the yellow fader's threshold corresponds to the lowest sounds, the red fader corresponds to the mid-level threshold, and the blue fader is reserved for the loudest zone. If you look at the Volume icon immediately below each fader, you'll see what I mean. You'll notice that the thresholds cannot cross each other, so it's important to choose your samples *before* you load them into the faders. In this case, let's see what we get when we replace the softer sounds with a closed hi-hat sample and the louder sounds with an open hi-hat. Here's how it's done:

1. Using the same method that you used with the previous tracks (previous Steps 5–7), assign the desired fader to the yellow fader. (Remember, this is the sound that you want for the softest sounds.) If you're following the example session, there's a sample called Replacement Closed Hi-Hat in the SoundReplacer Files subfolder of the Chapter 6e session.

2. Bring the yellow fader down until it marks *all* of the significant trigger points, even the loud ones. If you're following the example session, your SoundReplacer window should look something like Figure 6.22.

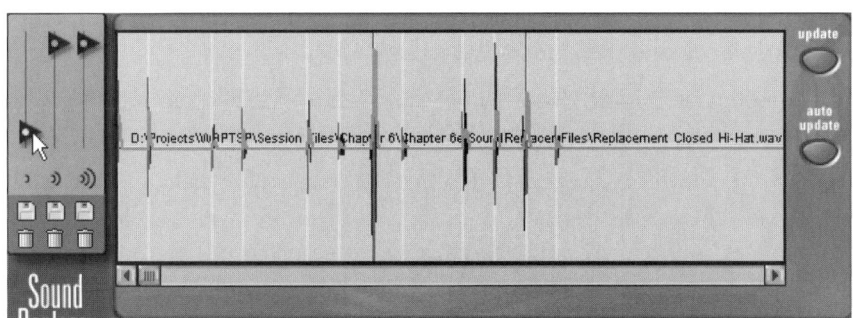

Figure 6.22
Setting your low amplitude threshold

3. Now, click the disk icon below the *red* fader. You'll see a familiar-looking navigation window, and here you'll choose your next louder sound. In this case, you should choose an open hi-hat sound, such as the Replacement Open Hi-Hat file in the SoundReplacer Files subfolder of the Chapter 6e session.

143

4. Now bring the red fader until it intersects only the louder peaks that you want to trigger this second sample. The lower you go, the more peaks will be assigned to this second sound, and the relevant triggers will turn red to let you know that they are going to trigger the second sound. When you're finished, your SoundReplacer window might look like Figure 6.23.

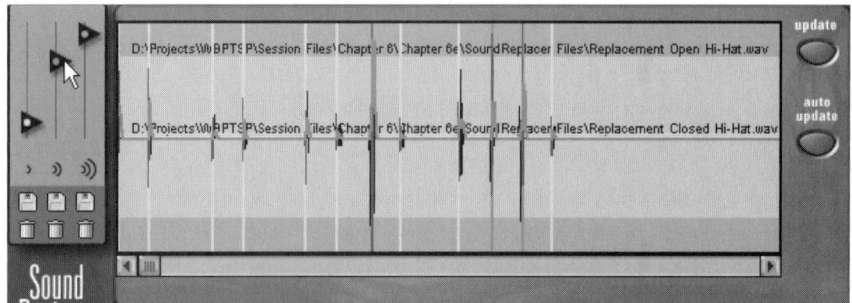

Figure 6.23
Setting your mid-amplitude threshold

In many cases, you would continue this process one more time and assign even louder sounds to the blue fader. This would effectively give you three separate velocity zones. In the case of the open versus closed hi-hat sound in this example, a third threshold isn't really necessary, and there's no need to use all three levels if three sounds aren't appropriate for the job.

So what's a common situation in which you'd use all three thresholds, you ask? Personally, I use all three volume thresholds when working with any drum that changes timbre (tonal color) based upon the velocity with which it is struck. Take the snare drum, for example: I would assign a softly played snare sample to the yellow fader, a medium snare to the red fader, and an aggressively struck snare sound to the blue fader. I would then configure the individual fader levels so that the appropriate original peaks are assigned to the appropriate sound.

Before we close out our discussion on SoundReplacer, there are a few other things to touch on that will make your drum replacement work even better!

- **The Crossfade button.** In many cases (such as the snare example we just talked about), you will want to emulate the sound of an instrument throughout its entire dynamic range, and that's where the Crossfade button (shown in Figure 6.24) comes in. When it is enabled (signified by a green color), markers that fall somewhere between two thresholds will trigger a proportional blend of the appropriate two sound files. For example, if a marker is exactly between the yellow (low) threshold and the red (middle) threshold, you will hear an equal amount of the corresponding two sounds. If the marker is closer to one threshold or another, the balance between the two sounds will be correspondingly biased.

  The Crossfade button is very commonly left active (its default state), but there are some times when you will want to make sure that it is deactivated, and this hi-hat situation is a perfect example. If you've been following along with this example, try previewing it with the crossfade active—you'll immediately notice that the majority of triggers are a mix of open and closed hi-hat sounds, which wind up sounding pretty muddy. Now deactivate the crossfade and listen again—you'll hear that the yellow lines trigger closed hi-hat only and the red ones trigger only the open hi-hat sound. In this case, this crossfade-disabled mode is the right one for this situation.

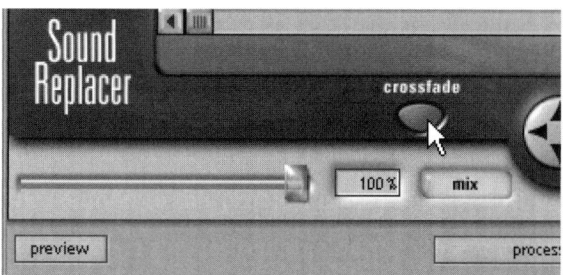

Figure 6.24
The Crossfade button

- **The Dynamics slider.** We've previously discussed the function of the Dynamics slider, and if you're following along with this example, you'll be able to hear it in action. If you preview the dynamic ratio at its default 1:1 ratio, you'll hear that the open hi-hat sounds pretty darn loud! Moving the Dynamics slider to the left (as shown in Figure 6.25), you'll find that the result is much more manageable. Beware of going too extreme, though—if the dynamic range is too narrow, the result can sound too mechanical.

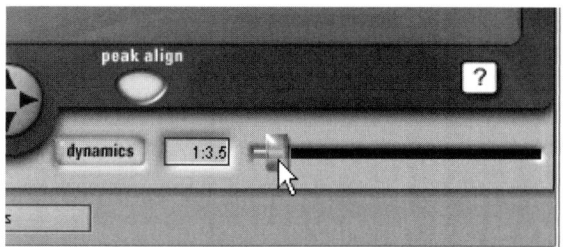

Figure 6.25
Taming a dynamic track with the Dynamics slider

- **Continuous files.** In the previous examples, we've chosen to create individual files and regions because that gives us the ability to manipulate and reposition individual segments. In the case of the hi-hat track, though, this mode will work against us because our Strip Silenced regions are so short that the replaced sounds would be cut short if they were constrained to these individual region boundaries. The solution to this problem is to choose Create Continuous File mode in the upper-left corner of the SoundReplacer window, as shown in Figure 6.26.

CHAPTER 6 ■ Mixing Beats

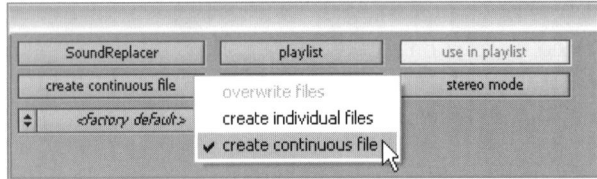

Figure 6.26

Creating a continuous file with SoundReplacer

With this mode chosen, you will create one large region that contains all of the hi-hat sounds (both closed and open). After you click the Process button in the lower-left corner of the SoundReplacer window, a new file will be created, looking something like Figure 6.27.

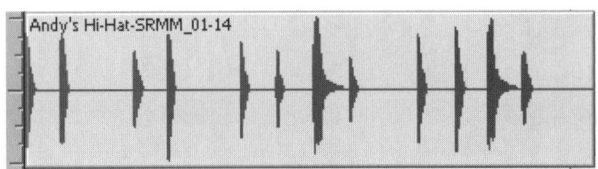

Figure 6.27

The replaced hi-hat track

> **NOTE**
>
> For your convenience, a completed version of this session has been included on your book's disc. If you launch the Chapter 6e — Finished session, you'll hear the result of SoundReplacer. Each track also has an alternate Edit Playlist of the original audio.

Working Smarter in the Mix Window

The last few versions of Pro Tools have seen some impressive improvements to the way mixing is done in this already impressive DAW. In particular, Pro Tools 7.3 (the latest version of Pro Tools at the time of this writing) has significantly upgraded the way Pro Tools LE users work, more than doubling the power of the Mix window over version 6.

Though there are too many mix improvements to discuss in the few pages we have here (again, I'd recommend Brian Smithers' *Mixing in Pro Tools: Skill Pack* for that level of study), there are a couple of things to talk about that will help you get the most out of the LE Mix window.

> **NOTE**
>
> This section will focus (though not exclusively) on new automation features in Pro Tools LE version 7.3. If you're a longtime Pro Tools HD user, you've seen many of these features already in Pro Tools 7.2. If you're using a version of Pro Tools prior to 7.3, many of these features and windows won't apply to your specific system.

Mix Groups

If you've done much mixing, you've probably used mix groups (also commonly referred to as "fader" groups). If you haven't, mix groups are a way that you can link together volume faders, so that you can adjust the volume levels of multiple tracks by simply moving one member's fader. Mix groups are an indispensable part of many kinds of mixing work and certainly impact working with beats and drums.

With the advent of Pro Tools LE 7.3 (and Pro Tools HD 7.2), the way you can work with groups has changed, giving you new power and flexibility. Here's the process of creating a group using Pro Tools LE 7.3:

> **NOTE**
>
> To follow along with these images, open session Chapter 6f.

1. Click the Group List pop-up button (shown in Figure 6.28), and you'll see a menu of group-related options from which to choose. Pick the New Group menu item. For users of previous Pro Tools versions, you don't have to pick your group members before creating a group. The Create Group window will appear.

Figure 6.28
Creating a group

> **TIP**
>
> The shortcut for creating a group is Ctrl+G (PC) or Apple+G (Mac).

2. In the Name field, type a descriptive name for your group.
3. Next, select the tracks that you want to include in the group from the Available column. If you hold the Shift key, you can select contiguous blocks of tracks. Holding the Ctrl (PC)

or Apple (Mac) key while selecting will allow you to select multiple noncontiguous tracks. When your desired member tracks are selected, press the Add button, as shown in Figure 6.29. The selected tracks will move to the Currently in Group column.

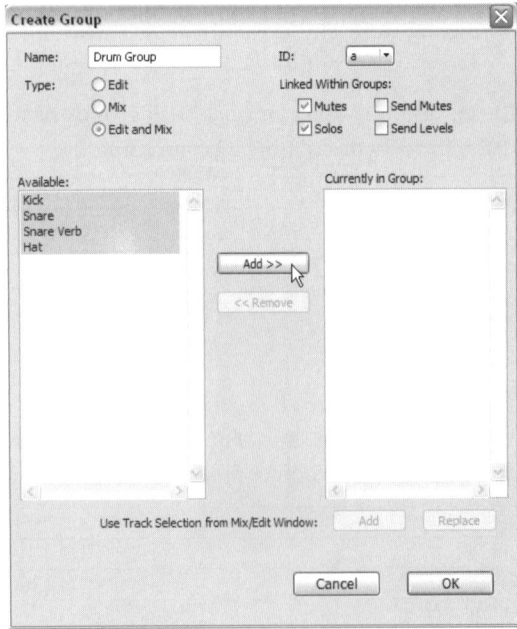

Figure 6.29
Choosing group members

If you take a look at the upper-right area of the Create Group window, you'll see four check boxes, which will let you choose the aspects of the tracks (in addition to volume) that will be grouped. By default, Mutes and Solos are checked, but you can disable these as you wish and even add some send grouping in the form of Send Levels and Send Mutes.

Not only has the method of grouping changed somewhat, but the number of groups you have at your disposal has increased substantially. Prior to Pro Tools 7.3 (Pro Tools 7.2 for HD users), you had a maximum of 26 groups (corresponding to the 26 letters of the alphabet), but now you have four times that amount, for a grand total of 104! You can easily access these additional groups in the Create Group window by clicking the ID drop-down menu, as shown in Figure 6.30. You will see that you have four banks of 26 letters from which to choose.

> **TIP**
>
> You can activate or deactivate a group in the Mix window by pressing the corresponding letter on your computer's keyboard. This shortcut only applies to the first bank of groups.

Working Smarter in the Mix Window

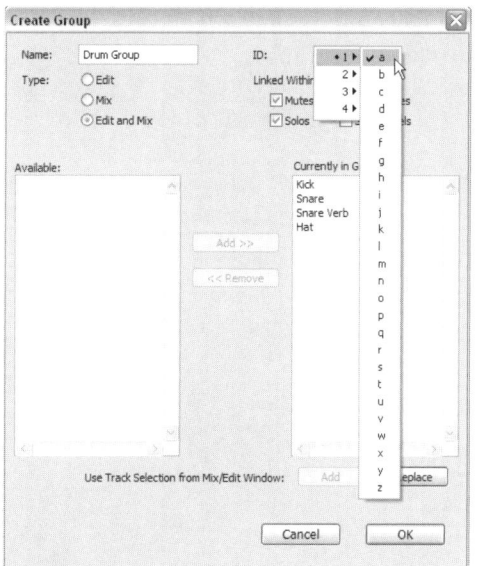

Figure 6.30
Choosing a group letter

> **NOTE**
>
> The Create Group window for Pro Tools HD is a bit more complex than its LE counterpart (see Figure 6.31) and gives you more groupable options and the ability to selectively group individual sends. The process of creating groups and selecting tracks is functionally identical in both versions.

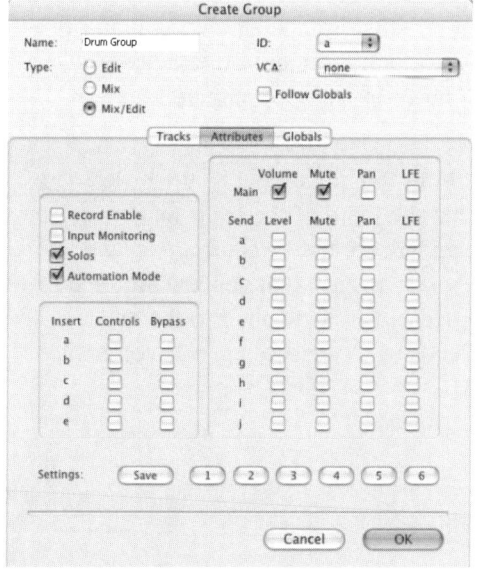

Figure 6.31
The Pro Tools HD Create Group window

149

If you need to change a group's members or attributes after its creation, simply right-click on the group name as shown in Figure 6.32 and choose the Modify menu item.

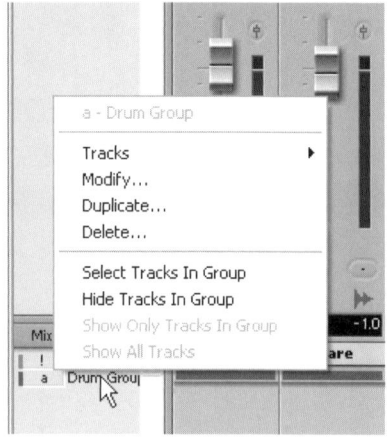

Figure 6.32
Changing a group

Subgroups

Actually, the topic of subgroups is one that we've covered already in the process of controlling a multitrack drum kit's stereo image earlier in this chapter. (See the "Ambient Tracks and Panning" subsection earlier in this chapter.) Subgroups bear a brief mention here as well because they relate closely to mix groups.

An audio subgroup is a way of funneling the output of a number of tracks and routing it to the input of an additional Auxiliary Input track. This has a similar effect to a mix group in that it provides easy control over a number of tracks from a single track, but there are other advantages to subgroups as well. In the case of drums, the smart use of subgroups can not only be a convenience, but it can also help conserve precious CPU resources.

Figure 6.33 shows an example of how this would be done. Note that the output of the Kick, Snare, Snare Verb, and Hat tracks has been set to Bus 3–4, and that the input of the Drum Subgroup Aux track is also set to Bus 3–4. With this configuration, you have complete control over the total volume of the drum tracks from the Aux track. Additionally, any plug-in that you instantiate on the Aux track (for example, the Compressor shown in the figure) will be applied to the entire drum kit, which takes a fraction of the CPU power it would've required to put a compressor on each individual track!

Working Smarter in the Mix Window

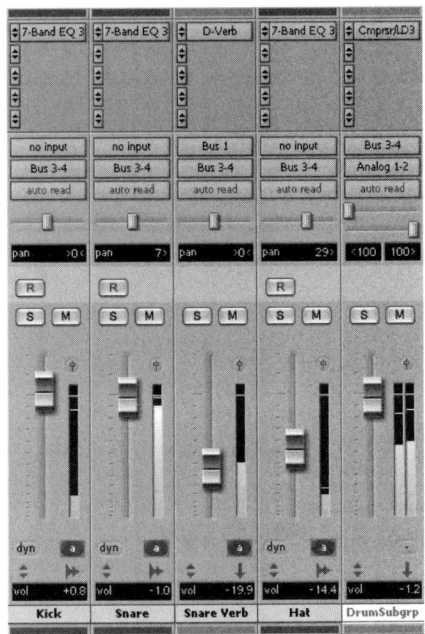

Figure 6.33

A subgroup

> **NOTE**
>
> To view a session showing the mix group and subgroup processes described here, take a look at the Chapter 6f – Finished session.

Automation

In some cases, a neater approach to addressing noisy tracks is to employ the use of Pro Tools automation. For Pro Tools LE, there have been recent improvements in how you can view automation as it is written. Pro Tools LE 7.3 (and Pro Tools HD 7.2) now uses a red line to show automation as it is being written in real time, as shown in Figure 6.34.

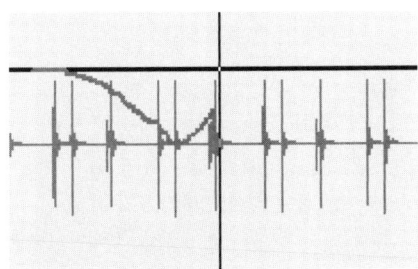

Figure 6.34

Real-time automation display

CHAPTER 6 ■ Mixing Beats

With Pro Tools HD version 7.2 and later, there are additional ways to view automation trim data. Pro Tools HD has long had an additional automation mode called *Trim mode*, which allows the user to modify the scale of preexisting automation in real time. Now, you have the option of viewing not only trim automation, but the original automation line and the resultant automation line. This is shown in Figure 6.35. The bottom line (with the automation breakpoints shown) is the original automation data. The yellow automation line (the straight line in this case) represents the trim automation pass, and the light blue automation line is the resultant automation level.

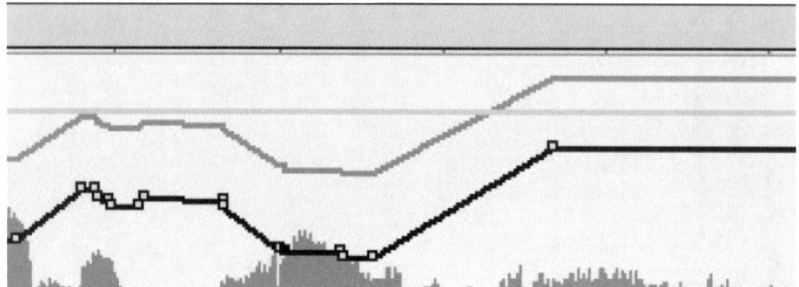

Figure 6.35

Trim automation display in Pro Tools HD

Workflow Ideas

Before we close the chapter on mixing, here's some food for thought!

Filter Sweeps

Here's an easy way to get that classic frequency swept sound.

> **NOTE**
>
> To follow along with this example, please launch the Chapter 6g session.

1. If your beat includes multiple tracks, create an audio subgroup using buses and an Aux track.
2. On the Aux track, instantiate a simple EQ, such as Digidesign's 1-band EQ 3.
3. Set a very narrow filter Q and a fairly high gain, such as the settings shown in Figure 6.36.
4. Enable the Frequency parameter for automation. This is easily done by holding down Ctrl+Start+Alt (PC) or Control+Apple+Option (Mac) and clicking on the Freq knob. From the menu that appears, choose Enable Automation for Frequency.

Workflow Ideas

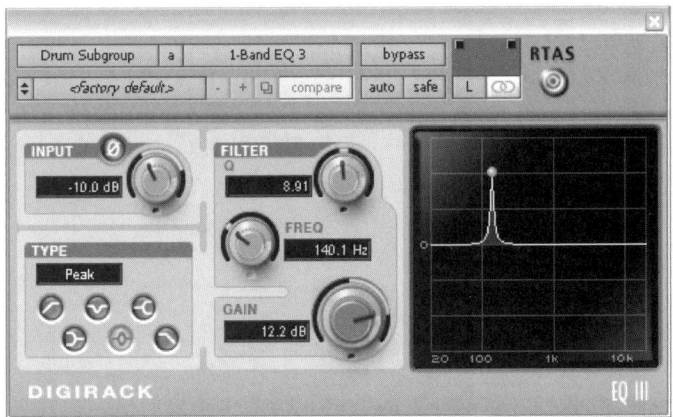

Figure 6.36
Typical filter sweep settings

5. Change your Aux track's automation mode to the desired mode. (I typically choose Touch mode.)
6. Begin playback at the desired location.
7. Move the Frequency knob to start sweeping the frequency. You might need to make a few automation write passes to get the desired effect.
8. After you've written your automation, you can view and edit your frequency sweep by choosing the appropriate track view format, such as the view shown in Figure 6.37.

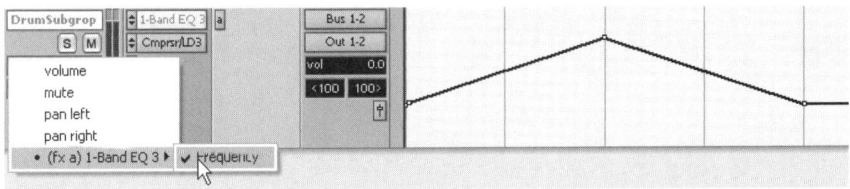

Figure 6.37
Viewing your plug-in automation playlist

> **NOTE**
> To view these steps in their completed form, check out the Chapter 6g – Finished #1 session.

> **TIP**
> Filter sweep effects, such as those shown here, can also be applied to individual drum tracks or any sound at all. Experiment!

153

CHAPTER 6 ■ Mixing Beats

Side-Chain and Signal Generator

Now, let's add a little more "thump" to the kick! Basically, the idea behind this process is to create a signal generator with a nice low frequency, then follow it with a noise gate. The noise gate will then be set up to open whenever a sufficient signal is routed to a Side-Chain input. It's pretty easy to do once you see the process, so read on:

> **NOTE**
>
> If you want to follow along, you can just reopen the Chapter 6g session.

1. Create an Aux track and instantiate a Signal Generator plug-in on the first insert.
2. Set your Signal Generator appropriately. A classic sound is a sine wave at a very low frequency, such as the one shown in Figure 6.38.

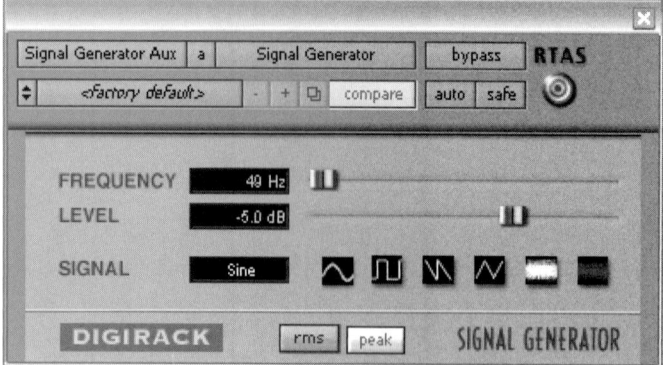

Figure 6.38

Signal Generator settings

3. In an insert *after* the one you used for your Signal Generator plug-in, instantiate a Noise Gate plug-in, such as Digidesign's Expander/Gate Dyn 3 plug-in.
4. The next step in the process is to somehow route a copy of the kick track's output to a bus. The recommended way to do this is to use a send and to make the send a *pre-fader* send, so that any changes you make to the kick track's volume won't affect the level going to the bus.
5. In the gate plug-in, set the key input to match the bus that you've just assigned to the kick's send. If you're using the Digidesign Expander/Gate Dyn 3 plug-in, you'll find the Key Input Selector button immediately below the Preset Menu button. (It has a key icon immediately to its left, as shown in Figure 6.39.)

Workflow Ideas

> **NOTE**
> To view these steps in their completed form, check out the Chapter 6g — Finished #2 session.

6. Next, enable the Side-Chain input to follow the key input. In the Expander/Gate Dyn 3 gate, it is the small key button in the Side-Chain, shown in Figure 6.39.

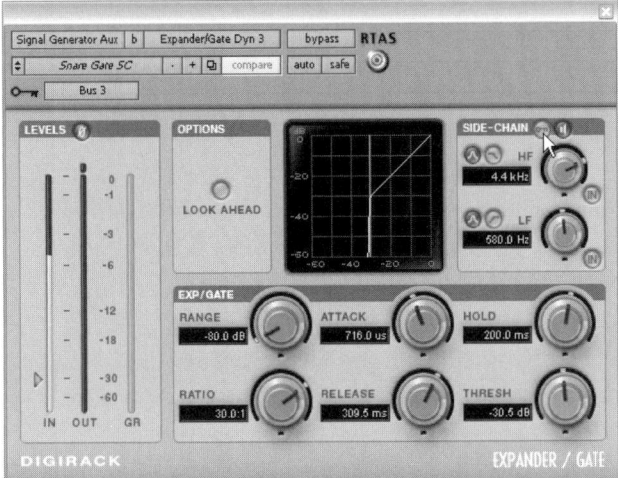

Figure 6.39
Gate settings

7. While playing your session, adjust the gate so that it opens with the kick track. This will take some adjustment of the threshold and release times. You'll also notice that there is a hard attack (something of a click sound, actually) as the gate immediately opens. Very often, I'll increase the attack time, allowing the gate to open more slowly, to smooth out the attack somewhat, as shown in Figure 6.39.

"New York" Compression

This popular technique is known by a number of different names. If you've heard of "parallel compression," "upward compression," or even "invisible compression," you've heard about "New York compression" as well. Whatever the name, though, the process and the effect are as effective as they are easy to use.

This kind of technique is made a lot easier if you understand the idea behind it. Consider traditional compression: As we talked about earlier in this chapter, compression narrows a dynamic range by "compressing" signals that are above a certain threshold. On the positive side, this gives your audio a more manageable audio level and can add punch to your drums. Sometimes, though, the audio can sound a bit flat and overly processed.

The New York compression technique combats this crushed kind of sound by effectively pushing *upward* rather than downward. How does that get done? Simple—a completely "dry" track is layered with a traditionally compressed track. (Very commonly, this compressed track is pretty aggressively compressed.) The combination of the two tracks together can give you the punch of compression plus the openness of an uncompressed track. Here's how you do it:

> **NOTE**
>
> If you want to follow along, you can just reopen the Chapter 6g session.

1. If your beat includes multiple tracks, create an audio subgroup using buses and an Aux track.
2. Duplicate the Aux track and instantiate a compressor on the second Aux track. Different situations will demand different compressor settings, but in general, don't be afraid to be a little more aggressive with your compression than you would be normally.
3. Bring the compressed Aux track's fader down so you can hear only the dry Aux track. Gradually, bring up the compressed Aux's level until you get the desired amount of "punch" while retaining the open feeling of the dry track. At the end of the process, your mix window might look something like Figure 6.40.

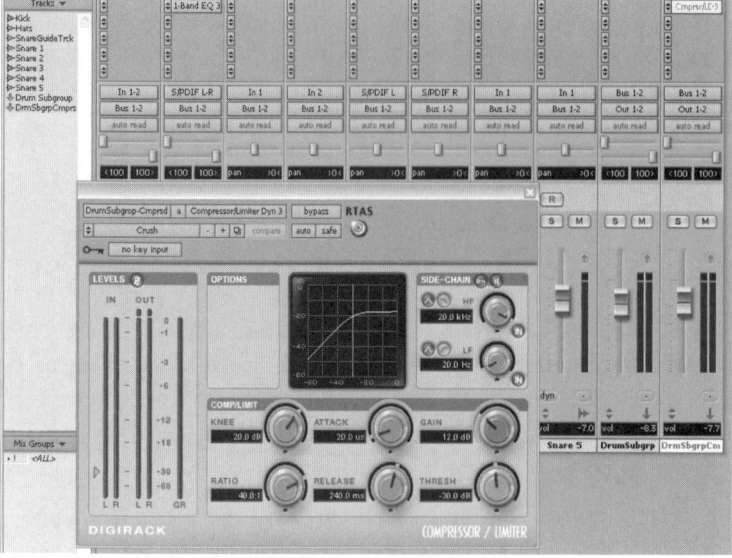

Figure 6.40

A Mix window showing a typical New York compression setup

> **NOTE**
> To view a multitrack drum setup with New York compression, check out the Chapter 6g – Finished #3 session.

> **TIP**
> If you're running a Pro Tools HD system, you'll want to make sure that you've enabled Automatic Delay Compensation (from the Options drop-down menu) to avoid differences in timing between the dry and compressed track due to DSP latency. If you've got a Pro Tools LE system, this is not an issue in most cases. (If you do happen to use an RTAS plug-in with processing latency, you can manually compensate for that delay with Digidesign's Time Adjuster plug-in.)

That's it for our discussion on mixing. Hopefully you've gotten some ideas to work with. Remember, the art of mixing can only be perfected through attentive practice, so experiment with these techniques and let your ears be your guide!

Tying It All Together

We're almost at the end of our discussions, and I do hope that you've found a few tidbits you can use to boost your creativity when working with drums and beats. A professional photographer friend of mine once told me, "If you get one really good shot out of a roll of film [this was a while ago!], the money that you spent for that roll was well spent." I hope that this book has given you a few "good shots" and new ways to look at creative challenges—if it has, my work is well-rewarded.

In the last few pages that remain, I'd like to touch on just a few final ideas that didn't fit neatly into the book. In this chapter we'll talk about:

- Stutter and glitch edits
- A new way to work with looped regions
- A workaround to the zero-crossing editing rule

Stutter and Glitch Edits

For those not familiar with the term, a *stutter edit* is generally defined to be the repetition of an isolated segment of a transient hit. This is obviously easy to do, using the tools that we've already discussed:

1. Isolate the desired transient with the Selector tool. For stutter edits, values of 16th notes or 32nd notes are commonly used.
2. Separate the selected area to form its own region.
3. Copy the region to the desired previous time (for example, one beat before the hit originally occurred).
4. Repeat the small region up to the point where the original note sounds.

159

CHAPTER 7 ■ Tying It All Together

There are some points to keep in mind when you do stutter edits:

- Because stutter edits sound best when they're rhythmically aligned, it's very helpful to make sure that your MIDI tempo (and hence your MIDI grid) matches your audio's tempo. There are two tools that will help you do this—Strip Silence (see Chapter 4) and Beat Detective (Chapter 5). Beat Detective will take more time, but will allow your small regions to follow the groove of the beat. (Just generate Bar|Beat markers, and then quantize the regions to a musical grid, as you did in Chapter 4.)
- Adding a little space between the slices can make them a bit more distinct. Again, using a musical grid with the Trim tool can be quite helpful.

Figure 7.1 shows a typical drum track (top), then a 32nd note stutter with no space (middle) and with 64th note spaces (bottom).

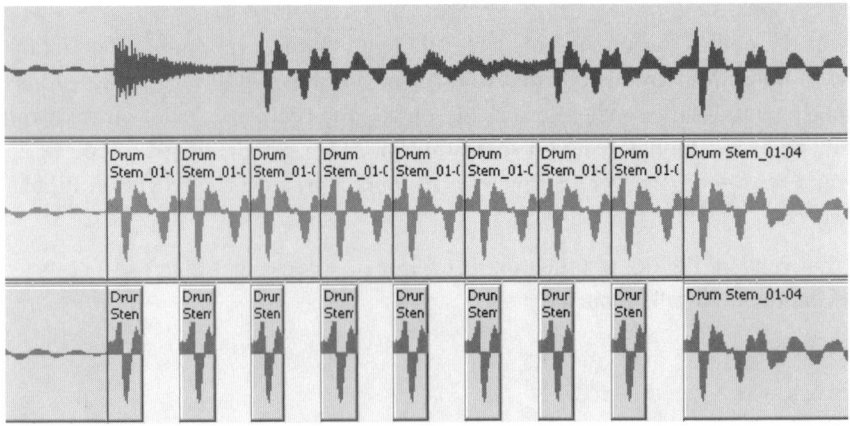

Figure 7.1
Two different stutters

> **NOTE**
>
> To listen to these examples, open the Chapter 7a – Finished (Stutter) session.

Essentially, a *glitch edit* is similar to a stutter edit, but with significantly smaller slices. At some point, slices become so small that they effectively become periodic oscillations that can be heard as pitches. The smaller the slices, the higher the pitch, as shown in Figure 7.2.

> **NOTE**
>
> To listen to these simple examples of glitch edits, open the Chapter 7a - Finished (Glitch) session.

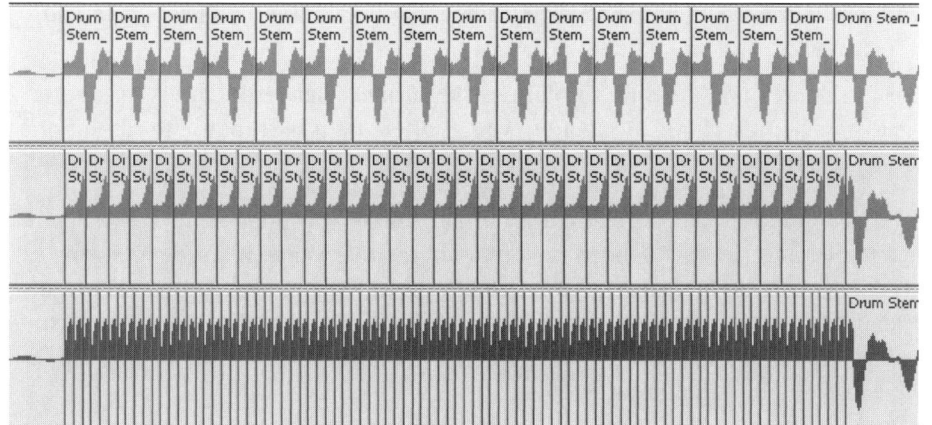

Figure 7.2
Three levels of glitch

Stutter and glitch edits aren't especially difficult to achieve, but they can be time-consuming and they demand some trial-and-error practice. I'd further challenge you to make the actual edit itself simply the foundation of the sound, embellishing the sound with pitch changes, filter sweeps, or whatever process you can imagine!

Loop Trim Polyrhythms

Human beings are very pattern-sensitive and tend to respond to all kinds of repetition. As the Stravinsky quotes in this book's introduction can attest, the regularity of beats is at the heart of our attraction to them.

A *polyrhythm* is defined as the simultaneous use of contrasting rhythms. In a sense, most music employs some degree of polyrhythm in that there is commonly more than one drum used to convey the musical style. Typically, though, the term *polyrhythm* is reserved for situations in which strikingly different grooves are combined to create a complex musical texture.

Pro Tools' region looping feature gives you a new opportunity to easily create and experiment with polyrhythms with the use of the Trim tool. In Chapter 4, we talked about using the loop trim process, but limited that discussion to the more traditional bar- or beat-related trimming. Now, let's break with tradition and see what can be done with some unconventional thinking.

> **NOTE**
>
> To experiment with this idea, you can open the Chapter 7b session included on this book's disc.

CHAPTER 7 ■ Tying It All Together

1. Set up two loops in the traditional manner (meaning that they share the same tempo and work well together).
2. Set your grid value to a non-measure resolution. The smaller your resolution is, the more polyrhythmic possibilities will be available to you. (I often use a sixteenth-note resolution.)
3. Select the Trim tool.
4. Moving the Trim tool to the lower-right corner of a region of your looped track (see Figure 7.3), change the duration of each looped region to an irregular value. If you're following along with this session, an individual region size of 1720 yields some interesting results. It's recommended that you do this during playback, so that you can hear the interaction of the two tracks. As you learned in Chapter 4, the changes you make to this single region will be mirrored throughout all of the looped regions.

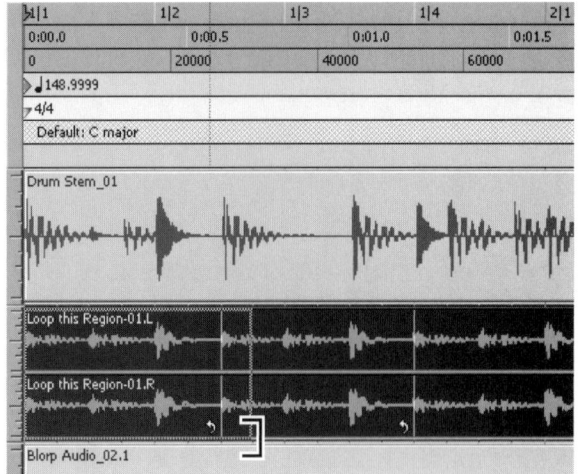

Figure 7.3
Creating a polyrhythm

> **NOTE**
> To see just one of the multitudes of possibilities, take a listen to the Chapter 7b - Finished session.

This is one of those processes that will sometimes bear fruit and sometimes won't, depending on the rhythms with which you're working. That being said, it has always been one of my favorite ways to create a more complex tapestry of rhythm!

"Breaking" the Zero-Crossing Rule

> **NOTE**
> For a refresher on the zero-crossing rule, read the note at the end of the "Separating Regions" section of Chapter 4.

A few years ago, I came across an interview article with a producer whom I highly respect. This person pioneered many of the beat techniques that have become part of our creative toolboxes, and I was particularly looking forward to his comments.

Overall the interview was great, but there was a section that kind of struck me as odd. I'm paraphrasing (like I said, this interview was some years ago), but the gist of what he said was, "You can forget about that cutting on the zero-crossing rule!" I was a little surprised to hear him say this, not only because it flew in the face of conventional wisdom, but also because I'd never heard any of the telltale clicks and pops that are the hallmark of not cutting on the zero-crossing.

After reading more of his interview, I understood what he was trying to say. His point was that there was a way to cut a drum hit closer to the peak of the transient (to get more punch) and then apply a very quick fade-in to the region. The important part—what makes the whole process make sense—is that the creation of the fade is itself creating a zero-crossing point. He wasn't breaking this rule of physics, but actually adhering to it in a whole new way. Brilliant!

As a result of this creative approach, a new technique has emerged that can give you more punch out of your drum hit samples. Here's how it works:

Figure 7.4 shows you a typical snare drum sound with traditional zero-crossing cutting.

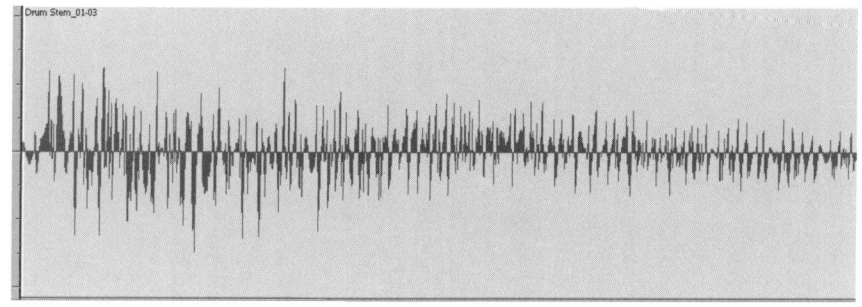

Figure 7.4
A typical snare

1. Identify the initial peak of the sound.
2. Trim the region within a few samples of the peak, as shown in Figure 7.5. Don't worry if you're not trimming to a zero-crossing point.

CHAPTER 7 ■ Tying It All Together

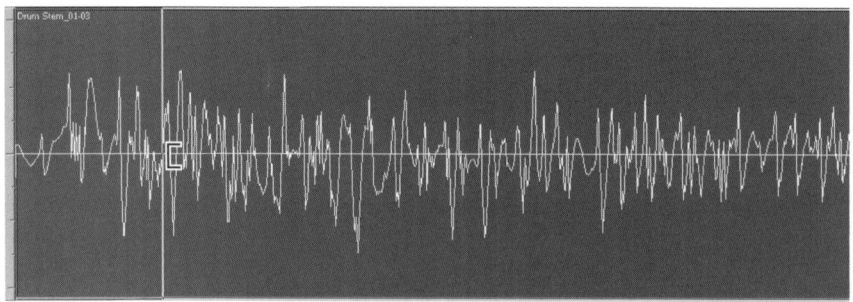

Figure 7.5
Trimming to the peak—almost

3. Now you're going to *create* a zero-crossing with a fade. My personal weapon of choice with this sort of work is the Smart Tool, as shown in Figure 7.6.

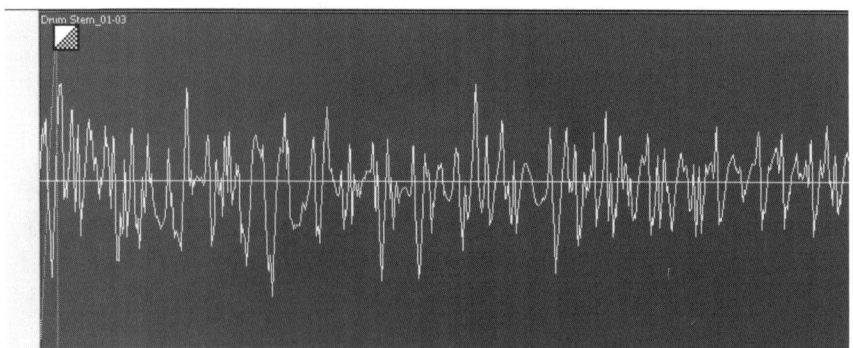

Figure 7.6
Creating a very quick fade

This technique can create a more explosive attack of the hit. Don't worry if your fade-in is only a couple of seconds long, just as long as you don't hear a telltale click! This technique is particularly useful for acoustic drums.

> **TIP**
> This same process can be effective with multiple drum hits as well. Using Strip Silence (with a high threshold and no start padding) can help to trim multiple regions. Once that's finished, select a number of regions and apply a very quick batch fade-in. Many times individual tweaking is also necessary, but these larger-scale processes can give you a good starting point.

Good Luck and Have Fun!

We're at the end out our explorations, and I hope that I've given you some nutritious food for thought.

Remember, the process of making music is cumulative, involving the combination of many different elements to achieve something really inspiring. In the microcosm of working with your beat tracks, always keep an eye open for opportunities to combine different techniques we've discussed to create new workflows of your own and achieve your own unique results.

Once that's finished, I hope that the beats you create will then be combined with other musical elements to create a final result that fully expresses your artistic vision. That's what it's all about in the end, and if you have half as much fun doing it as I do, you're lucky indeed!

Thanks for reading!

Appendix: Recommended Shortcuts

The following is a list of some recommended Pro Tools 7 shortcuts, printed with permission from Digidesign, that you might find useful in your work with beats. They are broken into platform, beginning with PC shortcuts followed by those for the Mac OS. Enjoy!

Pro Tools 7.0 Keyboard Shortcuts, for Pro Tools|HD, Pro Tools LE, and Pro Tools M-Powered Systems on Windows

Edit Modes and Tools

Shuffle mode	F1 or Alt+1 (on QWERTY keyboard)
Slip mode	F2 or Alt+2 (on QWERTY keyboard)
Spot mode	F3 or Alt+3 (on QWERTY keyboard)
Grid mode	F4 or Alt+4 (on QWERTY keyboard)
Zoomer tool	F5 or Ctrl+1 (on QWERTY keyboard)
Trimmer tool	F6 or Ctrl+2 (on QWERTY keyboard)
Selector tool	F7 or Ctrl+3 (on QWERTY keyboard)
Grabber tool	F8 or Ctrl+4 (on QWERTY keyboard)
Scrubber tool	F9 or Ctrl+5 (on QWERTY keyboard)
Pencil tool	F10 or Ctrl+6 (on QWERTY keyboard)
Smart Tool	F6+F7, F7+F8, or Ctrl+7 (on QWERTY keyboard)
Cycle through Edit modes	Single open quote (') key, located above the Tab key
Cycle through Edit tools	Escape (Esc) key

APPENDIX ■ Recommended Shortcuts

Edit Selection, Definition, and Navigation

Locate cursor to next region boundary/sync point	Tab (if Tab to Transients button is enabled)
Locate cursor to previous region boundary/sync point	Ctrl+Tab (if Tab to Transients button is enabled)
Go to song start	Start+Return
Extend selection to song start	Shift+Start+Enter
Extend selection to next region boundary	Shift+Tab
Extend selection to previous region boundary	Ctrl+Shift+Tab
Extend selection to include next region	Start+Shift+Tab
Extend selection to include previous region	Start+Shift+Ctrl+Tab
Return to start of session	Enter
Go to end of session	Ctrl+Enter
Extend selection to start of session	Shift+Enter
Extend selection to end of session	Ctrl+Shift+Enter
Link Timeline and Edit selection	Shift+Forward Slash (/)
Set selection start/end during playback	Down/Up Arrow keys
Set selection start/end to incoming time code while stopped	Down/Up Arrow keys
Select entire region in Edit window	Double-click with Selector Tool
Select entire track in Edit window	Triple-click with Selector or single-click in track and press Ctrl+A
Select all regions in all tracks in Edit window	Enter, then press Ctrl+A
Extend cursor or selection across all tracks	Enable "All" Edit group and Shift-click on any other track

Edit Menu Controls

Undo	Ctrl+Z
Redo	Ctrl+Shift+Z
Cut	Ctrl+X
Copy	Ctrl+C
Paste	Ctrl+V
Clear	Ctrl+B
Select All	Ctrl+A
Paste Special Merge	Alt+M
Paste Special Repeat to Fill Selection	Ctrl+Alt+V
Paste Special to Current Automation Type	Ctrl+Start+V
Match Edit Selection to Timeline Selection	Alt+Shift+5 (on numeric keypad)
Match Timeline Selection to Edit Selection	Alt+Shift+6 (on numeric keypad)
Play Edit Selection	Alt+[
Play Timeline Selection	Alt+]
Duplicate Selection	Ctrl+D
Repeat Selection	Alt+R
Shift Selection	Alt+H
Insert Silence	Ctrl+Shift+E
Trim Region to Selection	Ctrl+T
Trim Region Start to Insertion	Alt+Shift+7
Trim Region End to Insertion	Alt+Shift+8
Separate Region at Selection	Ctrl+E
Heal Separation	Ctrl+H
Strip Silence	Ctrl+U
Consolidate Selection	Alt+Shift+3
TCE Edit to Timeline Selection	Alt+Shift+U

APPENDIX ■ Recommended Shortcuts

Mix Group List and Edit Group List

Temporarily isolate channel strip from groups	Start-right-click applicable Group function
Suspend all groups	Ctrl+Shift+G or Ctrl-click on Groups pop-up menu
Rename group	Double-click to far left of Group name in Group List
Group enable/disable	Click the Group List Keyboard Focus, then type the letter corresponding to desired group
Select all tracks in group	Click to the left of a Group name in Group List
Show group members only	Right-click on Group(s) in Group List

Region Menu Controls

Mute/Unmute Regions	Ctrl+M
Lock/Unlock Regions	Ctrl+L
Bring to Front	Alt+Shift+F
Send to Back	Alt+Shift+B
Group Regions	Ctrl+Alt+G
Ungroup Regions	Ctrl+Alt+U
Regroup Regions	Ctrl+Alt+R
Loop Region	Ctrl+Alt+L
Capture Region	Ctrl+R
Identify Sync Point	Ctrl+Comma (,)
Quantize Region to Nearest Grid	Ctrl+0

Event Menu Controls

Open Time Operations window	Alt+1 (on numeric keypad)
Open Tempo Operations window	Alt+2 (on numeric keypad)
Open MIDI Operations window	Alt+3 (on numeric keypad)
Grid/Groove Quantize (in MIDI Operations window)	Alt+0 (on numeric keypad)
Change Duration (in MIDI Operations window)	Alt+P
Transpose (in MIDI Operations window)	Alt+T
Select/Split Notes (in MIDI Operations window)	Alt+Y
Open MIDI Event List window	Alt+Equal (=)
Open Beat Detective window	Ctrl+8 (on numeric keypad)
Identify Beat	Ctrl+I
All MIDI Notes Off	Ctrl+Shift+Period (.)

Window Menu Controls

Toggle Mix and Edit windows	Ctrl+Equal (=)
Show Task Manager window	Alt+Apostrophe (')
Show Workspace browser	Alt+Semicolon (;)
Show Project browser	Alt+O
Bring to Front	Alt+J
Send to Back	Alt+Shift+J
Show Transport window	Ctrl+1 (on numeric keypad)
Show Big Counter window	Ctrl+3 (on numeric keypad)
Show Automation Enable window	Ctrl+4 (on numeric keypad)
Show Memory Locations window	Ctrl+5 (on numeric keypad)
Machine Track Arming window	Ctrl+6 (on numeric keypad)
Universe window	Ctrl+7 (on numeric keypad)
QuickTime Movie or Avid Video window	Ctrl+9 (on numeric keypad)

Zoom

Horizontal zoom in or out	Ctrl+] or [
Vertical zoom in or out (Audio)	Ctrl+Alt+] or [
Vertical zoom in or out (MIDI)	Ctrl+Shift+] or [
Fill window with selection	Alt-click on Zoomer tool or Alt+F
View entire session	Double-click on Zoomer tool or Alt+A
Zoom vertical and horizontal axis	Hold down Ctrl key while dragging the Zoomer tool
Zoom to previous orientation	Alt-click on any Horizontal Zoom In or Out button, or Audio or MIDI Zoom In or Out button
Maximum zoom before waveform drawn from disk	Ctrl-click on Zoomer tool (faster drawing from RAM)
Zoom Toggle	Start+E
Zoom presets 1–5	Start+Zoom preset number (1, 2, 3, 4, or 5 on QWERTY keyboard) or Zoom preset number (1, 2, 3, 4, or 5 on QWERTY keyboard, in Controls Keyboard Focus)

APPENDIX ■ Recommended Shortcuts

Mixing

Make track active/inactive	Ctrl-Start-click Track Type icon in Mix window
Set all faders to their automation null points	Alt-click on either AutoMatch indicator
Reset a control to default value	Alt-click on control
Volume/Peak/Channel Delay amount	Ctrl-click on Track Volume/Peak/Channel Delay indicator
Clear peak or clip-hold from meter	Click on indicator
Bypass plug-in insert	Ctrl-click on insert name in Inserts view
Bypass send mute	Ctrl-click on send name in Sends view
Toggle send display between "All" and "Individual"	Ctrl-click on Send selector

Controls Keyboard Focus Mode

Copy Edit selection to Timeline selection	O (on QWERTY keyboard)
Center Timeline selection start	Q
Center Timeline selection end	W
Zoom Toggle	E
Zoom Out horizontally	R
Zoom In horizontally	T
Snap start (of selected region) to playhead	H
Move Edit selection up	P
Move Edit selection down	Semicolon (;)
Tab forward	Apostrophe (')
Play Edit selection	[
Trim Start to Insertion	A
Trim End to Insertion	S
Fade to Start (available if no selection)	D
Fade (without showing Fades dialog)	F
Fade to End (available if no selection)	G
Undo	Z
Cut	X
Copy	C
Paste	V
Separate	B
Timeline Insertion follows Playback (disable/enable)	N
Nudge back by Nudge value; Nudge Timeline selection (Link Timeline and Edit Selection disabled) or Nudge region (Link Timeline and Edit Selection enabled)	Comma (,)
Nudge forward by Nudge value; Nudge Timeline selection (Link Timeline and Edit Selection disabled) or Nudge region (Link Timeline and Edit Selection enabled)	Period (.)

Pro Tools 7.0 Keyboard Shortcuts, for Pro Tools|HD, Pro Tools LE, and Pro Tools M-Powered Systems on Macintosh

Edit Modes and Tools

Shuffle mode	F1 or Option+1 (on QWERTY keyboard)
Slip mode	F2 or Option+2 (on QWERTY keyboard)
Spot mode	F3 or Option+3 (on QWERTY keyboard)
Grid mode	F4 or Option+4 (on QWERTY keyboard)
Zoomer tool	F5 or Command+1 (on QWERTY keyboard)
Trimmer tool	F6 or Command+2 (on QWERTY keyboard)
Selector tool	F7 or Command+3 (on QWERTY keyboard)
Grabber tool	F8 or Command+4 (on QWERTY keyboard)
Scrubber tool	F9 or Command+5 (on QWERTY keyboard)
Pencil tool	F10 or Command+6 (on QWERTY keyboard)
Smart Tool	F6+F7, F7+F8, or Command+7 (on QWERTY keyboard)
Cycle through Edit modes	Single Open Quote (') key, located above the Tab key
Cycle through Edit tools	Escape (Esc) key

APPENDIX ■ Recommended Shortcuts

Edit Selection, Definition, and Navigation

Locate cursor to next region boundary/sync point	Tab (if Tab to Transients button is enabled)
Locate cursor to previous region boundary/sync point	Option+Tab (if Tab to Transients button is enabled)
Go to song start	Control+Return
Extend selection to song start	Shift+Control+Return
Extend selection to next region boundary	Shift+Tab
Extend selection to previous region boundary	Option+Shift+Tab
Extend selection to include next region	Control+Shift+Tab
Extend selection to include previous region	Control+Shift+Option+Tab
Return to start of session	Return
Go to end of session	Option+Return
Extend selection to start of session	Shift+Return
Extend selection to end of session	Option+Shift+Return
Link Timeline and Edit selection	Shift+Forward Slash (/)
Set selection start/end during playback	Down/Up Arrow keys
Set selection start/end to incoming time code while stopped	Down/Up Arrow keys
Select entire region in Edit window	Double-click with Selector
Select entire track in Edit window	Triple-click with Selector or single-click in track and press Command+A
Select all regions in all tracks in Edit window	Return, then press Command+A
Extend cursor or selection across all tracks	Enable "All" Edit group and Shift-click on any other track

Edit Menu Commands

Undo	Command+Z
Redo	Command+Shift+Z
Cut	Command+X
Copy	Command+C
Paste	Command+V
Clear	Command+B
Select All	Command+A
Paste Special Merge	Option+M
Paste Special Repeat to Fill Selection	Command+Option+V
Paste Special to Current Automation Type	Command+Control+V
Match Edit Selection to Timeline Selection	Option+Shift+5 (on numeric keypad)
Match Timeline Selection to Edit Selection	Option+Shift+6 (on numeric keypad)
Play Edit Selection	Option+[
Play Timeline Selection	Option+]
Duplicate Selection	Command+D
Repeat Selection	Option+R
Shift Selection	Option+H
Insert Silence	Command+Shift+E
Trim Region to Selection	Command+T
Trim Region Start to Insertion	Option+Shift+7
Trim Region End to Insertion	Option+Shift+8
Separate Region at Selection	Command+E
Heal Separation	Command+H
Strip Silence	Command+U
Consolidate Selection	Option+Shift+3
TCE Edit to Timeline Selection	Option+Shift+U

APPENDIX ■ Recommended Shortcuts

Mix Group List and Edit Group List

Temporarily isolate channel strip from groups	Control-click applicable Group function
Suspend all groups	Command+Shift+G, or Command-click on Groups pop-up menu
Rename group	Double-click to far left of Group name in group list
Group enable/disable	Click the Group List Keyboard Focus, then type the letter corresponding to desired group
Select all tracks in group	Click to the left of a Group name in group list
Show group members only	Control-click on Group(s) in group list

Region Menu Commands

Mute/Unmute Regions	Command+M
Lock/Unlock Regions	Command+L
Bring to Front	Option+Shift+F
Send to Back	Option+Shift+B
Group Regions	Command+Option+G
Ungroup Regions	Command+Option+U
Regroup regions	Command+Option+R
Loop Region	Command+Option+L
Capture Region	Command+R
Identify Sync Point	Command+Comma (,)
Quantize Region to Nearest Grid	Command+0

Recommended Shortcuts

Event Menu Commands

Open Time Operations Window	Option+1 (on numeric keypad)
Open Tempo Operations Window	Option+2 (on numeric keypad)
Open MIDI Operations Window	Option+3 (on numeric keypad)
Grid/Groove Quantize (in MIDI Operations Window)	Option+0 (on numeric keypad)
Change Duration (in MIDI Operations Window)	Option+P
Transpose (in MIDI Operations Window)	Option+T
Select/Split Notes (in MIDI Operations Window)	Option+Y
Open MIDI Event List Window	Option+Equal (=)
Open Beat Detective Window	Command+8 (on numeric keypad)
Identify Beat	Command+I
All MIDI Notes Off	Command+Shift+Period (.)

Window Menu Commands

Toggle Mix and Edit Windows	Command+Equal (=)
Show Task Manager Window	Option+Apostrophe (')
Show Workspace Browser	Option+Semicolon (;)
Show Project Browser	Option+O
Bring to Front	Option+J
Send to Back	Option+Shift+J
Show Transport Window	Command+1 (on numeric keypad)
Show Big Counter Window	Command+3 (on numeric keypad)
Show Automation Enable Window	Command+4 (on numeric keypad)
Show Memory Locations Window	Command+5 (on numeric keypad)
Machine Track Arming Window	Command+6 (on numeric keypad)
Universe Window	Command+7 (on numeric keypad)
QuickTime Movie or Avid Video Window	Command+9 (on numeric keypad)

APPENDIX ■ Recommended Shortcuts

Zoom

Horizontal zoom in or out	Command+] or [
Vertical zoom in or out (Audio)	Command+Option+] or [
Vertical zoom in or out (MIDI)	Command+Shift+] or [
Fill window with selection	Option-click on Zoomer tool or Option+F
View entire session	Double-click on Zoomer tool or Option+A
Zoom vertical and horizontal axis	Hold down Command key while dragging the Zoomer tool
Zoom to previous orientation	Option-click on any Horizontal Zoom In or Out button, or Audio or MIDI Zoom In or Out button
Maximum zoom before waveform drawn from disk	Command-click on Zoomer tool (faster drawing from RAM)
Zoom Toggle	Control+E
Zoom presets 1–5	Control+Zoom preset number (1, 2, 3, 4, or 5 on QWERTY keyboard), or Zoom preset number (1, 2, 3, 4, or 5 on QWERTY keyboard, in Commands Keyboard Focus)

Mixing

Make track active/inactive	Command-Control-click Track Type icon in Mix window
Set all faders to their automation null points	Option-click on either AutoMatch indicator
Reset a control to default value	Option-click on control
Volume/Peak/Channel Delay amount	Command-click on Track Volume/Peak/Channel Delay indicator
Clear peak or clip-hold from meter	Click on indicator
Bypass plug-in insert	Command-click on insert name in Inserts view
Bypass send mute	Command-click on send name in Sends view
Toggle send display between "All" and "Individual"	Command-click on Send selector

Commands Keyboard Focus Mode

Command	Key
Copy Edit selection to Timeline selection	O (on QWERTY keyboard)
Center Timeline selection start	Q
Center Timeline selection end	W
Zoom Toggle	E
Zoom Out horizontally	R
Zoom In horizontally	T
Snap start (of selected region) to playhead	H
Move Edit selection up	P
Move Edit selection down	Semicolon (;)
Tab forward	Apostrophe (')
Play Edit Selection	[
Trim Start to Insertion	A
Trim End to Insertion	S
Fade to Start (available if no selection)	D
Fade (without showing Fades dialog)	F
Fade to End (available if no selection)	G
Undo	Z
Cut	X
Copy	C
Paste	V
Separate	B
Timeline Insertion follows Playback (disable/enable)	N
Nudge back by Nudge value; Nudge Timeline selection (Link Timeline and Edit Selection disabled) or Nudge region (Link Timeline and Edit Selection enabled)	Comma (,)
Nudge forward by Nudge value; Nudge Timeline selection (Link Timeline and Edit Selection disabled) or Nudge region (Link Timeline and Edit Selection enabled)	Period (.)

Index

+ (plus) sign, moving regions, 73
- (minus) sign
    Grabber tool, 102
    regions, moving, 73
5ms Trigger Pads, 107

A

Absolute Grid mode, 71. *See also* Grid mode
absolute time linearity, 58
accessing Conform modes, 109
Accuracy slider, 32
ACID files, 16
Action section, 43
activating Tab to Transient buttons, 13
Add All Current Triggers to Collection option, 14
Add Bar|Beat Markers dialog box, 67
Add Only Unique Triggers to Collection option, 114
Advanced Instrument Research. *See* A.I.R.
A.I.R. (Advanced Instrument Research), 7
aligning, Peak Align button, 140
alternate edits, creating, 22–24
alternate tracks, creating, 24–25
ambient tracks, mixing beats, 126–129
amplitude thresholds, setting, 144
Analyze button, 99–100
analyzing
    beats, changing emphasis, 100
    Collection mode, 113–115
    MIDI Detective, 119–121
    waveforms, 95. *See also* Beat Detective
applying
    compressors, 129–132
    crossfades, 88
    DAE Playback Buffer, 39
    Dynamic Transport, 91–92
    Edit Playlists, 21–22
    gates, 132–133
    Mix window, 146–150
    playlists on MIDI drum tracks, 25–27
    Quantize feature, 47–53
    Rex files, 16–19
    SoundReplacer, 135–146
    TCE Trim tool, 30
    Tempo editor, 10
    transients, 12–16
areas
    Edit Selection, 13
    Operation (Beat Detective), 108
    Resolution (Beat Detective), 101
arrows, Grid Value Arrow, 71
artifacts, 30–35
audio
    Beat Detective, 95. *See also* Beat Detective
    beats, identifying, 65–70
    conforming, 110
    importing, 18
    intelligent, 16
    previewing, looping in browsers, 92–93
    quantizing, 105–119
    regions, separating, 77–79
    Sound Accuracy preset, 34
    TCE Trim tool, optimizing, 30–35
    tracks. *See also* tracks
        editing regions, 82–84
        quantizing, 96
Audio Files folder, 25
AudioSuite
    processing options, 140
    TCE plug-ins, 28
    Time Compression plug-in, 30
    Time Shift plug-in, 35
automation
    overview of, 25
    playlists, 153
    viewing, 151–152
Average Location Analysis mode, 120

B

bars, 4
    viewing, 7
Bars:Beats ruler, 4

Index

Beat Detective
    Analyze button, 99–100
    audio, quantizing, 105–119
    beat triggers, 101–103
    Collection mode, 113–115
    Edit Smoothing, 110–111
    Emphasis menu, 100
    groove templates, creating, 116–119
    multitrack beats, 112
    optimizing, 112
    overhead tracks, 113
    overview of, 95–97
    Pro Tools LE, 115–116
    regions
        conforming, 108–110
        creating, 107–108
        selecting, 97–99
    Resolution area, 101
    room tracks, 113
    selections, consolidating, 111
    tempo maps, creating, 97–105
beats
    Beat Detective. *See* Beat Detective
    changing, 16
    conforming, 96
    Dynamic Transport, 91–92
    identifying, 65–70
    MIDI, 41
        overview of, 7–8
        Quantize feature, 47–53
        Real-Time Properties, 54–58
        session linearity, 58–60
        single note height, 42–46
        track offsets, 60–63
        velocity, 53–54
    mixing, 123–124
        ambient tracks, 126–129
        applying compressors, 129–132
        applying gates, 132–133
        applying Mix window, 146–150
        applying SoundReplacer, 135–146
        cymbals, 126
        drum by drum, 124
        filter sweeps, 152–153
        hi-hats, 126
        kick drums, 124–125
        layering tracks, 133–135
        manipulating sound, 129
        New York compression, 155–157
        panning, 126–129
        Side-Chain input, 154–155
        Signal Generator, 154–155
        snare drums, 125
        toms, 126
        viewing automation, 151–152
    multitrack, 112
    notation, 4–7
    overview of, 1
    tempo, 2–3
    ticks, 6
    triggers, 100, 101–103
        changing values of, 104–105
        Collection mode, 113–115
        deleting, 102
        promoting, 103
    viewing, 7
BPM (beats per minute), 2
breaking the zero-crossing rule, 163–164
browsers
    looping in, 92–93
    updating, 137
buffers, changing, 39
buttons
    Analyze, 99–100
    Capture Selection, 99
    Conductor, 3, 8
    Crossfade, 145
    Edit Selection, 115
    Enable, 67. *See also* Conductor button
    Extract, 78
    Grid Value, 29
    Link Edit and Timeline, 36
    Link Track, 115
    MIDI Output, 45
    Mirrored MIDI Editing, 63
    Peak Align, 140
    Playlist Selector, 22
    Rename, 78
    Scroll Next, 102
    Separate, 78
    Strip, 78
    Tab to Transient, 13
    Tap End B|B, 99
    Time Base Selector, 82
    Value, 56

Index

C

Capture Region option, 14
Capture Selection button, 99
changing. *See also* **editing**
    beats, 16
    DAE Playback Buffer, 39
    data as it plays, 54–58
    emphasis, 100
    grids, 70
    groups, 150
    MIDI
        output, 44
        Quantize feature, 47
    Mirrored MIDI Editing button, 63
    modes, 14
    perspective, 129
    between playlists, 24
    Real-Time Properties, 56
    regions (TCE Trim tool), 28
    session linearity, 59
    tempo, 8–10, 18
    track output to a bus, 127
    values
        of beat triggers, 104–105
        in volume, 12
    versions, 23
check boxes, Show Trigger Time, 102
child tracks, 46
Choose Loop Preview, 92
chorus, tempo changes, 8
Clear All Triggers from Collection option, 114
clutching, Grid mode, 75–77
Collection mode (Beat Detective), 113–115
color-coding tracks, 46
columns, Real-Time Properties, 55
combining regions, 80
commands, Separate Region, 15
comparing sessions, 68
compensating for MIDI latency, 62
components
    regions, trimming loops, 90
    separating, 136
compression
    New York, 155–157
    tracks, 131
compressors, applying, 129–132
Conductor button, 3
    tempo changes, 8

configuring
    5ms Trigger Pads, 107
    amplitude thresholds, 144
    Beat Detective selections, 98
    filter sweeps, 153
    grids, 71
    mid-amplitude thresholds, 145
    Noise Gate plug-in, 154–155
    Nudge values, 73
    Signal Generator, 154–155
    thresholds, 78
conforming
    audio, 110
    beats, 96
    grooves, 109
    notes to a grid, 49
    regions
        Beat Detective, 108–110
        quantizing, 82
consolidating
    regions, 38–39
    selections (Beat Detective), 111
Constant option, 9
Contains menu, 99
contiguous tracks, grouping, 84
Continuous File mode, 145
controlling
    meter, 5
    tempo, 3
copying
    regions, 74
    tracks, 130
Create Continuous File mode, 145
creating. *See* **formatting**
Crossfade button, 145
crossfades, applying, 88
cutting. *See also* **editing; separating**
    crossfades, 88
    regions, 81
Cymbal region, 79
cymbals, mixing beats, 126

D

DAE Playback Buffer, changing, 39
defaults
    beats per minute (BPM), 2
    Strength option, 52
deleting beat triggers, 102
detecting mixdowns, 116

Index

determining tempo, 106
dialog boxes
    Add Bar|Beat Markers, 67
    Duplicate Tracks, 130
    Extract Groove Template, 117
    Identify Trigger, 104
    MIDI Operations, 43
    MIDI Quantize, 47
    Preserve Tempo After Selection, 9
    Realign Session, 104
    Region Looping, 87
    Select/Split Notes, 44
    Shift, 73
Digidesign, 7
disabling Real-Time Properties, 56
displays. *See also* browsers; interfaces
    real-time automation, 151
    tempo, 3
    Trim automation, 152
    updating, 137
Do You Like This One Better folder, 25
dragging. *See also* moving
    grids, 71
drawing options, 11
drums
    Edit Playlist, creating alternate, 24–25
    grouping, 85
    Identify Beat function, 65–70
    on Instrument tracks, 42
    kick
        mixing beats, 124–125
        replacing tracks, 141
    MIDI, applying playlists on, 25–27
    multitrack, mixing beats, 124
    previewing, looping in browsers, 92–93
    snare, mixing beats, 125
    velocity, 53
Duplicate Tracks dialog box, 130
duplicating
    playlists, 23
    regions, 74
    tracks, 130
Dynamics slider, 140, 145
Dynamic Transport, 91–92

E

edit density, 38
editing
    beats, identifying, 65–70

glitch edits, 159–161
Grid mode, 68, 70–71
    clutching, 75–77
    Relative Grid mode, 71–75
healing, 81
matrix drum, 42
Mirrored MIDI Editing button, 63
overview of, 65
regions, 16, 38–39, 77
    Audio tracks, 82–84
    Dynamic Transport, 91–92
    groups, 84–87
    looping, 87–91
    looping in browsers, 92–93
    new features, 84
    quantizing, 82
    separating, 79–81
    starting, 68
    Strip Silence, 77–79
stutter edits, 159–161
timelines, 36
transients, 12–16
editors, viewing Tempo Editor, 10
Edit Playlists
    alternate edits, creating, 22–24
    alternate tracks, creating, 24–25
    applying, 21–22
    MIDI drum tracks, applying on, 25–27
    TCE Trim tool, 28–35
Edit Selection areas, 7, 13
Edit Selection button, 115
Edit Smoothing, 110–111
eighth notes
    nudge value of, 7
    values, 6
Emphasis (Beat Detective), 100
Enable button, 67
Enable Crossfade (Region Looping dialog box), 87
enabling
    Dynamic Transport, 91–92
    Real-Time Properties, 56
end points, setting, 68
entering data (Pencil tool), 11
Event drop-down menu, 9
Exclude Within option, 52
Extract button, 78
Extract Groove Template dialog box, 117
extracting grooves, 117

Index

F

fades
   creating, 164
   crossfades, applying, 88
   regions, creating on groups, 85
   two-measure, 27
features
   Beat Detective. *See* Beat Detective
   new, 84
   regions, 84
Feel Injector
   Templates menu item, 49
   16th Shuffle, 49
files
   ACID, 16
   Continuous File mode, 145
   Create Continuous File mode, 145
   previewing, looping in browsers, 92–93
   Rex
      applying, 16–19
      importing, 18
   sessions, importing, 92
filter sweeps, 152–153
First Note Analysis mode, 120
folders. *See also* files
   Audio Files, 25
   Do You Like This One Better, 25
   Plug-In Settings, 34
   Root Settings, 34
formatting
   alternate edits, 22–24
   alternate tracks, 24–25
   fades, 164
   global MIDI offsets, 60
   grids, 30
   groove templates, 116–119
   groups, 147
   maps, tempo, 96, 97–105
   MIDI output, 45
   playlists, 25
   polyrhythms, 162
   regions (Beat Detective), 107–108
   static tempo, 106
   TCE presets, 32
   values, 30
four-bar regions, 66
Free Hand option, 11

frequencies, optimizing TCE Trim tool, 30–35
functions, Identify Beat, 66–70

G

gates, applying, 132–133
glitch edits, 159–161
global MIDI offsets, formatting, 60
Grabber tool, 53, 73
   beat triggers, creating, 102
Grid mode
   editing, 68, 70–71
      clutching, 75–77
      Relative Grid mode, 71–75
   regions, changing, 28
grids
   configuring, 71
   formatting, 30
   modifying, 70
   Offset Grid By option, 49
   Quantize, 48
   Randomize option, 50
   values, 7
Grid Value Arrow, 71
Grid Value button, 29
Groove Clipboard, 117
Groove mode, 109
Groove Quantize feature, 54
grooves
   conforming, 109
   extracting, 117
   Quantize feature, 49
   quantizing, 118
   templates
      creating, 116–119
      saving, 118
Group menu, 86
groups
   changing, 150
   letters, selecting, 149
   members, selecting, 148
   Mix window, 147
   regions, 84–87
   subgroups, 150–151

H

half note values, 6
Heal Separation feature, 80

Index

height, single note, 42–46
hiding
    tracks, 46
    Transport window, 3
High Emphasis (Beat Detective), 101
Highest Note Analysis mode, 120
hi-hats
    beats, mixing, 126
    TCE trim tool, 34

I

Identify Beat function, 66–70
identifying beats, 65–70
Identify Trigger dialog box, 104
Ignition Pack, 17
importing
    files into sessions, 92
    Rex files, 18
Include Within option, 51
increasing DAE Playback Buffer, 39
input, Side-Chain, 154–155
insertion, timelines, 15
Instrument tracks
    drum kits on, 42
    MIDI output, changing, 44
    velocity, 53
    viewing, 26
intelligent audio, 16
interfaces
    looping in, 92–93
    updating, 137

K

keys, Tab, 13
kick drums
    mixing beats, 124–125
    tracks, replacing, 141
Kick tracks (TCE trim tool), 34

L

Last Note Analysis mode, 120
latency (MIDI)
    compensating for, 62
    measuring, 61
launching. *See* opening; starting
layering tracks, 133–135
letters, selecting groups, 149
limitation of playlists, 25

linearity of sessions, 58–60
Line option, 11
linking edit and timeline selections, 36
Link Track button, 115
listening to tracks, 45
loading replacement sounds, 138
locations. *See* saving; storage locations
Loop Length (Region Looping dialog box), 87
loops
    cutting, 81
    playback (Dynamic Transport), 91–92
    previewing, 17
    regions, 87–91
        looping in browsers, 92–93
        trimming, 89
    rhythm tracks, pulling from, 13
    Tabs to Transient button, 14
    trim polyrhythms, 161–162
Loop Until End of Session (Region Looping dialog box), 87
Loudest Note mode, 121
Low Emphasis, 101
Lowest Note Analysis mode, 120

M

Main Counter, 6
    viewing, 7
managing tempo, 8–10
manipulating sound, 129
Manual Tempo slider, 3
maps, creating tempo, 96, 97–105
marking transients, 139
matrix drum editing, 42
measures, 4
    meter of, 4
    two-measure fades, 27
measuring MIDI latency, 61
melodic structure, 4
members, selecting groups, 148
menus
    Contains, 99
    Emphasis, 100–101
    Event drop-down, 9
    Group, 86
    Track View Selector, 26
meter
    controlling, 5
    of measures, 4

Index

Meter ruler, 5
mid-amplitude thresholds, setting, 145
MIDI
   beats, 41
      identifying, 65–70
      overview of, 7–8
      Quantize feature, 47–53
      Real-Time Properties, 54–58
      session linearity, 58–60
      single note height, 42–46
      track offsets, 60–63
      velocity, 53–54
   Detective, 119–121
   drum tracks, applying playlists on, 25–27
   latency
      compensating for, 62
      measuring, 61
   Mirrored MIDI Editing button, 63
   Operations dialog box, 43
   output
      changing, 44
      formatting, 45
   Quantize dialog box, 47
   Rex files, 16–19
   volume, selecting, 27
Min:Sec timeline, 58
minus (-) sign
   Grabber tool, 102
   regions, moving, 73
Mirrored MIDI Editing button, 63
mixdowns, detecting, 116
mixing beats, 123–124
   ambient tracks, 126–129
   applying compressors, 129–132
   applying gates, 132–133
   applying Mix window, 146–150
   applying SoundReplacer, 135–146
   cymbals, 126
   drum by drum, 124
   filter sweeps, 152–153
   hi-hats, 126
   kick drums, 124–125
   layering tracks, 133–135
   manipulating sound, 129
   New York compression, 155–157
   panning, 126–129
   Side-Chain input, 154–155
   Signal Generator, 154–155
   snare drums, 125
   toms, 126
   viewing automation, 151–152
Mix slider, 139
Mix window
   applying, 146–150
   New York compression, 156
modes
   changes, 14
   Collection (Beat Detective), 113–115
   Conform, accessing, 109
   Continuous File, 145
   Create Continuous File, 145
   Grid
      clutching, 75–77
      editing, 68, 70–71
      Relative Grid mode, 71–75
   Groove, 109
   MIDI Detective, 120
   Select/Split Notes, 43
   Slip, 73
   Standard conform, 109
modifying. *See also* **changing**
   beats, 16
   grids, 70
   groups, 150
moving
   regions
      clutching, 75–77
      by grid values, 71–75
   Rex files, 18
   timeline insertions, 106
multiple regions, grouping, 84–87
multitrack beats (Beat Detective), 112
multitrack drums
   grouping, 85
   mixing beats, 124
muting regions, 46

N

naming playlists, 23
navigating
   beat triggers, 102
   Quantize feature, 48
new features, regions, 84
New menu items, 24
New York compression, 155–157
Noise Gate plug-in, 154–155

Index

notation
    beats, 4–7
    tempo, 2
notes. *See also* specific notes
    MIDI Quantize feature, 47
    quarter, 5
    single note height, 42–46
    splitting, 43
    values, 6
nudge values, 7
    setting, 73
Number of Loops (Region Looping dialog box), 87
number of ticks per beat, 6

O

objects, trimming loops, 89
Offset Grid By option, 49
offsets, tracks, 60–63
opening
    Beat Detective, 98
    MIDI Detective, 119
    output windows, 128
    Relative Grid mode, 75
    SoundReplacer, 137
Operation area (Beat Detective), 108
Operation tab, 15
optimizing
    Beat Detective, 112
    SoundReplacer, 143
    TCE Trim tool, 30–35
options
    AudioSuite processing, 140
    Capture Region, 14
    Collection mode, 114
    Constant, 9
    drawing, 11
    Exclude Within, 52
    extraction, 117
    grids, Quantize, 48
    Include Within, 51
    Instrument tracks, viewing, 26
    Offset Grid By, 49
    Pencil tool, 11
    Randomize, 50
    Rex file import, 18
    Separate Region, 14
    Separate Regions, 15
    Straight Line, 27
    Strength, 52
    Swing, 51
    Tuplet, 49
output
    MIDI
        changing, 44
        formatting, 45
    tracks to a bus, changing, 127
    windows, opening, 128
overhead tracks (Beat Detective), 113

P

panning, mixing beats, 126–129
Parabolic option, 11
parent tracks, 46
Peak Align button, 140
Pencil tool, 11
perspective, changing, 129
Pitch Criteria section, 43
pitches, separating tracks, 43
playback
    DAE Playback Buffer, changing, 39
    editing during, 74
    loops (Dynamic Transport), 91–92
playlists. *See also* Edit Playlists
    automation, viewing, 153
    changing between, 24
    creating, 25
    duplicating, 23
    limitation of, 25
    naming, 23
Playlist Selector button, 22
Play Start Marker, 91
plug-ins. *See also* tools
    AudioSuite Time Compression, 30
    automation playlists, viewing, 153
    Noise Gate, 154–155
    searching, 33
    TCE, 28
    Time Shift AudioSuite, 35
    Xpand!, 7
Plug-In Settings folder, 34
plus (+) sign, moving regions, 73
polyrhythms
    formatting, 162
    loop trim, 161–162
preferences, 14. *See also* options
Preferences window, 15

Index

Pre-Separate Amount window, 15, 79
Preserve Tempo After Selection dialog box, 9
presets
    selecting, 34
    Sound Accuracy, 34
    TCE Trim tool
        formatting, 32
        saving, 31
previewing
    audio, looping in browsers, 92–93
    loops, 17
processing AudioSuite options, 140
Project browser, looping in, 92–93
promoting beat triggers, 103
properties, Real-Time Properties, 54–58
Pro Tools HD
    Create Group window, 149
    Trim automation display, 152
Pro Tools LE, applying Beat Detective, 115–116
pulling loopable regions from rhythm tracks, 13
pulse of the rhythm. *See* beats

Q

Quantize feature, 47–53
quantizing
    audio, 105–119
    Audio tracks, 96
    grooves, 118
    real-time, 56
    regions, 82
quarter notes
    beats, 5
    Quantize feature, 51, 52
    values, 6

R

Randomize option, 50
Realign Session dialog box, 104
real-time automation display, 151
Real-Time Properties, MIDI, 54–58
real-time quantization, 56
re-analyzing audio, 100
Region End pad slider, 78
Region Looping dialog box, 87
regions
    absolute time linearity, 58
    Beat Detective
        conforming, 108–110

        creating, 107–108
        selecting, 97–99
    beats, identifying, 65–70
    Capture Region option, 14
    consolidating, 38–39
    cutting, 81
    Cymbal, 79
    drums, splitting, 43
    duplicating, 74
    editing, 16, 77
        Audio tracks, 82–84
        Dynamic Transport, 91–92
        groups, 84–87
        looping, 87–91
        looping in browsers, 92–93
        quantizing, 82
        separating, 79–81
        starting, 68
        Strip Silence, 77–79
    Edit Playlists, 21–22. *See also* Edit Playlists
    fades, creating on groups, 85
    four-bar, 66
    moving
        clutching, 75–77
        by grid values, 71–75
    muting, 46
    new features, 84
    nudging, 73
    Real-Time Properties, 56–58
    Rex files, importing, 18
    Separate Regions option, 14, 15
    separating, 108
    sync points, 134
    TCE Trim tool, 28
    timelines, 16
    timing, shifting, 73
    trimming, 89
    Trim Region option, 14
Relative Grid mode, 71–75
remapping, 76
Rename button, 78
renaming tracks, 46
repetition, loop trim polyrhythms, 161–162
replacement sounds, loading, 138
replacing tracks, kick drums, 141
Resolution area (Beat Detective), 101
Rex files
    applying, 16–19
    importing, 18

Index

rhythm, 4. *See also* beats
    tracks, pulling loopable regions from, 13
room tracks (Beat Detective), 113
Root Settings folder, 34
rulers
    Bars:Beats, 4
    Meter, 5
    Tempo Ruler, 8, 10–11, 67
Ruler view, 5
rules, zero-crossing, breaking the, 163–164

S

sample-based regions, 82
Save Effect Settings As window, 31
saving
    groove templates, 118
    TCE presets, 31
Scroll Next button, 102
S-curves option, 11
searching plug-ins, 33
segments, selecting, 106
Select Bars:Beats, 71
selecting
    audio (Beat Detective), 106
    Beat Detective, consolidating, 111
    groups
        letters, 149
        members, 148
    loopable, 13
    presets, 34
    regions (Beat Detective), 97–99
    segments, 106
    TCE plug-ins, 33
    timelines, 35–38
    transients, separating, 15
    volume, MIDI, 27
selectors, Instrument tracks, 45
Select/Split Notes dialog box, 44
Select/Split Notes mode, 43
Sensitivity slider (Beat Detective), 100
Separate button, 78
Separate Region command, 15
Separate Regions option, 14, 15
Separate Region submenu, 79
separating
    components, 136
    Heal Separation feature, 80
    pitches, 43

regions, 79–81, 108
tracks, 77–79
Trigger Pads, configuring, 107
sessions
    comparing, 68
    editing during, 74
    Edit Playlists, 22. *See also* Edit Playlists
    files, importing, 92
    linearity, 58–60
    Realign Session dialog box, 104
    tempo, managing, 8–10
settings
    5ms Trigger Pads, 107
    amplitude thresholds, 144
    Beat Detective selections, 98
    end points, 68
    filter sweeps, 153
    mid-amplitude thresholds, 145
    Noise Gate plug-in, 154–155
    Nudge values, 73
    Signal Generator, 154–155
    thresholds, 78
Shift dialog box, 73
shifting timing of regions, 73
Show Trigger Time check box, 102
Side-Chain input, 154–155
Signal Generator, 154–155
signatures, time, 4
single note height, 42–46
sixteenth notes
    grid value of, 7
    Quantize feature, 49
    Randomize option, 50
    Swing option, 51
    values, 6
    velocity, 54
sliders
    Accuracy, 32
    Dynamics, 140, 145
    Manual Tempo, 3
    Mix, 139
    Region End pad, 78
    Sensitivity (Beat Detective), 100
    Tempo, 8
Slip mode, 73
Smart Tool, 10, 86
smoothing, Edit Smoothing, 110–111
snare drums, mixing beats, 125

Index

snare hits, tracks with no, 23
software, Sibelius, 2
Solo-safe, 46
sound, 129. *See also* audio
    replacement, loading, 138
Sound Accuracy preset, 34
SoundReplacer, applying, 135–146
Speaker icon, 92
speakers, 19
speed. *See also* velocity
    of musical pieces, 2. *See also* tempo
    Rex files, 18
splitting notes, 43
Standard conform mode, 109
starting
    Beat Detective, 98
    Dynamic Transport, 91–92
    MIDI Detective, 119
    regions, editing, 68
    Relative Grid mode, 75
    SoundReplacer, 137
static tempo
    click tracks, 8
    creating, 106
stereo images, focusing, 128
storage locations
    plug-ins, 33
    presets, 32
Straight Line option, 27
Strength option, 52
Strip button, 78
Strip Silence, 77–79
stutter edits, 159–161
subgroups, 150–151
submenus, Separate Region, 79
sweeps, filter, 152–153
Swing option, 51
switching
    Audio tracks to tick-based, 82
    playlists, 24
sync points, regions, 134

T

Tab key, 13
tabs, Operation, 15
Tab to Transient button, 13
Tap End B|B button, 99
tapping out tempo, 3

TCE Edit tools, selecting timelines, 35–38
TCE (Time Compression/Expansion), 28
TCE Trim tool presets
    formatting, 32
    saving, 31
templates (grooves)
    creating, 116–119
    saving, 118
tempo, 2–3
    changes in, 8–10
    controlling, 3
    determining, 106
    display, 3
    drawing, 11
    drum tracks, Identify Beat function, 65–70
    maps, creating, 96, 97–105
    MIDI Quantize feature, 47
    Rex files, 18
    static, creating, 106
    tapping, 3
    values, getting exact in tempo, 11
Tempo Editor, viewing, 10
Tempo Operations window, 9
Tempo Ruler, 8, 10–11
    Enable button, 67
Tempo slider, 8
thirty-second note values, 6
thresholds
    amplitude, setting, 144
    mid-amplitude, setting, 145
    setting, 78
ticks
    Audio tracks, editing regions, 82–84
    beats, 6
    linearity, 59
    viewing, 7
time
    absolute time linearity, 58
    AudioSuite Time Compression plug-in, 30
    beat triggers, viewing, 102
    MIDI, 7–8
        latency, 62
        Quantize feature, 47
    regions, shifting, 73
    sample-based regions, 82
    signatures, 4
Time Base Selector button, 82
Time Compression/Expansion. *See* TCE

Index

timelines
    editing, 36
    insertion, 15
    insertions, moving, 106
    Min:Sec, 58
    regions, 16
    selecting, 35–38
Time Shift AudioSuite plug-in, 35
toggling between Grid modes, 72
toms, mixing beats, 126
tools. *See also* **options**
    Beat Detective. *See* Beat Detective
    Grabber, 53, 73, 102
    Mirrored MIDI Editing button, 63
    Pencil, 11
    Smart Tool, 10, 86
    Straight Line, 27
    TCE Trim, 28–30
        formatting presets, 32
        optimizing, 30–35
        saving presets, 31
    Trim, 10
tracks
    alternate, 24–25
    audio
        modifying, 82–84
        quantizing, 96
    child, 46
    color-coding, 46
    compressing, 131
    drum, applying playlists on, 25–27
    duplicating, 130
    editing, identifying beats, 65–70
    Edit Playlists, 21–22. *See also* Edit Playlists
    hiding, 46
    Instrument tracks. *See* Instrument tracks
    kick drums, replacing, 141
    layering, 133–135
    listening to, 45
    multitrack beats (Beat Detective), 112
    with no snare hits, creating, 23
    offsets, 60–63
    output to a bus, changing, 127
    overhead (Beat Detective), 113
    parent, 46
    pitches, separating, 43
    previewing looping in browsers, 92–93
    regions, grouping, 84–87

    renaming, 46
    rhythm, pulling loopable regions from, 13
    room (Beat Detective), 113
    separating, 77–79, 79
    static-tempo click, 8
    TCE trim tool, 34
Track View Selector menu, 26
transients
    applying, 12–16
    Beat Detective, 95. *See also* Beat Detective
    marking, 139
    overview of, 12
    regions, separating, 80
    selections, separating, 15
transitions, crossfades, 88
Transport window
    tempo, 2, 8
    viewing, 3
Trigger Pads, setting, 107
triggers (beats), 100, 101–103
    changing values of, 104–105
    Collection mode, 113–115
    deleting, 102
    promoting, 103
Trim automation display, 152
trimming, 89. *See also* **cutting**
trim polyrhythms, loops, 161–162
Trim Region option, 14
Trim tool, 10
troubleshooting
    MIDI latency, 62
    SoundReplacer, 142
Tuplet option, 49
two-measure fades, 27
types of region groups, 85–86

U

unaltered tracks, Quantize, 48
unit of musical measurement, bars, 4
updating interfaces, 137

V

Value button, 56
values
    beat triggers, changing, 104–105
    formatting, 30
    grids, 7, 71–75
    Grid Value Arrow, 71

Grid Value button, 29
notes, 6
nudge, 7, 73
tempo, getting exact, 11
ticks, 6
velocity, MIDI, 53–54
versions, changing between, 23
viewing
    automation, 151–152
    Instrument tracks, 26
    Main Counter, 7
    playlists, 153
    Real-Time Properties column, 55
    Rex files, 17
    tempo, 3
    Tempo Editor, 10
    Transport window, 3
    trigger time, 102
views, Ruler, 5
voltage, 12. *See also* **volume**
volume
    changes in, 12
    MIDI, selecting, 27
Volume browser, looping in, 92–93

W

waltzes, number of beats, 5
waveforms, 95. *See also* Beat Detective
whole note values, 6

windows
    Add Bar|Beat Markers dialog box, 67
    Mix
        applying, 146–150
        New York compression, 156
    output, opening, 128
    Preferences, 15
    Pre-Separate Amount, 15, 79
    Pro Tools HD Create Group, 149
    Save Effect Settings As, 31
    Strip Silence, 78
    Tempo Operations, 9
    Transport
        tempo, 2, 8
        viewing, 3
Workspace browser, looping in, 92–93

X

Xpand! plug-in, 7

Z

zero-crossing rule
    breaking, 163–164
    regions, cutting, 81

INTERACTIVE TRAINING
for serious musicians
Cool School Interactus™ CD-ROMs

If you prefer an interactive, hands-on style of learning, check out our *CSi Starters* and *CSi Masters* on various topics including:

ACID | Pro Tools | Cubase SX | Nuendo | Digital Performer | Logic
GarageBand | Reason | SONAR | Sound Forge | Audio Plug-Ins | Waves Plug-Ins

Find these CD-ROM tutorials and more at www.courseptr.com/csi.

CSi STARTERS=Beginning to intermediate training ■ CSi MASTERS=Intermediate to advanced training

To order, visit www.courseptr.com or call 1.800.648.7450.

THOMSON
COURSE TECHNOLOGY
Professional ■ Technical ■ Reference

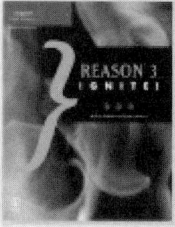

License Agreement/Notice of Limited Warranty

By opening the sealed disc container in this book, you agree to the following terms and conditions. If, upon reading the following license agreement and notice of limited warranty, you cannot agree to the terms and conditions set forth, return the unused book with unopened disc to the place where you purchased it for a refund.

License:
The enclosed software is copyrighted by the copyright holder(s) indicated on the software disc. You are licensed to copy the software onto a single computer for use by a single user and to a backup disc. You may not reproduce, make copies, or distribute copies or rent or lease the software in whole or in part, except with written permission of the copyright holder(s). You may transfer the enclosed disc only together with this license, and only if you destroy all other copies of the software and the transferee agrees to the terms of the license. You may not decompile, reverse assemble, or reverse engineer the software.

Notice of Limited Warranty:
The enclosed disc is warranted by Thomson Course Technology PTR to be free of physical defects in materials and workmanship for a period of sixty (60) days from end user's purchase of the book/disc combination. During the sixty-day term of the limited warranty, Thomson Course Technology PTR will provide a replacement disc upon the return of a defective disc.

Limited Liability:
THE SOLE REMEDY FOR BREACH OF THIS LIMITED WARRANTY SHALL CONSIST ENTIRELY OF REPLACEMENT OF THE DEFECTIVE DISC. IN NO EVENT SHALL THOMSON COURSE TECHNOLOGY PTR OR THE AUTHOR BE LIABLE FOR ANY OTHER DAMAGES, INCLUDING LOSS OR CORRUPTION OF DATA, CHANGES IN THE FUNCTIONAL CHARACTERISTICS OF THE HARDWARE OR OPERATING SYSTEM, DELETERIOUS INTERACTION WITH OTHER SOFTWARE, OR ANY OTHER SPECIAL, INCIDENTAL, OR CONSEQUENTIAL DAMAGES THAT MAY ARISE, EVEN IF THOMSON COURSE TECHNOLOGY PTR AND/OR THE AUTHOR HAS PREVIOUSLY BEEN NOTIFIED THAT THE POSSIBILITY OF SUCH DAMAGES EXISTS.

Disclaimer of Warranties:
THOMSON COURSE TECHNOLOGY PTR AND THE AUTHOR SPECIFICALLY DISCLAIM ANY AND ALL OTHER WARRANTIES, EITHER EXPRESS OR IMPLIED, INCLUDING WARRANTIES OF MERCHANTABILITY, SUITABILITY TO A PARTICULAR TASK OR PURPOSE, OR FREEDOM FROM ERRORS. SOME STATES DO NOT ALLOW FOR EXCLUSION OF IMPLIED WARRANTIES OR LIMITATION OF INCIDENTAL OR CONSEQUENTIAL DAMAGES, SO THESE LIMITATIONS MIGHT NOT APPLY TO YOU.

Other:
This Agreement is governed by the laws of the State of Massachusetts without regard to choice of law principles. The United Convention of Contracts for the International Sale of Goods is specifically disclaimed. This Agreement constitutes the entire agreement between you and Thomson Course Technology PTR regarding use of the software.